Beyond Chaos

The Expert Edge in Managing Software Development

Larry L. Constantine

ADDISON-WESLEY

Boston • San Francisco • New York • Toronto • Montreal
London • Munich • Paris • Madrid
Capetown • Sydney • Tokyo • Singapore • Mexico City

Chapters 1 through 44 first appeared in The Management Forum, a column created and edited by Larry Constantine and appearing regularly in *Software Development* Magazine. Copyright © 1997, 1998, 1999, 2000, 2001 *Software Development* Magazine, CMP Media Inc. Reprinted with permission.

The publisher offers discounts on this book when ordered in quantity for special sales. For more information, please contact:

Pearson Education Corporate Sales Division
One Lake Street
Upper Saddle River, NJ 07458
(800) 382-3419
corpsales@pearsontechgroup.com

Visit AW on the Web: www.awl.com/cseng/

Library of Congress Cataloging-in-Publication Data
Constantine, Larry L.
    Beyond chaos : the expert edge in managing software development / Larry L. Constantine.
      p. m.
    Includes bibliographical references and index.
    ISBN 0-201-71960-6 (pbk.)
      1. Computer software—Development—Management.   I. Title.

  QA76.76.D47 C654 2001
  005.1'068—dc21

                                                2001022852

ISBN 0-201-71960-6
Text printed on recycled paper
1 2 3 4 5 6 7 8 9 10—CRS—0504030201

First printing, June 2001

*To Jack C., Ken M., Ray W., Larry O.,
and Lucy L.—managers all.*

Contents

PART IV QUALITY REQUIRED   185

PART V PROCESSES AND PRACTICES   249

PART VI LEADERSHIP AND TEAMWORK   329

Preface

Chaos. Not the inchoate state of the early universe, not the ill-behaved subject of a specialized branch of mathematics, not the mid-revolutionary fragmentation of a society in transition, but coding chaos—the everyday reality of projects that develop software applications for computers and the World Wide Web.

Countless managers struggle for control and stability, for accountability and predictability amidst this chaos. From the project leaders, who provide the day-to-day oversight and guidance all the way up to the CIOs, whose charge is strategic direction and corporate-wide coordination, they struggle to understand and manage technology and processes of enormous complexity made all the more complex and unmanageable by the relentless and accelerating pace of technological change.

Herding squirrels. Corralling cats. Taming the mongrel hordes. Whatever the metaphor, the challenges of managing software development are legend. The stories are alarmingly similar for projects of every scope and size, whether staffed by the arrayed forces of thousands of programmers and testers or tackled by a small team of freelancers. The budget may be blown by a hundred percent or more and deadline upon deadline may be passed like so many exits on a freeway. Rarely do software development projects meet budget constraints, technical objectives, and delivery schedules—if indeed recognizable constraints, objectives, and schedules exist. Applications that are far more complex than a high-rise office building have sometimes been launched with little more planning than a sketch on the back of a napkin.

Some managers simply give up and accept this uncontrolled chaos as the state of affairs, an unchangeable reality and the unavoidable price of dealing with a highly paid and poorly understood profession. They accept the reality of seeking discipline among the undisciplined, of perpetually pushing the envelope of the possible, or of seeking certainty where specifications are little more than executive fantasies and deadlines are the arbitrary impositions of uninformed marketing managers.

Some managers seek refuge in mind-numbing manuals of procedure and in the step-by-step details of elaborately defined processes. They rationalize the investment in expensive systems that promise predictability through the imposition of regulation and regimentation.

Some managers, defining defeat as success, instead celebrate unmanageable chaos as the crucible of creation, the necessary and desired context in which to unleash the powers of the digital genie that will transform life on earth.

Beyond chaos, however, beyond surrender or celebration, is another view of software development—the view that software development projects and software developers are indeed manageable, that chaos is not an inevitable condition or concomitant. In this view, salvation dwells in the details, success lies in subtle insights, and control is achieved through thoughtful attention and planning.

The expert edge is the difference. Compiled in this book are the insights, inspiration, practical pointers, and provocative thinking of an elite assemblage of working managers and practicing consultants—the recognized experts who contributed monthly to The Management Forum. The Forum, a regular feature in the respected industry publication *Software Development,* occupied the prestigious inside back page of the magazine and proved to be one its most popular features.

Written for busy working managers, the Forum featured pragmatic, provocative essays by the leading thinkers and doers in software and Web development, software engineering, and technical management, including such industry luminaries as Ed Yourdon, Capers Jones, Meilir Page-Jones, Steve McConnell, and Jim Highsmith. The column set high standards for the clarity and quality of both the writing and the thinking it expressed. Every guest columnist was charged with the twin tasks of providing something that a working manager could put to use tomorrow and of offering something to think about for the next week.

Not surprisingly in light of the diversity of contributors, the discussions reprinted in this volume represent diverse views grounded in a variety of backgrounds and experiences. What they have in common, however, are common and positive threads—that software development and software developers are manageable, and that better management in this economically and technologically critical field is sorely needed.

The essays span such diverse topics as dealing with difficult people, managing from the bottom-up, coping with project failure, sustaining teamwork, and building software to throw away. Managers will find among the chapters the distilled essence of experience and the hard-won wisdom of those who have fought in the trenches of technical management, and won.

Highly focused analyses and specific suggestions are combined with provocative arguments and thoughtful perspectives. The essays have been edited and organized by broad subject matter and arranged to form a logical progression, finishing with what I hope will stand as a challenge and a look to the future of management and of software development.

Larry Constantine
Rowley, Massachusetts
March 2001

Acknowledgments

First credit for the existence and substance of this book must go to Barbara Hanscome, former editor of Software Development, who persuaded me to return to the magazine and helped me to hatch the idea of the monthly Management Forum, the source for all but one of the chapters in this volume. She adroitly shepherded the column through its launch and early days and set the stage for a smooth handover to Alexa Weber Morales, my adept and ever adaptable editor over the rest of the column's history.

This volume may be among the most thoroughly edited of books on management. As column editor, I worked with authors to pound their raw material into creditable shape, often guiding an initial contribution through several rounds of rewrites. Then I would edit and send the "final" manuscript off to the magazine, where Barbara, Alexa, and their assistants would finish what I had started. Over the four-year run of the column, Julie Fadda, Theresa Gonzales, Rosaclaire Baisinger, and Tamara Carter were among those whose subtle and skillful editorial improvements pervade this entire anthology. In due time, I collected the individual columns and edited them one "final" time before Chrysta Meadowbrooke, copy editor supreme, truly finished the job under the able leadership of production coordinator Elizabeth Ryan. If there remain mistakes or malapropisms, let it not be said we didn't try!

Naturally, my greatest debt is owed to the guest columnists themselves—those writers who lent their names and ideas to a collective endeavor and who rose to the challenge when I kept at them to write with more punch and precision. I am proud to call them colleagues and friends. Among them is my partner, my best and first editor Lucy Lockwood, who not only contributed her own work but helped vet all the rest.

Last credit must go to Peter Gordon, my perspicacious and persevering editor at Addison-Wesley, who saw the potential in this collective work and let me push ahead with the project while still owing him a manuscript for another book. That, too, shall come!

My appreciation also goes to Regina Ridley of CMP Media Inc., a manager whose authority and integrity ultimately made this collection possible. For permission to use previously published material, I am grateful. For her support and friendship over many years of working together, I am doubly grateful.

PART I

It's about People

Well, of course it is. Nearly everything in this book is about people to one degree or another, but in this section the people issues take center stage. Here we deal with some of the messier and more personal matters, such as handling difficult people and situations, improving communications, maintaining balance in relationships, and creative problem solving.

Chapter 1

Dealing with Difficult People: Changing the Changeable

Larry Constantine

Software development is hard enough without the added challenge of managing difficult people. The whole planet would be an easier place to live were it not inhabited by so many difficult human beings. Most of us do not think of ourselves as the difficult ones, of course; it is those others, always those others—the loudmouths and the recalcitrants and their sundry kin—who make life harder than it needs to be.

Reams have been written already on dealing with difficult people, primarily by pop psychologists and management consultants, primarily predicated on analyzing personality problems or on mastering techniques for manipulating people. I am duly hesitant to add to this genre of glib prescriptions. Instead, this chapter offers a way of thinking about difficult people and situations that seems to have helped many technical managers over the years.

—Editor

For years, editors, clients, and conference organizers asked me to teach classes or conduct workshops or write articles on how to deal with difficult people, as if I were some sort of expert. I confess to having been somewhat suspicious of these requests. Did they assume I have some expertise because I myself am difficult? There must be some other explanation, however, because friends and colleagues who know me well will tell you that I am a pussycat, as easy to handle as an Isotoner glove, except, of course, on those occasions when I am being difficult.

TIME AND PLACE

Difficult people come in many shapes and forms. They are our bosses and our subordinates, our coworkers and our friends. They include the attention grabbers who must always be at the center of meetings and the whining negativists for whom contentment seems to lie in discontent. On the one hand are those creative prima donnas who could not possibly restrict themselves to routine programming; on the other are the plodding plan followers who seem incapable of thinking outside the box. Difficult people range from sycophantic suck-ups who hang on your every word to crusty critics whose greatest joy seems to lie in finding fault with everyone else's work.

Of course, some people actually appreciate a well-trained toady, and some count curmudgeons among their most likable colleagues. Being difficult is not necessarily a trait of temperament, but, like beauty, it rests largely in the experience of the beholder. The ignorant oaf who might try my patience to the limit could be the pliable peon of your dreams.

This perspective shifts the focus from the other person—that jerk who is being a pain or that lazy analyst who is exploiting my easygoing nature—to me. I am, after all, the one having difficulty, the one for whom a particular person is difficult. Even more importantly, I have no real control over anybody else. The only person whose behavior I can change is yours truly. Rather than wasting time trying to turn a jackass into a genial genius, I can concentrate on figuring out what I can do differently to make the situation work better for me.

> *You have no real control over anybody else. The only person whose behavior you can change is you.*

I am reminded of an American tourist we kept running into while on a consulting trip in Rome. He was having a miserable time. Wherever he went, whether having dinner in a *trattoria* or buying tickets at the railway station, he got terrible service and met with uncooperative resistance. No doubt he went home concluding that Italians were all difficult. How strange, then, that we found the exact same waiters and ticket clerks to be friendly and helpful. Could it be that he did something that assured he would encounter so many difficult situations?

Finding a way to make difficult situations better begins with questions. In my experience, asking the right question is the greater part of getting a useful answer. Instead of wondering why some person is so difficult, I find it more useful to ask myself why I am having difficulty with that person. It is, of course, usually far easier to spot the mote in a colleague's eye than to see the macaroni in your own, but every frustrating encounter with a difficult person is an opportunity to learn more about yourself. Over the long term, you may find yourself meeting fewer and fewer people who are difficult for you to handle.

Without waiting for the next difficult person to come along, I can ask myself what kind of people I find most difficult. Why are they, in particular, difficult? I would have to place near the top of my own list those people who seem rigid and immovable. Why? What's my problem? Maybe I pride myself overly in being a flexible and collaborative colleague. I can feel at a disadvantage with someone unwilling to negotiate, or be responsive, or consider other ways. And how do I usually cope with such immovable persons? I try to get them to move. Does it work? Hardly ever. From this sort of self-inquiry it becomes clear that I need to learn alternative ways to cope with rigid people. If I am having difficulty dealing with someone, it is really because I have not yet found another way to handle the situation.

Most difficult encounters are challenging and frustrating precisely because they drag on. For anything to keep happening between people, there must be some level of collaboration or complicity. For all I know, I am being difficult for the other person, too, like that American tourist in Rome who was difficult for the Italians and so found them difficult. My first rule, then, for dealing with so-called difficult people is:

■ Do Something Different

Do something different from what you have been doing so far or different from what you have done before. It need not be particularly clever or inspired. Doing almost anything different changes the interaction, changes your experience of the other person as well as his or her experience of you. Offer that angry ogre a sweet or a cup of coffee. Ask that bloody bore if he would help you review a design diagram you have been puzzling over. I can't give you a set menu of options or a top ten list of brilliant moves because I don't know what you usually do. The most important thing is that you make a move that breaks from your own usual patterns of behavior.

> *Difficult encounters can make you feel like you are caught in an infinite loop of frustrating interaction leading nowhere. The important thing is to make a move that breaks from your own usual patterns of behavior.*

Difficult encounters can make you feel like you are caught in an infinite loop of frustrating interaction leading nowhere. It can seem as if you have already tried everything and can think of nothing different to do. Next time that happens, try making a physical move of some kind. Walk to another place in the room. Sit down if standing, get up if seated. You might, for example, come out from behind your desk and sit in a side chair or rise and pace a bit before leaning on the credenza.

A remarkable thing happens as you shift your position and survey the scene from a new perspective: you see things differently. At the very moment you feel most stuck, you move, taking you to a new position that offers a new perspective. Inevitably, a change in position changes the interaction. Standing when someone else is sitting changes the relationship. Standing side by side to study a chart with your client conveys a different message than if you were to leave the chart on the table between you. Once unstuck, you can pause to study the situation, perhaps just listening and watching for a while before thinking about what you might do next that could help make the situation work better for everyone.

BAD LANGUAGE

Some things you might do are only likely to make the situation worse. Shouting at an angry colleague is likely to lead to an even more heated exchange, for example. I think of such actions as "escalators" because they are styles of communication or language that tend to escalate situations from merely difficult to potentially impossible or even dangerous. Escalators invite defensive or antagonistic responses because they can make people feel bad: trapped, belittled, threatened, or misunderstood. At best, they are unhelpful; at worst, they can set off even the most congenial and cooperative of coworkers.

> *Language that makes people feel bad invites defensive or antagonistic responses, escalating the difficulty.*

One example of an escalator is **categorical language**, which puts everything and everybody in boxes. In categorical language, the world is black or white, without shadows or shades of gray. Questions have only right or wrong answers. There is only one correct way to do something or only one way to view the situation. ("Absolutely nobody programs that way anymore.") What I call "limit-stop language," a close relative of categorical language, carries every distinction to the extreme. ("You always take the most inefficient approach possible." "I can't imagine in my wildest nightmare a more fouled-up architecture." "You never have anything useful to offer.")

Judgmental language is blaming and accusatory. It puts a personal spin on discussions that can twist the knife in an open wound. ("It's clear from the design that you didn't have much time to work on it." "The problem is not the compiler; the problem is you don't know how to use it.") The judgment can be merely implied. Spoken in just the right tone, "Do you *really* want to do it that way?" can imply the other person is unintelligent, misguided, and lacking in judgment.

Dissociative language, the refuge of those who wish to deny their own responsibility or participation in a process, is another way of shifting blame. ("It's policy. I don't make the rules." "Objectively, it is obvious and unambiguous which logic is superior.")

Escalators not only fail to help us deal with difficult people and situations, they also can turn us into difficult people ourselves. In other words, in dealing with anyone you find difficult:

■ *Avoid Being Difficult Yourself*

I find it productive to think of situations, rather than the people in them, as being difficult. This perspective shifts the focus from trying to fix the person to fixing the process—that is, the situation taking place between us. Even the most difficult person is not difficult all the time and in every circumstance. Being difficult is contextual. Everyone is difficult sometimes. Everyone is difficult for somebody. No one is difficult all the time for everyone.

Remembering this, you start thinking about what you can do to make a difficult situation easier for the other person rather than concentrating on what he or she could do to make it easier for you. You become more creative, making room for the other person to consider other options.

SMALL TALK

So-called influencers, at the other end of the spectrum from escalators, are language that can help transform difficult situations into successes and difficult people into winners. **Inclusive language** draws people together to meet a common challenge. ("We are having problems in our meetings. Perhaps we can come up with ways to make them more productive.") Inclusive language recognizes the situation as a shared difficulty, acknowledging that you also take a share of the responsibility. It is neither the "royal we" of imperious leaders nor the phony "we" of comedy nurses. ("So, how are we feeling today?")

Speculative language poses possibilities and raises questions. ("I wonder what might be done to speed up the process." "Maybe it is possible to merge these approaches into a common design for the database." "What might be done to enhance performance in this subsystem?") Speculative speech is neither manipulative questioning nor a form of interrogation, both of which usually escalate tensions. It is, instead, an honestly tentative and conditional mode of expression that creates a verbal vacuum to draw others into a dialogue.

Progressive language, which builds involvement and commitments by small and easily taken steps, can be especially effective with people you find uncooperative. It starts with getting agreement on the smallest and least arguable matter and builds from there. ("Is it possible that this technique could work, even if it is not the approach you would prefer?" "Would you have any objection to our considering this approach just for the sake of discussion?" "Might it be nearly as good as the alternative under some circumstances?") And so it goes.

Often the most influential language of all is silence. As long as I am talking, I am not learning anything new. If I listen well, the other person is more likely to feel heard and, feeling heard and understood, will be less likely to be so difficult. "Active listening" or "reflexive listening" is widely known, but many people who think they have mastered it forget the point. The point of listening actively is not to persuade others by your repetition and paraphrasing that you are a good listener and have heard them correctly. You reflect what you hear to help understand it yourself and to engage others in helping you understand what they are trying to say or to accomplish.

> *Often the most influential language of all is silence. If you listen well, the other person is more likely to feel heard and less likely to be so difficult.*

BIGGER VOCABULARY

Although any of us can be difficult at times, some people are more difficult, more often, for more people than the rest of us are. They are the ones most likely to be labeled "difficult." Typically, we describe such people in extremes or even exaggerations. Difficult people are, basically, just like the rest of us, but they act "that way" all the time or do it to a fault. Often, what makes an employee difficult for colleagues and coworkers is fairly ordinary, even acceptable behaviors carried to an extreme or continued without pause or variation.

Being difficult is a form of impoverished vocabulary. In my experience, many chronically difficult people do not know any other way to act. Especially if they work for you or are otherwise in your charge, part of your long-term job is to coach them in building larger repertoires of behaviors. The payoff can be that a brilliant but very irritating programmer becomes merely brilliant. In the shorter term, it can be helpful during a difficult encounter to think how you might expand alternatives for the other person. ("Maybe we can brainstorm some other course of action here." "Perhaps you would feel better dealing with another agent.")

Regrettably, not every person or situation is salvageable. Part of dealing effectively with difficult people is knowing when to give up or back off. It is important not to throw in the towel too soon, but it is equally important not to cling tenaciously to false hopes that the unchangeable might suddenly change. It can be a good tactic to start off assuming that a relationship can be made to work or that a troublesome employee can become a productive and appreciated contributor, but there may come a point when that working assumption needs to be questioned.

Ironically, the very act of giving up can sometimes be a breakthrough. One manager told an engineer that she was considering reassigning him. His constant carping and crushing criticism in meetings was wearing on the entire team. He was astonished. He had considered it part of his job to point out problems and had never thought of it as a problem for other people. With some private coaching, he was able gradually to overcome some habitual ways of expressing himself that had not only been making it difficult for his coworkers but also had contributed to his being on the downsizing list more than once.

Much the same principle applies to those of us trying to deal more effectively with difficult people. The more choices we have for our own behavior, the greater the range of styles we have in communicating, the more likely we are to find an effective response that makes it easier for us to work with those people.

Chapter 2

Avoiding Feedback Traps: Improving Customer and Client Communication

Naomi Karten

In my other life, when I was teaching psychotherapy, one of the high-lights of the training year was feedback. We scheduled it late enough in the program to have some real experience to base it on but early enough for there to be time to do something about it. After all, feedback is a route to improvement, if not of the soul then of the persona, if not of the heart then of the technique.

In our formula, feedback always came in two parts, assets and things to work on, not because we wanted a spoonful of sugar to help the medicine go down but because change—whether it is software process improvement or the nurturing of the healer—requires retaining and building on strengths and assets even as we overcome weaknesses and improve on shortcomings. We need reminders of which is the baby and which the dirty bathwater lest we discard too much as we strive to improve our programming processes or ourselves.

Another rule about feedback was never to give it without also inviting it. This two-way street between faculty and trainees was the road to improving the process as well as the people in it.

When we develop computer software, we often do a lot more than pound code into the keyboard. We pour something of our souls into those products. We stay late and sweat the details. We crank up on cof-fee or Jolt cola and run like hell to meet impossible deadlines. Who wants to be told they screwed up? Who wants an "unsatisfactory" rat-ing from a whinging client? Who needs this? Who needs them anyway?

Well, we do need them, and they need us. Feedback is one way we can keep improving the process as well as the products.

—Editor

11

This was one project that had progressed smoothly and concluded successfully, Paul thought as he opened the customer satisfaction survey. As project manager, he had done everything right, and he expected a glowing report from Carl. From the very start of the effort, Paul had sent written status reports to Carl every week, just as requested, and had continued to send them even after he realized they were piling up, unread, in Carl's in-box. He had supplied duplicate information whenever Carl asked, even when it covered matters already included in the weekly reports.

To his surprise, Paul discovered the feedback was negative. A note in Carl's handwriting complained that he never knew the status of the project!

This experience, related in a recent seminar, aptly illustrates some of the common traps encountered in obtaining customer feedback. Paul had relied on a deficient feedback process that left him baffled about where he had gone wrong. The good news is that you can avoid these traps and, by so doing, generate a more satisfying outcome for your customers and yourself.

Here are some of the feedback traps that Paul fell into and how to avoid them.

■ Trap #1: Assuming That No News Is Good News

Customers and clients may have a collective reputation of being cranky, but many customers never complain, even when dissatisfied, unless they are specifically asked for their feedback. This may be hard to believe if you are on the receiving end of continuous complaints, but some customers can turn weak-kneed and crackly-voiced at the very thought of lodging a complaint. Some fear their complaints could trigger anger, resentment, or retribution. Others still believe that if you can't say something nice, you shouldn't say anything at all. Some actually feel forced to use products or services they dislike. Convinced that complaints will get them nowhere, they swallow their frustrations and doggedly cope with ill-suited software or inept reports.

> *Unless specifically asked for feedback, many customers will never complain, even when dissatisfied.*

The absence of complaints does not mean the presence of happy customers. Indeed, the absence of complaints may merely be the icy tip of massive problems lurking beneath placid waters.

Whatever their reasons for suppressing grievances, many dissatisfied customers say nothing until they are asked. Asking gives them permission to say something negative they might otherwise never mention to you. Not that they don't tell others—many of the customers I interview on behalf of software developers sound off with great intensity. They may also regale their friends and coworkers with stories of faulty products and shoddy service. But tell you? No way.

Paul's client was a case in point: Carl was dissatisfied by what he perceived as a lack of information about the project status. He could have raised the issue at any time during the project, but for reasons we'll never know, he said nothing until the project was complete, and then only when he was handed a post-project survey form.

If you multiply the number of complaints you do receive by ten (or some other two-digit number of your choice), you might approximate the number of mumbled complaints from those who grumble under their breath but never tell you out loud because you never asked. If you want to know what your customers think, don't wait for them to come to you with their complaints. Go to them. Ask for their feedback. Tell them that it's important to you to know what is working well and what needs attention. Identify grievances before they escalate into cacophonous complaints.

And when customers do come to you with their complaints, consider yourself lucky. Without asking, you've received valuable feedback and a chance to work with your customers to resolve problems.

■ *Trap #2: Requesting Feedback Only After the Job Is Done*

Most feedback is solicited, if at all, after a project has been completed or the system has been delivered. Who benefits from negative feedback that is deferred until after the fact? Not the customers, whose silent suffering may have been accompanied by plots to take their business elsewhere; certainly not the software development group, whose only means to satisfy the customer at that point may be through costly concessions. Sure, you benefit by being able to apply to the next project the lessons learned in the last one, but is a trail of dissatisfied customers in the wake of each project worth the lessons learned?

If after project completion is not the best time to check in with your customers, when should you assess customer satisfaction? You should be asking for and getting feedback regularly throughout the course of the project, whether it is developing a system or delivering consulting services. If you have not been requesting feedback from your customers regularly, right now is the time to begin. It is likely that if Paul had periodically met with Carl to discuss how things were going, he would have been able to identify Carl's concerns sooner and could have taken steps to prevent later problems.

Holding feedback sessions regularly is more important than holding them frequently. The sessions need not be lengthy. For Paul's project, even a brief 15-minute meeting every other week would have been better than nothing. Paul could have used one of these meetings to ask Carl about the unread status reports. He might have learned early why Carl didn't know the status of the project and taken steps to rectify the situation.

> *Holding feedback sessions regularly is more important than holding them frequently.*

Every software development manager knows it is important to focus not just on the project and the product but on the process as well. This process includes regularly scheduled feedback sessions to which both parties commit right from the beginning. These meetings ensure that both parties are in sync and that concerns are addressed sooner rather than later. You may not be able to resolve every concern your customers raise in these meetings, but you don't stand a chance of resolving problems if you don't even know about them.

■ Trap #3: Obtaining Feedback That Is Not Useful

Written surveys and questionnaires are the most common methods of assessing customer satisfaction. They can be an effective means of quickly gathering information from a large customer population. Too often, though, survey questions invite answers that provide few clues to what needs to change and what should stay the same. For example, the survey that Carl was given asked him, among other things, what aspects of the project he was dissatisfied with. Open-ended survey questions tend to elicit more meaningful and useful feedback than mere ratings do. Nevertheless, Carl's response, that he never knew the project status, was mystifying to the project manager. Unfortunately, the survey itself did not request any clarifying information, and the feedback process did not include any follow-up procedure to gather it.

Of course, Paul could have called or e-mailed Carl, explaining that the comment about project status was puzzling since written status reports had been sent regularly. Any explanation Carl offered might shed light on the origins of the problem.

Whether or not you can hold follow-up sessions with customers, make sure the feedback you receive from written surveys is as useful as possible. Include space for comments after each survey question. If you use a rating format, follow each item to be rated with a request for further explanation. This additional information tells you what is really on the customer's mind.

For example, it is not useful in itself merely to know that a customer rates your responsiveness as, say, 4 on a scale of 10. It doesn't sound like your customer is ecstatic, but it remains unclear exactly why, and it is impossible to say what you should do. For ratings to be useful, they need to be followed with "Please explain the reason for this rating" or "Please describe an experience that will help us understand your reason for this rating." The comments that customers supply can turn nebulous ratings into a firm basis for action: information that helps you understand what went wrong and what you need to do to correct the situation.

> *The comments that customers supply when asked to explain can turn nebulous ratings into a firm basis for action.*

Software development managers are commonly concerned that no one will respond to requests for written comments. The concern is understandable but generally unfounded. To the surprise of many managers, customers often respond to such requests at length. Not everyone writes a dissertation, of course, but many supply more details than might be expected.

Clarifying comments are just as important when a rating is high as when it is low. Knowing you rated a 10 out of 10 is gratifying but still not informative. It is far more instructive to understand what contributed to this level of satisfaction so that you either continue to do what has worked well or at least understand the potential risk if you choose to change it.

■ Trap #4: Misinterpreting Customer Comments

We fall into this trap because we are often quick to jump to conclusions when interpreting what customers mean by their comments. Paul's blood pressure shot up when he read that Carl never knew the status of the project. How could Carl not know the status? Paul not only had prepared the written progress reports but also had done so in response to Carl's request. In Paul's view, Carl's admission that he never knew the project status was proof that the reports had been deliberately ignored.

Was Paul's interpretation correct? We may never know, but other interpretations are certainly possible. For example, Carl might have meant that the status reports were poorly written or unorganized. Perhaps he had trouble making sense of the terminology. Such possibilities would put Carl's statement in a very different light. In fact, Carl's frequent questions about items already addressed in the status report might have been a clue that the reports were unclear, rather than that he hadn't read them.

Another possibility is that Carl had something different in mind when he requested status information, so Paul's reports were not helpful. Maybe the reports were in narrative form, whereas Carl was a graphs-and-charts sort of guy who liked knowing the score without having to wade through text to find out. Maybe the reports were too lengthy and Carl wanted something concise and to the point. Or maybe they were too brief and lacked the details Carl desired.

Misinterpreting and misconstruing are easy enough when we are face-to-face, but when communication is written, the potential misses multiply. Whenever feasible, written feedback should be supplemented with face-to-face feedback (or at least voice-to-voice) to resolve uncertainties and flush out ambiguities. The question, "Can you help me understand what you meant by this comment?" is a vital one in truly understanding the customer perspective.

> *When communication is written, the potential for misinterpreting and misconstruing multiplies. Written feedback should be supplemented with face-to-face feedback.*

■ Trap #5: Getting but Not Giving Feedback

Paul expected Carl's feedback during the project and in the survey, but he didn't see it as his responsibility to give feedback about his own satisfaction level to Carl. When he noticed the status reports piling up in his client's in-box, he said nothing.

When we discussed this trap in my seminar, Paul confessed that he didn't know how to let Carl know of his concern. After all, how could he accuse his client of not reading the reports? How could he indicate that Carl's questions were covered in last week's report without embarrassing Carl?

This is a reasonable concern and an important one. Just as many customers don't complain because they don't know how, the same is true of many developers. Paul didn't know how to give feedback. Given improperly, the feedback could have offended his client and created an awkward situation for Paul and his organization.

Paul, though, had several reasonably safe options for expressing his concern. For example, he might have said to Carl, "I was wondering if you've had a chance to read my status reports, because I'd like to know if I'm providing the kind of information you want." Or when Carl raised a question that had already been addressed in the status report, Paul might have said, "I commented on that in last week's report, but maybe I wasn't clear. Let me answer your question, and then maybe you can help me make sure I'm writing the reports the way you'd like." Or during a review meeting, Paul might have said, "I know you asked for a weekly written status report when we started out, but now that we're well into the project, maybe there are other methods you'd prefer. What would be the best way to keep you informed about the status?"

None of these suggested approaches accuses Carl of wrongdoing. In each, Paul makes a judgment-free observation, emphasizes his responsibility to Carl, and requests Carl's assistance in helping him do a good job. All three options help to minimize any awkwardness Carl might otherwise feel about expressing his dissatisfaction. Allowing customers to save face is crucial for obtaining useful customer feedback. If Carl did think the status reports were a muddled mess, an appropriately inviting opener might give him permission to say, for example,

"Well, now that you mention it, I've been really swamped, so would you limit those reports to a single page of highlights?"

Had Paul raised the issue in a nonthreatening and nonblaming way, he would have provided Carl with an excellent communication model. In so doing, he might have cut through Carl's concealed dissatisfaction about the status reports and avoided the complaint in the final survey.

Never underestimate the psychological impact of gathering feedback. Using a noncombative method of asking customers for feedback and then doing something about the problems they cite tells them that you are listening. The very process of requesting feedback helps to raise the satisfaction level expressed in that feedback.

The traps Paul fell into are common ones, yet each is easily avoided if you incorporate a well-conceived feedback process into your projects. Ask customers for feedback regularly. Give them face-saving ways to respond. Make sure you understand what they tell you and show evidence of having listened. Both you and your customers will benefit.

Chapter 3

These Are Trained Professionals: Beyond Training to Transformation

Larry Constantine

Software development is a business founded on the work of trained professionals whose training is almost continuously rendered obsolete. As in modern medicine, staying current in software development requires continuous retraining [Constantine, 1995a]. Our industry annually invests enormous sums in seminars, courses, and conferences in an endless effort to sustain currency and competitiveness; some will argue that even this may not be enough.

Unfortunately, too many managers squander their usually limited training budgets and waste scarce staff time on training that will have no impact on either the process or the end product. They train the wrong people in the wrong things, then entrust the outcome to the fickle fates and wonder why they do not see immediate results. Getting more out of training depends on what you do before and after class, not just what happens during the course.

—Editor

It was Monday morning of a week-long seminar for applications development professionals within a major financial institution, and my partner and I wanted some sense of just whom we were teaching. As we asked around the group, one gentleman said without hesitation, "I'm a database administrator. I was told last night to show up for class this morning. No one said the subject was user interface design. I have no idea why I am here." The man on his right said, "Me too!"

So what were these two fellows doing in this seminar? Apparently, their managers had a quota to fill. Someone from each group had to attend the training, and the database administrator could be spared. A business analyst working on a system redesign might have made immediate use of the material we were teaching, but she could not be spared. Unfortunately, we see this sort of thing all the time, as opportunities to improve performance and quality are lost among the small and quick decisions of everyday project management.

The outcome of training should be more than just another line on someone's résumé or an added paragraph in a corporate profile. Investing in even the best of training by the best of trainers is not enough if managers fail to take the extra steps needed to ensure that their investment will pay off for their developers and for the organization.

All too often, skills and techniques are taught to developers who are in no position to put them into practice. After one particularly frustrating and seemingly fruitless class, Meilir Page-Jones, a leading consultant on object-oriented analysis and design, opined that technical training without management consulting to help translate learning into change should, perhaps, be regarded as a form of professional malpractice.

> *Technical training without follow-up to help translate learning into change is a form of professional malpractice.*

Who is to blame, then, for widespread malpractice? Some training companies may be more interested in selling seats in classes than in delivering results, but most consultants and trainers only reluctantly serve clients who will pay for training but not for the coaching or consultation that will make it work.

I long ago lost count of how many classes I have taught in the thirty-plus years since I first stood up in front of a group of developers to train them in LISP programming. However, through the successive revolutions of structured methods, object technology, and software usability, I can count on my fingers how many classes have been coupled with adequate management preparation and follow-up. Where once I may have started with the illusion that a teacher was responsible for teaching classes, I soon came to realize that accountability stretches far beyond those easily defined boundaries.

Managers should, of course, take care that they are getting effective training from competent trainers, but even more important than what happens during class is what takes place before and after. Training is often at the wrong time or for the wrong people. Sometimes methods or technologies are introduced that simply cannot be put into practice under established policies and procedures. More often than not, there is no subsequent support for graduates trying valiantly to apply what they have learned.

BEFORE WE BEGIN

Training starts before the first day of class. It starts with the choice of participants and the scheduling. Training the wrong people or the right people at the wrong time can be a complete waste of everyone's time and money. The managers who shop around for affordable courses or request competitive bids from training companies often ignore the fact that the fully burdened costs of staff time are typically much larger than the training fees. They frequently overlook the fact that it costs just as much to train the wrong person as the right person.

Who is the right person to train? The answer depends on what the training is intended to accomplish, but, in general, participants in training should be people who can make use of what they learn—people who, by virtue of where and how they work and on what, can put into immediate practice whatever is being taught. The best learners are often those who can see an immediate application for what they are learning, those who are starting a new project or entering a phase where new knowledge can be applied. People who will not use the material in the foreseeable future are hardly prime candidates for training.

> *The best learners are often those who have an imminent need where new knowledge can be applied in immediate practice.*

Participants in training should be chosen with a creative eye toward both practical and strategic objectives. Most candidates probably should be selected based on their immediate needs: the just-in-time training (JITT) model. Some may be chosen because they are technical leaders. People might be invited because of their enthusiasm for the subject or even for their skepticism, but ordering professionals into class over their objections benefits no one.

It is not hard for the experienced trainer to spot the people who do not want be there. They glower from the back of the room with their arms crossed, or they take every opportunity to belittle anything new. They are the bane of trainers and of other students because they seldom learn much themselves and often make learning more difficult for everyone. They also tend to give low marks to the instructor and the course.

Some who begin as active resisters can be won over by good material and good trainers, and that is a win for everyone. Managers should know their own staff well enough to be able to guess the probable outcome. Most people do not learn what they do not want to learn, so some creative managers budget a certain amount of training for everyone but leave the choice of subject to the individual.

One kind of person you do want in training is someone who will grab onto new ideas and run with them. Even one such enthusiast in a class of twenty can make the whole process worthwhile. A would-be evangelist who is also a quick study can take even introductory material and put it to immediate use. I once was asked to review the work of a man who had attended a two-hour workshop I had given at a conference. On the basis of that brief introduction, he had his entire team designing more usable software.

WHY BOTHER?

In order to answer questions about whom to train and when, managers will also have to consider the question of why. Training can serve many purposes apart from imparting knowledge or building skills. Training can build teamwork and promote collaboration. When members of a project team go through training together, their experience with each other outside the normal job setting can contribute to a sense of identification and a spirit of cooperation. The shared vocabulary and common perspective on technical issues they acquire can also facilitate more effective teamwork.

Training is a form of communication that can convey a message beyond the content of the course. An investment in training can itself demonstrate that an organization values its staff members and takes an interest in their long-term professional development. Training can also communicate and promote specific technical values and objectives. A course in defect prevention can show—far more effectively than posters and imprinted coffee mugs—that management takes the matter of software quality assurance seriously. Of course, the message received may not always be the message intended. If management contracts for training, then fails to free participants from their other duties, it sends a clear message that the subject matter is of low priority.

Most managers want to see results from the money spent on training. If training is effective, it should change how developers work. To know whether anything has changed, to determine whether training has made a difference, you need to know concretely about the state of affairs before training. A skills inventory or benchmark before training can help management gauge progress and impact afterwards. An assessment can be as rough and rapid as a show of hands at a meeting to survey the level of interest, awareness, or knowledge regarding a subject, but more formal and systematic measurement has advantages. Upper management loves to see numbers. If you can show that a course made possible a 37% reduction in redundant data fields in a redesigned system, the odds of getting your next training budget approved are much improved.

> *If training is effective, it should measurably change how developers work.*

An assessment or benchmarking exercise before training commences becomes yet another part of the message. Measuring anything increases awareness and begins to affect the process. Measuring software defect injection rates draws the attention of developers to how mistakes are being made. Counting excess screen changes highlights the role of screens and context switching in user interface design. So, you should measure what you are interested in improving, then provide the training to improve it.

WHAT NEXT?

The most important day in any training program is the following Monday, when it begins to be clear whether the class was merely a change of pace or the prelude to change. What happens next is far and away the most important part of the entire training process. In my experience, training without effective follow-up seldom achieves more than a fraction of its intended or potential impact.

To make effective follow-up happen, you need to plan, schedule, and allocate resources. Many different forms of follow-up can be effective, but the most important rule is: do something! Training that is followed by business as usual or management indifference is training that is going nowhere.

Training should be followed up at intervals. Within the first week or two, managers should find some excuse for contacting all participants, if only to thank them for their participation or to remind them that more follow-up is to come. Within the first six months following training, all participants should be brought together at least once or twice for milestone meetings to review progress, raise questions, and explore areas for further training. If possible, the original trainers should return to answer questions at these meetings. Trainers can also be useful during inspections or walk-throughs and as presenters or facilitators at an experience-sharing workshop.

The benchmarking and measurement process that began before the training should continue after training. Not only should you be looking for a measurable impact, but the very process of monitoring sends, once more, a message: We are watching this, it matters to us, and we expect you to use what you learned.

Focused reviews, inspections, and walk-throughs are among the most powerful and efficient forms of follow-up to training. They should be started as soon as there is work to review. Group inspections and reviews can be focused on almost anything relevant from training. If the course was a program on user interface design, collaborative usability inspections of paper prototypes are appropriate; if the training covered component reuse in C++, code walk-throughs are the ticket.

Inspections and reviews accomplish multiple goals in a single process, keeping attention focused on the subject of the training while making it easier for groups to monitor their own success and progress in translating training into practice. Inspections and reviews expose problems in application and encourage the sharing of solutions and experiences. Inspections and reviews also provide a form of self-paced training since they help groups to correct errors and improve systems.

By including less-experienced participants, inspections and reviews can also serve to spread the wealth, exposing junior staff and others to new and better methods. To make a real difference in how software is developed in an organization, the skills and knowledge gained through training need to be deployed and dispersed—to be put into regular practice and gradually diffused through the organization. Like inspections and reviews, the most successful and cost-effective follow-up activities contribute to the spread of knowledge as well as its application.

Once some experience has been accumulated, it can be useful to hold a workshop to share it. The primary purpose of an experience workshop is to swap stories and trade troubles among those who have been trying to put training into practice. Such workshops help developers crystallize what they have learned about the pitfalls and the payoffs of the new practices and about what works and what does not. By gathering the training participants, you also recognize and support the community of practitioners and underscore the significance of what they know and are trying to accomplish. At the same time, you can spread the word and build momentum by inviting some newcomers and outsiders who did not take part in the training.

AND ON AND ON

If the size of your organization and the scope of the new practices warrant, you can start a newsletter or online discussion forum on the subject. Companies have created internal electronic or paper publications on things as varied as C++, object-oriented design, software metrics, and user interface design. Once training with a new language or tool is completed, you can launch an in-house user group or interest group or help connect graduates to ones outside. Groupware can be effective for promoting discussions, compiling FAQs, or posting calls for assistance. All such freelance and free-form channels promote communication and raise the visibility of the subject within the organization.

Official organizational sponsorship of workshops, conferences, publications, and interest groups reinforces the message that the training was not an end in itself but a means to improve processes and products. Not every group can organize a conference on applying usability metrics, for example, but even the smallest company can hold lunchtime discussions on the outcome of training. Reading groups that meet regularly to discuss books and articles on a subject can, for some people, help sustain interest over the long term and keep raising the level of knowledge.

It should be evident that training is not over when the last PowerPoint slide is done. Many questions will not arise until participants try to practice what has been preached. Managers who want to get the most from training should insist that trainers provide follow-up consultation to answer outstanding questions and to address the perplexities of real-world application. Trainers can take part in special meetings or workshops and meet with project teams to provide ongoing mentoring and monitoring.

In the long run, the goal of all legitimate teachers and consultants is to work themselves out of a job. In the long run, expertise in new technologies and practices needs to be internalized within your own organization. As a manager, one of your most important contributions to training success will be in identifying, enabling, and exploiting the internal evangelists and experts who develop. You need to find the nascent mentors who will pick up where the training left off and will continue to spread the word and the skills.

> *You need to identify, enable, and exploit the nascent mentors and evangelists who will pick up where training leaves off and will continue to spread the word and the skills.*

Once again, official acts backed by real resources communicate far more effectively than words. If you are trying to improve the usability and user interface design of your products, locate the most enthusiastic new expert on usage-centered design and make her the new Usability Czar or Usability Assurance Officer. Free her of half her duties, then turn her loose to wreak change.

The same rules apply to managing official structures. Take a careful look at organizational barriers and impediments to putting new learning into practice. If current procedures specify screen layout as part of the requirements definition, long before the newly trained usability engineers even see a project, then change the procedures. If you want to make usability testing an integral part of development, build it into the life cycle before you build the lab to do it. If you want to promote greater reuse of designs and components, then stop rewarding developers for reinventing the wheel.

In the end, the real measure of successful training is not knowledge acquired but knowledge applied.

Chapter 4

Maintaining Balance: Managing Working Relationships

Sue Petersen

I once wrote a column [Constantine, 1992] about "coding cowboys," those rebellious programmers who reject design discipline and eschew all modeling and methods. It was to become one of the most cited and controversial pieces I have ever written. Later, I gave a presentation at the Software Development Conference on how to manage such unmanageable mavericks. In the audience was Sue Petersen, who politely pointed out that this was not strictly a male-oriented phenomenon and then acknowledged being a coding cowgirl herself. I knew, or at least suspected, that the story was somewhat more complex than her public confession suggested. Although we had not met before, I knew Sue by reputation from exchanges in online forums, where she was a frequent and insightful contributor regarding the people side of programming. In the final analysis, Gantt charts and COCOMO and version control systems aside, software development management is about people—about the people we manage and about ourselves as people. In this chapter, Sue Petersen takes the stage herself to share some of her realizations about the balancing act that good managers, as people, must learn.

—Editor

There will always be some tension in the relationship between employer and employee, between boss and subordinate. Management wants workers who will be as productive as possible while consuming as few company resources as possible. Employees—"human resources" in business-speak—want to feel productive, appreciated, and well compensated. These goals do not necessarily conflict, but the potential is always present. As managers, we work where the rubber meets the road. How we balance the competing forces in this eternal tension will affect the management–employee relationship as well as the company bottom line.

Unfortunately, most of us have plenty of bad examples to follow. I once worked for a "screamer" who took out his aggressions on whomever was around whenever he felt like throwing a tantrum. He burned through almost as many secretaries as Murphy Brown! And he was certainly a big contrast to my first boss, who was nice to everybody regardless of the circumstances. Unfortunately, he went broke when some of his workers learned they could stretch their breaks to half a day. He laid them off eventually, of course, and he even managed to hang on for a few more years, but the damage was done, and he never did recover financially. Since then, I've worked with other managers who complimented me to my face, then cut me behind my back to anyone who would listen. They always seemed to wonder why their employees lacked motivation. I've also worked in places where everybody tried hard, but the structure of the organization was just wrong. People were unhappy, conflicted, and found themselves in battles that seemed to blow up out of nowhere. And, I must confess, I've done most of these things myself at one time or another.

Despite dramatically different styles, none of these managers was as effective as he could have been. Fortunately, I've also worked for and with people who told me what they really thought in ways that I could hear. They understood what they wanted out of our relationship and what they needed to provide me so that I could carry out my side of the bargain. They communicated clearly, without blaming or whining. They listened to my needs and wishes. They carried through on their commitments and made sure that I was made aware as soon as a potential problem arose. These experiences, although rare, have shown me that such relationships are possible, and I've even managed to emulate them a time or two.

Despite the titles of some graduate seminars, management is no science, and it may never be possible to create an Asimov-style psychohistory of management, but some basic psychological rules of thumb do govern how most people interact most of the time. Once I started to notice these principles in action, I found it easier to create working relationships that really worked, along with organizational structures that flowed rather than prevented work. In particular, I've found four lessons to be helpful.

DON'T GET TRIANGULATED

When things are tense at work, people often seem unwilling or unable to say the difficult things directly to others. Instead, they will tell a third party, who then will pass on the message to the intended recipient. In theory, this saves face and prevents hurt feelings or difficult confrontations. In theory. The reality is somewhat different, of course.

When I was a kid, we played a party game where the first person in line whispered a message to her neighbor, who tried to repeat the exact same message to the person next to her, and so on down the line. The last person in line said the message out loud, and we all giggled at how distorted it had become. Well, it's considerably less funny when the game gets played at work, where people's reputations and feelings are at stake.

Even as a manager, I can't control what other people talk about when I am not there. But I can control what I will listen to. A few years ago, consultant and author Gerald Weinberg heard me talking about a difficult situation at work. He suggested that I could simply refuse to listen when someone tried to tell me what others in the office were saying about me behind my back. Since nothing else was working, I decided to try his suggestion.

> *You can't control what other people say when you are not there, but you can control what you listen to.*

When I got back from the workshop, I carefully explained my decision. Everybody nodded and looked wise. Putting advice into practice proved a lot harder than expected, though, especially harder on other people. In fact, some people—particularly my friends—seemed compelled to let me know what others were saying. For example, one morning a coworker was so upset that she came to my office specifically to tell me what someone had said. We discussed the fact that she was upset, and I told her that I was sorry she was upset, but I did not want to hear what someone else thought about me. She listened; she even agreed that I was wise. But she was *so* frustrated that, as she got ready to leave, she hovered near my door, blurted out the phrase, and then ran out the door and down the hall.

After I picked my jaw up off the floor, I started to think about what goes on when people repeat office gossip. A sociology professor of mine once defined politics as "the process of distributing scarce resources." Since very few organizations will ever have all the resources they will ever need, this means that office politics will always be with us. Whether we like it or not, people will disagree, people will compete, and people will form alliances against common enemies. Gossip is a very human attempt to highlight common goals and cement alliances.

Unfortunately, in the process, gossip can paralyze an organization. We can, however, minimize the harm it does by controlling the way we communicate. The parlor game we played as kids demonstrates how a message is distorted as it is passed from one person to another. If the message is important, if it really matters to me what someone thinks about me, I need to talk directly to that person. I simply cannot afford what happens when the message is passed through a third party.

It follows, then, that if I have anything truly important to say to someone, I need to communicate it directly. I once hired the friend of an employee as a new secretary. Although somewhat young and unsure of herself, she proved to be a good worker. When she started thinking about a raise, she went to her friend instead of to me. Her friend, in turn, came to me to tell me how upset my secretary was. This knocked me off balance, and I started to feel defensive because I had not noticed how long she'd been working for her starting salary. Luckily, I had by then had some practice in avoiding triangulation, and I was able to recognize the potential pitfalls in this situation. I checked my understanding of the message with my secretary directly and learned that she was more puzzled than angry. I pointed out the miscommunications to both coworkers and explained that I would not discuss my secretary's raise with anybody except her. This policy has done a lot to reduce misunderstandings in the office.

> *If you have anything truly important to say to someone, you need to communicate it directly.*

KNOW WHEN TO LET GO

Once we start to clear up the gossip and interpersonal problems, we are left with our own personal issues. Some people seem to believe that it is always someone else, somebody "out there," who is responsible for ensuring happiness. ("It's the boss's fault, the company's fault, my wife's fault. . . .") In my view, if I want to feel in control of my life, I need to take responsibility for my own job satisfaction. In one online forum, my colleague, consultant Dale Emery, offered a contemporary management variant on Fritz Perls's famous "Gestalt Prayer."

> I choose to be here.
> I will stay as long as working with you meets my needs.
> While I am here, I will try to support you.
> If I am not getting what I need, I will make a change.
> I may change myself in some way.
> I may ask you to change, and will respect and accept your response.
> I may choose to change our relationship and stop working with you.

The central element here is balance. In order to live by Dale's philosophy, I must be able to balance myself and my needs, the people around me and their needs, and the context, the world we all share. First, I must be aware of my own needs. As any frequent airline passenger knows, I must be able to take care of myself, without guilt or remorse, before I can take care of those around me. Then I must be aware of other people. I must be able to recognize, without feeling angry or threatened, when they have needs of their own. I must know how to negotiate fairly when our goals conflict. I must be willing to compromise when I can do so without undue cost to myself. And I must be willing to walk away, without blame or anger, when we are unable to resolve the conflict.

I've come close to this ideal a few times in my own life. It always seems to happen at those times when I am able to step back and separate my emotional reactions from what is going on around me. I remember times when something threatening happened and I reacted with fear and anger, but I was able to pause inside just long enough to realize that my anger wasn't helpful. Once I achieved that moment of balance, I could find a way to put my anger and fear aside and to react in a more useful, centered way.

> *You must be able to balance yourself and your needs with the people around you and their needs.*

PRACTICE THE PRESENT

It is easier to describe balance than it is to be balanced. Luckily, there are plenty of ways to practice balance. Practitioners of the martial arts call it "finding your center"; consulting guru Gerald Weinberg calls it being congruent. Aikido, tennis, horse riding, and many other sports can teach you how to center yourself physically. Once you learn the physical skills, the mental benefits can follow. My colleague Sharon Marsh Roberts explains it this way:

> When I ski, I focus better on what's happening "right now." I find that doubly true when I climb rocks. When I'm fifty feet from the ground, and I'm trying to place a piece of protection, I know what I'm doing and why.
>
> That's in opposition to much of life. I may drift from one future moment to another, not focused on the present. Or I may be in the past, reliving a conversation. But I'm not always here, now.
>
> Lesson? I get a lesson that being present, being balanced, allows one to tend to needs that truly exist, rather than ones which do not. I can better focus on what my team needs if I can hear what they tell me.

BROADEN YOUR BASE

One of the quickest ways to improve your balance is to widen your base of support. I work in a family business, and especially in this environment, it is fatally easy to start relying on just a few people for advice. After all, who else knows my world as well as my family and coworkers? The flaw in that reasoning is that the people closest to me every day are also the ones most likely to share my blind spots. Nine years ago I discovered CompuServe and then the Internet. There I met people from around the world who share many of the same problems, interests, and goals that I have. The very fact that my cyber-friends do not share my daily experiences makes them a better audience off of which to bounce my problems. Seminars, workshops, industry trade groups, and consultants can often serve the same purpose. So, to a certain extent, can books and trade magazines.

STAYING IN BALANCE

Balance is not a frozen posture. No matter how well I avoid being triangulated, learn how to let go, practice the present, and broaden my base of support, something will occasionally come along to knock me off center. But I'm slowly learning to celebrate these moments of uncertainty. As long as I remember how to waver and to recover, I can exploit the creativity and the potential for learning in the tension that surrounds me. And that's good for my company, it's good for my coworkers, and it's good for me.

Chapter 5

Job Qualifications: On Hiring the Best

Larry Constantine

Every software development manager knows that one way to get the best results is to start with the best people. According to recent figures from consultant Howard Rubin, the average productivity of American programmers is less than 8,000 lines of code per year, and if you look at actual delivered functionality, as measured by Function Points [Albrecht and Gaffney, 1983], it's declining. However, if you hire the very best, they could be 10 to 20 times as productive as the average developer—and, if you are lucky, they will command only twice the salary, or so the data suggest. But who are the best people and what are their qualifications? How do you know them if and when they walk in the door?

—Editor

When I interviewed at C-E-I-R in 1963, it was one of the leading consulting firms of the day. So how did the people there know to hire me? How was department head Jack Cremeans able to look at the brash college dropout sitting across from him and see not an overconfident and underexperienced programmer but a promising professional? I remember that he and Ken Mackenzie asked me more questions about good programming practice than about what languages I knew or what applications I had written. But what exactly were they looking for and how did they know whether I had it?

I also recall, with some embarrassment, that I tried to bluff my way through a question about an obscure variant of an instruction on the IBM 1401 that could be used to facilitate argument passing to subroutines. I hadn't a clue. Much later, I asked Jack why he had hired me even though he must have known that I was making it up as I went along. He said that he was more interested in the thought processes than the answer. He figured that I would learn the nitty-gritty quickly enough.

He was right, in part because I had good teachers. Under the tutelage of Ken, Dave Jasper, and Bud Vitoff, I did learn. I learned not only about the craft of programming but also about the value of thinking, particularly regarding the principles on which good programming is based. When I returned to MIT to resume my interrupted studies, I continued my investigations, trying to understand what constituted best practice and contributed to sound software.

FOUNDATION CLASS

These distant events may not, at first glance, seem to have much bearing on hiring and programming practices in software development today, but, as historian-commentator James Burke might argue, there is a connection. Perhaps I am in such a retrospective mood in part because of the twenty-fifth anniversary of the publication of a paper that was to alter my career and, some would say, the course of programming history.

In May 1974, the *IBM Systems Journal* published "Structured Design," the paper that summarized and finally gave a name to what I had learned about good programming and design and had spent more than a decade trying to make comprehensible [Stevens, Myers, and Constantine, 1974]. That widely reprinted and much cited article introduced an expanded audience to many of the basics of modern software development practice.

Structured design did not, however, spring suddenly from the ground, fully formed in 1974. The foundations had been laid much earlier. The basic methods, models, and concepts were already well developed when I presented a paper at the National Symposium on Modular Programming in 1968, the same year that the ACM published Edsgar Dijkstra's duly famed letter on the harmfulness of go–tos [Dijkstra, 1968]. In my archives are documents going back to 1966 describing notational innovations that have stood the test of time. Those little arrows indicating information flow in the recently minted Unified Modeling Language (UML), for instance, come from structured design by way of the Unified Object Notation developed by Meilir Page-Jones, Steven Weiss, and myself [Page-Jones, Weiss, and Constantine, 1990].

Is this truly ancient stuff still relevant today? The average shelf life of books in our field is just over two years. Can anything that is more than a quarter century old mean something to you as a development manager? Well, you can still find the book *Structured Design* in bookstores, unrevised after more than two decades. Why? Open almost any current textbook or popular book on programming, design, software engineering, or even development management, turn to the index, and the odds are that you will find references to coupling and cohesion even if you do not find mention of Constantine or Yourdon or Stevens or Myers. The fact that the terms are increasingly used without attribution or citation demonstrates that they have passed from coinages to become coin of the realm. Why?

Although it has been said that I invented structured design, it is more accurate to say that I invented a way of talking about design. In many respects, the concepts and techniques are simply software development best practices distilled. The best developers design their software systematically to increase the cohesion of individual components and reduce the coupling between them. This was true in 1963, and it is still true today.

In this age of object-orientation and the dawning of the so-called Unified Process, it is unlikely that many developers still practice orthodox structured design, and even fewer would admit it. But good developers will understand and apply the underlying principles, keeping the sundry parts of their programs distinct and independent, pulling together what is strongly related so these can be used as a coherent unit, and organizing the overall structure in a rational way that reflects the nature of the problem being solved. Whether you call the resulting collections subroutines or object classes, whether you write in Fortran or Java, this stuff is simple, basic motherhood and apple pie. Reduce coupling and enhance cohesion. Who could argue otherwise?

> *Good developers, now as ever, understand and apply underlying principles, keeping the sundry parts of their programs distinct and independent, pulling together what is strongly related to be used as a coherent unit, and organizing the whole in a rational way that reflects the nature of the problem.*

The core of structured design is, after all, design. You design what you build before you build it. You design it so the overall architecture makes sense. You design it so the pieces hide and encapsulate the appropriate bits of code and data. Except for the smallest and most uncomplicated problems, you cannot achieve this merely by cutting code, hoping to discover where to chop it up or how to connect it all together along the way. Architecture precedes carpentry, in software as well as buildings.

THE REDMOND WAY

Sooner or later, after enough failures and near disasters, nearly everyone learns these basic truths. In *Microsoft Secrets*, Michael Cusumano and Richard Selby

(1995) quote development manager Ben Slivka who, in recounting the sad consequences of complex interdependencies, finally added, "We should make all team members have practice at object-oriented design, focusing on data-hiding and minimal interfaces, to ensure that code will be modular, decoupled, and maintainable." Laudable sentiments indeed, if but they were practiced.

Slivka goes on to suggest brief training in these software engineering fundamentals, which leaves me wondering: Is the two to four weeks he advocates enough? And why didn't his developers know and practice these good practices in the first place? Which returns us to the issue of hiring the best people.

HIRING BIASES

Consultant and former Microsoft manager John Rae-Grant once told me that he first became aware of the tacit bias in Microsoft hiring practices when he took a workshop with an outside consulting group. He realized that Microsoft's interview style, which stressed quick, on-your-feet decision making and rapid-fire responses, tended to reject people who are more systematic, thoughtful, and thorough.

> *An interview style that stresses quick, on-your-feet decision making and rapid-fire responses tends to reject people who are more systematic, thoughtful, and thorough.*

I cannot attest to the accuracy of this characterization of their hiring methods—I've never applied for a position at Microsoft and there is good reason to doubt that they would be interested—but I can say that such practices would be in keeping with what I have learned about the working culture at Microsoft, a culture that is, by all evidence, strongly shaped from the top down.

In their book, Cusumano and Selby quote Bill Gates himself as saying, "There's no 'design,' in the sense of how the code works, that's ever done in program management." Another manager, Chris Peters, explained that Microsoft uses little or no design documentation. "A developer's job is to write code that we sell, not to spend time writing high-level design documents." And Gates confirms this, rejecting any "methodology where you have a document that's independent from the source code. . . . Going off and spending a lot of time on that—that's ridiculous. . . . One document. One. It's the source code."

So, does Microsoft design or not? What is "undocumented design?" The same Ken Mackenzie who played a role in hiring me in the first place—and then tried to teach me the difference between coding and software development—put it succinctly in the form of what he modestly called Mackenzie's First Law: If it isn't written down, it doesn't exist. Undocumented design is no design at all. You cannot design anything of nontrivial proportions without putting pencil to paper or mouse to pad. That is the fundamental reality behind every design notation and modeling tool from data flow diagrams all the way through to use cases and the UML.

As I write this, I realize, once again, that I leave myself open to charges of bashing Microsoft, but that is certainly not my intention. I point to Microsoft precisely because it is so often held up as the paragon of success. At conferences, developers often begin their questions or challenges with, "But Microsoft does such and such." Whole books have been written about the Microsoft way, about the methods of development and management that are the supposed secrets of its success. If the folks at Microsoft are so successful, it is argued, it must be because they are doing something right, so let's all emulate them.

In my opinion, however, Microsoft has been so successful largely because it has been in the right places at the right times and has ruthlessly and relentlessly pursued advantage, not because it produces great software and certainly not because it exemplifies best practices. Microsoft is about selling code more than it is about writing code, and there is no argument that they do a good job of selling. Hiring people to write code to sell is, of course, not necessarily the same as hiring people to design and build durable, usable, dependable software.

> *Hiring people to write code to sell is not the same as hiring people to design and build durable, usable, dependable software.*

Spending time designing and documenting design is "ridiculous" only if you do not count the time wasted later on trying to work around all the mistakes in partitioning the problem or fixing the thousands of bugs that might have been avoided in the first place by planning how things will fit together. It is time wasted only if you do not have to account for the thousands of hours wasted by your customers due to lost work or applications that freeze up several times a day. If what you are selling is code, not solutions, only the code counts. If what you are measuring and interested in is quick answers to coding questions, then the coders who crank out the most lines of code by going directly from concept to code are the ones you want.

In all fairness, even the Microsoft megalith is not a cultural monolith. Ben Slivka, the development manager quoted by Cusumano and Selby, seems to have learned his lesson, and a *Wall Street Journal* article on Windows 2000 honcho Jim

Allchin (4 February 1999, pages B1 and B10) suggests that, he, too, may be trying to create a more sober culture focused on sound architecture. We can only wish him well. Cultural change is a slow process, and he has to contend with the gung-ho hackers and commando coders (see Chapter 37) who already work there. Only time will tell if these are the best people for such an environment.

So, how do you pick the applicants who would be the best? What might I ask developers applying for a position with me? I would ask them about some of the latest hot topics in development, but I would also ask about "the old stuff." I would ask them how they know where to put the code for a particular feature or bit of functionality. I would ask them what they do to try to make their programs easier to debug, maintain, and modify. I would ask them how they decide upon and describe the architecture—the overall organization—of a large program. If they used the terms *coupling* and *cohesion,* I'd ask them to explain what those words meant to them. But even if they did not, I would expect them to understand and apply such fundamental ways of thinking in their work. I would want to see not only some of their code but also how they documented it.

I would probably give bonus points to candidates who said to some of my questions, "Let me think about that for a bit," or, "This is a complex issue with subtle trade-offs that need to be thoroughly considered." If they started sketching ideas on the whiteboard or doodling on my desk pad, I would probably hire them on the spot!

Chapter 6

Problem-Solving Metarules: Habits of Productive People

Larry Constantine

One way or another, most of us who work in software development are in the solution business. Our profession is problem solving. Of course, we may think of it differently. My company, for instance, specializes in product usability. However, whether we are creating the slides for a training program, designing the user interface for an industrial automation system, or organizing the content and navigation for an e-commerce site on the Web, our real job is solving problems. In our business of delivering usability solutions, we are often constrained by impossible and unalterable deadlines yet mandated to produce breakthrough solutions—on time and within budget. What do you do to produce genuine innovations on demand? It's all a matter of habit.

—Editor

Whatever you do often enough and well enough you will eventually learn at a level that goes beyond the boundaries of ordinary technical know-how or professional skill. The best problem solvers learn the tacit logic of creative problem solving itself, whether or not they are conscious of the axioms and rules of this logic. There are patterns in those processes that efficiently lead to good solutions, regardless of the nature of the problems or the domain within which they are being pursued. After years of building insight into complex problems and producing creative and practicable solutions, conscious practice is transformed into efficient habits—habitual styles and modes of working that spell the difference between those who are only good at something and those who are really good at it.

When I am asked about the secrets of our successes, I usually reply there are no secrets; it's problem solving, not rocket science. However, a few years ago I started turning some of the unconscious habits of productive problem solvers into aphorisms that might be shared with others. These are not so much rules for a particular method as they are metarules for effective problem solving in general. In the popular idiom of our day, we would cast these as "patterns" along the lines established by the so-called pattern movement. They would still be just metarules for problem solving, so I will not try to expand and rewrite them into something else. My hope is that they may help others become more effective solution providers. Because there are so many of these process metarules, I am going to focus this chapter on a particularly powerful subset: metarules that help keep us from wasting time when there is no time to waste.

GETTING UNSTUCK

Individuals and project teams can get stuck in numerous ways, but most commonly they are either stalled or spinning their wheels. It is important to understand the difference between these difficulties so you can pick the most effective tactics for getting unstuck.

You know you are stalled when you draw a blank, when no one has any ideas of where to start or how to proceed. Long silences around a conference table, serious doodling that threatens to wear through the paper, or blank stares at a display screen are all indicators of mental stall-out. Writer's block, which every columnist facing a deadline and every would-be Ellison or Vonnegut knows well, is a prime example, but you don't have to be a writer to be familiar with the feeling. Time slows, the tick of the clock—real or imagined—becomes the loudest sound in the room, and the sense of doom heightens with every passing minute.

When you are stalled in a car, you need to restart the engine. If the battery is dead, you need a jump start. The process metarule that applies to being stalled is simple.

■ *Start Somewhere*

It is easy for software people to become obsessive about starting at the beginning or doing things in the right order. However, when it comes to problem solving, doing anything—even the "wrong" thing—is almost invariably better than doing nothing. Authors who write for a living usually have a whole kit bag of personal tricks for overcoming writer's block. Word processing has ushered in an array of new tricks owing to the flexibility of the medium and the ease of editing and rewriting. If you are stuck for an opener, you can write the conclusion first, then construct the arguments that get you there. You can jump into the middle, even plunging into topics without knowing where they will ultimately fit. They can always be rearranged later to form the story you need to tell.

> *In problem solving, doing anything—even the "wrong" thing—is almost invariably better than doing nothing.*

Programming, software engineering, user interface design, and the sundry skills that come into play in producing software all have their variations for overcoming inertia. Despite what the advocates of process maturity and formal methodology will tell you, it is not always necessary that you start at the beginning. It *is* necessary that you start somewhere. If you fail to get the project moving, it will rapidly become irrelevant that you were stalled in the right place.

In usage-centered design [Constantine and Lockwood, 1999], for instance, the modeling process is "supposed" to begin with the roles users play in relation to a system. If that draws a blank, however, why not start with something you do know or understand? You can sketch out some tasks that you are confident must be supported by the system. Not only are you doing something, rather than doing nothing, but—surprise, surprise—you will often find yourself inspired to fill in some of the blanks regarding your users.

Because software developers love problems, they often tackle the really interesting and messy stuff first. It's more fun! As a rule, however, progress will be smoother and swifter if you proceed from areas you know and understand and push the boundaries slowly out or back into areas that are less well known or understood.

■ Begin With What You Know

Of course, there are situations in which you are so lost that there is no familiar ground on which to stand, no home base from which to launch your explorations. Then you have to create what you know out of thin air, and for that there are two preeminent techniques.

Brainstorming, familiar to nearly every citizen of the developed world, is the preferred and obvious way to jump-start a stalled problem-solving process. The freewheeling and uncensored atmosphere of tossing out ideas without debate or discussion is just what is needed. In fact, brainstorming incorporates into its procedures another of the great process metarules.

■ Create Before You Critique

Separating out the generation of ideas from their review and refinement accelerates problem solving of any ilk. Criticizing, highlighting the constraints and limitations, searching out the problems, and pointing out the downside are all important parts of producing good solutions, but when you are already standing still, slowing things down hardly makes sense. Besides, we are all better at critical analysis when we have something to critique. So build the ideas, the proposed solutions, before you start tearing them apart.

> *Build the ideas, the proposed solutions, before you start tearing them apart.*

I did say there were two jump-start techniques. Brainstorming is the lively right-brain variant, but there is also a more methodical technique to appeal to our logical faculties. Let's call it blank-filling. Blank-filling is like generating your own forms or checklists. To move ahead, you need to know what you don't know, so that is the starting point—you list what you don't know. You can structure the process by labeling two sheets with "What we don't know!" and "What we know!" After the lists are complete, you can either proceed from what you know or start filling in the blanks on the other sheet. Either way, you are no longer stalled.

CIRCLE GAME

If you watch software development professionals enough, you realize that we in this business have a tendency to spend a lot of time spinning our wheels. Wheel spinning can be a solo activity or a team sport. You can sit staring at your screen for hours as you go back and forth between alternative ways to resolve some programming problem, or you can join with coworkers and turn a half-hour design briefing into a three-hour shouting match. Time spent going in circles does not advance the project. Debates without resolution and discussions that lead nowhere do not bring the team closer to meeting its deadline.

Because so much of the work my company does is conducted under heavy time pressure, we often find ourselves invoking what we have come to regard as the foremost among process metarules.

■ *Don't Spin Your Wheels*

A car that is stuck on ice or up to its hubcaps in mud gets nowhere fast as long as the wheels are spinning. A project team caught in a go-round over the best way to organize the start-up screen is going nowhere.

You know you are spinning your wheels as soon as you start repeating yourself. When the same arguments are being met with the same counterarguments, when you find yourself reviewing the same materials without new insight or understanding, you know you are spinning your wheels. Under the pressure of modern accelerated, time-boxed development cycles, there is no time for spinning your wheels. So don't.

As soon as we recognize that we are spinning our wheels, we stop—and do something else. We move on without resolving the issue if the nature of the problem and the process allows. Or we switch streams and work on another problem or another part of the same problem. Or we switch gears, deliberately speeding up or slowing down the process in the effort to get a grip on the problem.

> **As soon as you recognize that you are spinning your wheels, stop. Then do something else.**

We often see wheel spinning when design teams first try to apply a new modeling technique to user interface design. Around and around they go, without stopping and without progress. When we recognize this state, we draw the team's attention to it and suggest the simple process metarule. Suddenly, a mental lightbulb is lit and progress can begin again.

Whatever you do when you and your teammates find yourself spinning your wheels, the essential thing is to stop spinning them and do something else. What we usually suggest, to continue the automotive similes, is to back up, shift gears, or try a different route. Sometimes your wheels are spinning now because of what you didn't do earlier. You need to backtrack and see what you can do to get more information or refine the work. Sometimes the wheels spin because you are going too fast or too slow. In complex problems, progress can often be achieved by ignoring details, by skipping over unresolved issues, or by practicing that grand technique we consultants call "suitable vagueness." But sooner or later the details need to be detailed and the unresolved issues resolved; otherwise you keep spinning your wheels in the muck.

Alternatively, you may be spinning your wheels because you are obsessing over minutiae or worrying a problem to a premature death. Then you need to speed up, leap forward over the piddling matters, and move on to the next solid issue.

Most often, however, the best course is to take another course. Attack a different problem, work on another model, explore an unrelated issue. If you are mired in the mud of trying to construct the narrative bodies of your use cases, you can work on the map that gives an overview instead. If your data model is being churned to death, work on the search strategies and algorithms.

Another time-waster is solving problems that are not part of the problem, which is especially undesirable when time and budget are tight. "Oh, we never do that," you are probably thinking. What about all those clever features you dream up to toss into the next release, features that are not in the specs and that nobody has requested? The truth is that programmers love to program, so they are more than happy to think up new things to program. Often without awareness, they will invent interesting challenges to be overcome.

■ Solve Problems, Don't Create Them

Some design teams are particularly adept at taking problems that are already difficult enough and expanding them through creative feature creep into bloated monsters. You may have seen some of their software.

> *Some teams are particularly adept at taking difficult problems and expanding them through creative feature creep into impossibly bloated monstrosities.*

Of course, sometimes the problems are already so enormous, so overwhelming in their complexity, that you have no idea at all where to start, much less what to add. Sometimes, faced with dead end after dead end, you can become so discouraged that you are ready to give up and walk away from it all. That urge to give up, to surrender in some way, sometimes points to the best way to cope. The last of our process metarules could be phrased in many ways—give up, go away, set it aside—but I'll express it in my favored mode.

■ Sleep on It

I do some of my best work at night—not in the evening marathons that are one of the exhilarating but exhausting hallmarks of running a multinational operation from a home office—but after I finally go to bed and fall asleep. I have come to trust the workings of all those unconscious search and retrieval functions, those irrational little engines of reasoning scattered around the brain. Time and time again, I have gone to sleep with an unsolved problem on my mind, only to awake the next morning with the dawn of a new idea or a fresh approach.

I now know that I can rely on background processing to solve the seemingly insoluble, so I will deliberately turn the toughest nuts to be cracked over to that network of little subprocessors that keep chugging away while I go about other business or get some sleep. How many times have you struggled to remember a name, given up, then ten minutes later suddenly gotten a mental priority interrupt when the name comes to you? In the interim, your myriad little concurrent processing demons have been scurrying around without supervision or awareness to get you the answer.

So, stuck without a solution, I will often assign it to the unconscious. I take a moment to review and restate the problem to myself, then I give it over to background processing. I do not puzzle over it or keep poking at it. I know that sometime in the next day or two I will be about to take a bite of lasagna or will awaken after a good night's sleep and there it will be—the solution or the germ of a solution.

Software specialists are skeptics, for the most part, distrustful of intuition or the unconscious. When working in a project team, I might just suggest that a difficult problem be put on the back burner, that we not worry about it now but see if anything turns up. It works. In the meantime, we are working on some other part of the problem and making progress there, so we can't lose.

In fact, you probably are facing a tough software problem right now. Maybe you should take a nap.

PART II

Project Management

Among the many aspects of managing software and Web development, project management issues loom largest. Will we finish on time? How will we ever finish? How far along are we? How much will it cost? How can we finish the project faster? Cheaper? Better? How can we tell when we are getting into trouble? Appropriately, this is the largest section of the book. It begins with a compact primer on project management basics and ends with how best we can learn our lessons when projects fail. In between, eleven leaders in the field offer project management perspectives on a full gamut of special issues, including sponsorship, productivity, data integrity, usability, creativity, collaboration, outsourcing, customer relations, and how to tell when failure looms on the horizon.

Chapter 7

First Things First: A Project Manager's Primer

Karl Wiegers

Shifting from problem solving to project management, in this chapter Karl Wiegers offers us a kind of McGuffey's Reader *for new software development managers. Like the authors of famous grammar-school texts of the nineteenth century, Wiegers sets a high moral tone, spelling out the basic virtues that effective software managers must master for long-term success and exhorting them to put first things first. Although addressed to the new manager, even those who have been through the mill of multiple projects may find in this primer a useful review of the important basics that may help them gauge their progress and fill in the gaps within their project management repertoires. If nothing else, there is much here to which we can all nod in enthusiastic agreement.*

—Editor

Everyone has to start someplace, even software development managers. You may have approached the prospect with anxiety or unalloyed anticipation, but one day you find yourself "promoted" from the engineering or programming staff to a software project lead or team leader position. Whether management is your chosen career path or you have only reluctantly agreed to give it a try, you have probably received little education in the arts of project and people management. In those first anxious days, it would be handy to have a primer that would help you put first things first and keep you focused on actions that will improve both your own effectiveness and that of your team.

SET PRIORITIES

First, you need to set your priorities as a manager. While you may be tempted to remain heavily engaged in software development activities, which may even still be in your job description, you now have a new set of responsibilities. Many new managers cannot resist the lure of staying technically active, which can lead them to neglect the needs of others on the project team who look to them for help.

Effective leaders know their top priority is to provide services to their team. These services include coaching and mentoring, resolving problems and conflicts, providing resources, setting project goals and priorities, and providing technical guidance when appropriate. Team members need to know you are always available to help them. I find it valuable to think of myself as working for the people I supervise, not the reverse. Team members who need something from you are a non-maskable interrupt over almost anything else you might be doing.

> *The top priority is providing services to your team, including coaching and mentoring, resolving problems and conflicts, setting goals, and providing technical guidance when appropriate.*

Your second priority is to satisfy your organization's customers. As a manager, you no longer personally provide the products and services that satisfy customers. Instead, you must create an environment that enables your team to meet the needs of customers effectively.

Your third priority should be to work on your own projects. These may be either technical projects or activities requested by your own managers, such as serving on planning committees. Be prepared to postpone these activities when they conflict with the two higher priorities.

Explicitly taking actions to please your own managers should be your lowest priority. Unless you work in a Dilbert-style organization, your managers will be thrilled if you are successful at the three most important priorities. Even if you are not so fortunate, at least strive to keep the most important responsibilities of your new job at the top of your list. Instead of going out of your way to satisfy those above you, focus on helping your team members be as effective—and as happy—as possible.

INTO THE GAP

Regardless of your preparation, you may perceive some gaps in your current leadership and management skills. Your strong technical background was probably a factor in your being selected for the leadership role, but you'll need some additional skills to be fully effective. Take an honest inventory of your strengths and shortcomings in critical people and project skills, and begin closing any gaps.

Software developers aren't usually noted for their superlative people skills. You may need to become more adroit at interpersonal relationships, conflict resolution, persuasion, and selling ideas. You'll have to be able to deal with varied situations, ranging from hiring and firing staff to negotiating schedules to having someone crying in your office during a performance review.

As technical team members, we may have enjoyed the luxury of energetically pushing our own agendas. However, effective management often requires a more collaborative and receptive interpersonal style. It took me awhile to learn how and when to channel my natural assertiveness. I found it valuable to start my management career with a listening-skills class. What I learned has been useful in many situations.

> *Team members may have the luxury of pushing their own agendas, but project managers need a more collaborative and receptive style.*

Next, you may need to step behind the podium and improve your presentation skills. If you are really uncomfortable with public speaking, a Dale Carnegie course might be helpful. Practice what you learn through such training, and you will find that your enhanced communication ability will serve you well in any job you hold in the future.

As a project leader, you are responsible for coordinating the work of others, for planning and tracking projects, and for taking corrective actions when necessary to get a project back on track. Take a training course in project management, and begin reading books and articles on project and risk management. Join the Project Management Institute (*www.pmi.org*) and read their monthly magazine, *PM Network*. The Software Capability Maturity Model (Software Engineering Institute, 1995) contains much useful advice on software project planning and project tracking. Your ability to set priorities, conduct effective meetings, and communicate clearly will have a substantial impact on your effectiveness as a manager.

QUALITY BY ANY NAME

Almost everyone takes quality seriously and wants to produce high-quality products. However, there is no universal definition of what quality means in software. Debates rage about "good enough" software versus more orthodox views of software quality. To help steer your group toward success, spend some time working with your team members and your customers to understand what quality means to them.

These two communities often do not have the same definition in mind, so it's easy to end up working at cross-purposes. A manager focused on the delivery schedule may be impatient with an engineer who wants to formally inspect every line of code. A customer to whom reliability is paramount won't be happy receiving a product piled with seldom used features and also riddled with bugs. A spiffy new graphical user interface might turn off a user whose fingers have memorized how to use the previous version of the product most efficiently.

> *Team members and customers often have different definitions of quality, so it's easy to end up working at cross-purposes.*

To better understand their views of software quality, customers, who were fellow employees, were invited with their managers to an open forum on this topic by my group back at Kodak. This forum showed where our group's ideas of quality did not match the perceptions of those who used our products. Understanding such differences can help you focus energy where it will yield the greatest customer benefit, not just where it will provide the greatest developer satisfaction.

Traditional interpretations of software quality include conformance to specifications, satisfaction of customer needs, and the absence of defects in code and documentation. The buzz phrase of "six-sigma quality" may set a very high bar for low defect density or frequency of failure, but it doesn't address other dimensions of quality, such as timeliness, usability, rich feature sets, and delivered value for the price. We might hope to maximize all of these characteristics in the products we produce and purchase, but trade-offs are always necessary.

During the requirements phase on one project, we listed ten quality attributes we thought would be important to users: qualities such as efficiency, interoperability, correctness, and ease of learning. We asked a group of key customer representatives to rate the desirability of each of these attributes. Once we understood which attributes were most significant, we could design the application to achieve those objectives. If you do not learn what quality means to your customers and then design to deliver that level of quality, you are simply trusting to luck.

One telling indicator of quality is that the customer comes back, but the product does not. Work with your customers and developers to define appropriate quality goals for each product. Once determined, make these quality objectives unambiguous priorities. Lead by example, setting very high personal standards for the quality of your own work. You might adopt the motto, "Strive for perfection, but settle for excellence."

RECOGNIZE PROGRESS

Recognizing and rewarding the achievements of your team members are important ways to keep staff motivated. Unless your group already has a recognition program in place, this should be one of your top priorities. Recognition can range from the symbolic (certificates, traveling trophies) to the tangible (movie coupons, restaurant gift certificates, cash bonuses). Presenting recognition of some kind says, "Thanks for what you did to help," or "Congratulations on reaching that milestone." By investing a small amount of thought and money in a recognition and reward program, you can buy a lot of goodwill and future cooperation. Remember to recognize people outside the development group, too, including customer representatives and support people who contribute in special ways to the project's success.

Talk to your team members to understand the sorts of recognition and rewards they find meaningful. Make recognition—for accomplishments large and small—a cornerstone of your team culture. Equally important is the implicit recognition of showing sincere interest in the work being done by each team member and doing all you can to remove obstacles to effectiveness. Recognition is one way to demonstrate to your team members that you are aware of and appreciate the contributions they make to the success of the team.

LEARN FROM THE PAST

It's possible that some of the projects undertaken by your group in the past were not completely successful. Even on successful projects, we can often identify things we would do differently next time. As you embark on your new leadership role, take some time to understand the struggles encountered in earlier projects, and plan to avoid repeating the same mistakes. Software development is too hard for each manager to take the time to make every possible mistake on his or her own. Jump-start your own success by learning from what has worked before—and from what has failed.

> *Take time to understand the struggles of earlier projects. There is not enough time for you to make every possible mistake on your own.*

Begin with a nonjudgmental assessment of the last few projects undertaken by your group, whether successful or not. Your goal is not to determine blame but to do a better job on future projects. Conduct a post-project review (sometimes called a *postmortem*) to learn what went well and what could have been done better. Lead the team in brainstorming sessions or use an impartial facilitator to analyze each current project in the same way at major milestones.

In addition, become well-acquainted with established software industry best practices. A good place to start is with Part III of the Jolt Award–winning book, *Rapid Development* [McConnell, 1996], which describes 27 such best practices. Beware of repeating the 36 classic software development mistakes McConnell describes. Your team members may resist new ways of working, but your role as leader is to ensure that the team consistently applies the best available methods, processes, and tools. Actively facilitate the sharing of information among team members so local best practices can become a part of every developer's tool kit.

IMPROVEMENT GOALS

Once you've conducted a retrospective analysis of previous projects and determined what "quality" means to your group, set some goals for both short- and long-term improvements. Goals should be quantified whenever possible, so you can select a few simple metrics that will indicate whether you are making adequate progress toward the goals.

For example, if you've determined that projects are often late because of volatile requirements, you might set a goal to improve the requirements stability by 50% within six months. Such a goal requires that you actually count the number of requirements changes per week or month, understand their origins, and take actions to control those changes. This will likely require alterations in the way you interact with those who supply the requirements changes.

Your goals and metrics make up part of the software process improvement program you should put into place. It's fashionable these days to disdain "process" as the last refuge of uncreative bureaucrats. The reality, though, is that every group can find ways to improve the work it performs. Indeed, if you continue to work the way you always have, you shouldn't expect to achieve any better results than you have before.

> *It's fashionable to disdain "process" as the last refuge of uncreative bureaucrats, but every group can find ways to improve the work it performs.*

There are two compelling reasons to improve your processes: to correct problems and to prevent problems. Make sure your improvement efforts align with known or anticipated threats to the success of your projects. Lead your team in an exploration of the strengths and shortcomings of the practices currently being used and of the risks facing your projects.

My group held a two-session brainstorming exercise to identify barriers to improving our software productivity and quality. In session one, the participants wrote their thoughts about this topic on sticky notes, one idea per note. A facilitator collected and grouped the ideas as they were generated. At the end, we had a dozen major categories, which we then recorded on large flip-chart sheets.

In the second session, the same participants wrote ideas for overcoming these barriers on more sticky notes and attached them to the appropriate flip charts. Further refinement led to a handful of specific action items that could be addressed in our effort to break down barriers and help team members achieve their software quality and productivity objectives.

Setting measurable and attainable goals brings a focus to your improvement efforts. Keep the goals a visible priority, and monitor progress with the group periodically. Remember that your objective is to improve the technical and business success achieved by your projects and company, not to satisfy the detailed expectations found in some process improvement book. You should treat improvement efforts as mini-projects, with deliverables, resources, schedules, and accountability. Otherwise, process improvement activities will always get a lower priority than the more enticing technical work.

START SLOWLY

Buffeted by the day-to-day pressures of managing, it can be a struggle just to keep your head above water. However, during this window of opportunity, the new manager has a critical role to play. You can't follow all the suggestions in this primer at once, but starting with a select few most appropriate for your situation can help shape the culture and practices of your software development group for the long term.

Of course, completing the next project on time and within budget is vital, but as a software manager you are responsible for doing more. You need to foster an environment of collaborative teamwork, leading the technical staff into forming a cohesive team that shares a commitment to quality. You want to promote and reward the application of superior software engineering practices while balancing the needs of your customers, your company, your team members, and yourself.

So, good luck with the new job!

Chapter 8

Money Bags and Baseball Bats: Sponsorship Rules

Rob Thomsett

I once worked with a woman who was a brilliant manager of people. Adept at drawing the very best from the people who worked for her, her major flaw as a manager was her difficulty with managing upward, *with dealing as effectively with her boss and those above as she did with the people below. Many software project managers whom I have met over the years share similar problems. Skilled as team leaders, they are often so focused on the management of the project team, the technical issues, and the schedule and resources that they forget to look up. They fail at the start to fully understand the larger picture and the perspective of upper management, then easily become lost in details once the project is under way.*

Like flying a plane under Visual Flight Rules, effectively managing a software project requires you to look up, down, and around; you can't just keep your eyes glued to the cockpit instruments. In this chapter, Australian consultant Rob Thomsett provides some of the flight rules for project managers when it comes to one of the most crucial aspects of managing upward: handling sponsors and sponsorship.

—Editor

On television, the mere mention of the word "sponsor" may be taken by viewers as an excuse to dive for the remote, but without sponsorship of one form or another, all television would resemble the low-budget amateurism that fills the cable public-access channels. Like television programs, good software programs depend on creative partnerships—among your team members, with your clients, with business associates, and, most importantly, with your project sponsor.

My consulting experience confirms what research by the Standish Group [1995] and others has shown. The effectiveness of the project sponsor role is the single best predictor of project success or failure. For you as a project manager, the relationship that you build with your sponsor is the most critical relationship in your project. Simply put, a project without the appropriate degree of executive sponsorship will fail.

For software developers and project managers facing another potential project disaster, here are a few simple rules that could turn you from a victim into a hero.

MONEY BAGS AND BASEBALL BATS

The first and most important rule is that the best sponsor for a project is the one with the biggest baseball bat and the fattest money bag, but what does this mean? Your project involves many stakeholders and service providers. You need a sponsor who can best assist in the resolution of the inevitable conflicts that arise throughout the project.

> *The first and most important rule is that the best sponsor for a project is the one with the biggest baseball bat and the fattest money bag.*

For example, a common area of conflict is project scope and objectives. In fact, I have seen this issue on every project with which I have been involved. In all projects, it is highly likely that each of the represented stakeholder groups will view the scope and objectives of the project differently. For example, your project team members, supported by the members of some other group of stakeholders, may agree that process and system documentation can be added after implementation and is therefore "out of scope." However, the internal audit and system support groups may strongly disagree with this position. Clearly, it is part of your role as manager to negotiate among these stakeholders and to find some resolution through compromise. However, should this fail, you must be able to then escalate or "push back" the problem to a person who can make a unilateral decision as to whether documentation is "in" or "out." This is where the "bag of money and the baseball bat" test becomes relevant.

The *bag of money* refers to the level of spending authorization available to the project sponsor. Basically, the larger the authorization level for spending available to the sponsor, the more corporate power the sponsor has to wield. If the project sponsor is actually paying for the project from her own budget, then she would typically have the authority and authorization to decide unilaterally whether documentation was required or not.

The *baseball bat* refers to the level of organizational and political clout available to the project sponsor. The bag of money and the baseball bat are typically linked, but the relationship is not always simple and direct. For example, although the project sponsor may not have financial authority, he may have organizational authority.

Organizational authority is typically associated with position or level in the management hierarchy, but additional organizational power may come through the sponsor's use of allies, powerful mentors, personal charisma, and the like. A rising star may have more power than others at the same level in the organization. What is important is the project sponsor's ability to use organizational power—the baseball bat—to assist you in resolving project conflicts.

An inappropriate level of delegation, where the actual sponsor delegates decisions to a weaker stand-in, inevitably leads to difficulties. At best, it will cause delays, as the surrogate sponsor passes decisions upward to the person with the right level of authority and power. At worst, it results in problems being left for you, the project manager, to solve. As many experienced project managers have found, attempts to solve boundary disputes without an effective power base typically result in the project becoming mired in a series of political battles among various stakeholder groups. Fortunately, I've learned that senior executives love using their baseball bats. All you have to do is to show them where to swing.

> *Inappropriate delegation, in which the sponsor delegates decisions to a weaker stand-in, inevitably leads to difficulties.*

THE PASSIVE CONDUIT

This rule is a corollary of the first. As a project manager, one of the most common and serious mistakes you can make is to compensate for inadequate sponsorship by taking on by yourself such major project decisions as scope, objectives, risk management, and quality expectations.

As a project manager, your job is to take the sponsor's concept for the project and then—through participative project management processes—define, refine, plan, and manage the development of the initial concept through to its successful implementation and support. You need to recognize that it is your responsibility to manage the realization of the concept, but it is not your concept; it belongs to your sponsor. In other words, you are the "passive conduit" through which the dreams of the sponsor flow.

In this context, *passive* refers to the ownership of the sponsor's concept. Project management is far from a passive process, and it is your responsibility to proactively negotiate, communicate, plan, enable, facilitate, and manage the project team, the stakeholder involvement, and so on. Should you come across differences of opinions among stakeholders as to the scope and objectives, quality requirements, or other key aspects of the project, it is your job to attempt to resolve the conflict using whatever organizational authority or personal power you have available. However, if you are unable to restore order, you must push the conflict back to your sponsor, explaining what you have done to resolve it and what decisions your sponsor needs to make to get the project back on track.

> *If you are unable to resolve differences among stakeholders regarding key aspects of the project, you must push the conflict back up to your sponsor.*

At this stage, you may find that your sponsor attempts to redelegate the problem to you by saying, "Oh! Thanks for letting me know. However, I'm a bit busy at the moment. Why don't you handle it?"

You are now facing the most critical decision you will make in the project. If you accept this behavior, you will violate the first rule and reap all the associated consequences. You must firmly and politely resist the redelegation. You will have to explain again what you have already done to resolve the conflict and the impact that the nonresolution of the problem may have on the project. Other tricks include using the "royal we," as in, "Thanks for the vote of confidence, boss, but unless we resolve this together, our project will tank."

Chris Wooley, of one of Australia's major insurers, is one of the most experienced and competent project managers I have ever met. He advises new project managers that, when asked for their opinions on major issues of scope or objectives for any project they are managing, they should always reply, "I have no opinion. I am just the project manager."

EDUCATE AND INFORM

During the 25-plus years I have been involved in project management education and consulting, I have been constantly amazed by the lack of project management education and support offered to senior business executives. In conducting seminars and tutorials for senior management, I have learned that the majority of senior business executives do not understand projects or project management or the kind of work involved!

All organizations engage in two distinct categories of work. The first is process work. This type of work is "business as usual" and has the following attributes:

- It repeats.
- It has a short time frame (usually measured in minutes).
- It is standardized, noncreative, and structured.
- It is documented.
- It is easily measured.
- It minimizes variation among people undertaking the work.
- It operates within the status quo.

This is the sort of work most frequently found in factories, offices, restaurants, airlines, construction sites, hospitals, banks, and so on. I would estimate that between 70 and 80 percent of all work belongs to this category.

The second category of work, project work, is the exact opposite of process work. It is designed to change "business as usual" and has several defining attributes.

- It is unique.
- It has a long time frame (usually measured in months).
- It is nonstandardized, creative, and generally unstructured.
- It is difficult to document.
- It is not easily measured.
- It maximizes variation among people undertaking the work.
- It changes the status quo.

Project work is found in all organizations but is most common within groups such as marketing, information technology, research, policy, and other specialist groups.

Typical executive-level sponsors will have had many years of experience in process work but not in project work. As a result, they are often quite ignorant of the dynamics of projects. More importantly, your sponsor is also probably ignorant of the roles and responsibilities of a project sponsor. This lack of insight explains much of the frustration that project managers experience with their sponsors.

> *Typical executive-level sponsors, having had more
> experience in process work than in project work,
> are often quite ignorant regarding both project
> dynamics and their own roles and responsibilities
> as sponsors.*

For example, in process work, it is accepted that great leaders should empower and delegate. Indeed, process work, by nature, operates in a machine-like and predictable fashion, so executives can generally leave the day-to-day operations to others and focus on strategic issues. Consequently, it can seem natural and normal to executives to delegate many of the critical decisions for their projects to their project managers. The problems described in the discussions of the first two rules are generally not the result of management stupidity or stubbornness but rather the result of years of practice and education. Therefore, as a project manager, one of your key roles is educating your business stakeholders and sponsor on the nature of project work.

DELAY-DIMINISHED HELP

The one project manager behavior that annoys senior business executives more than any other is the tendency for project managers and other intermediate managers to delay the delivery of bad news. This practice places the executive sponsor in the reactive position of cleaning up a mess rather than in the proactive position of taking action to avoid the mess in the first place.

For one of my company's clients, we were reviewing a high-profile and very expensive outsourced project. In the consulting company developing the software was a project manager who had a difficult relationship with the project manager at the company for which the software was being developed. Although the consultant project manager had documented the situation, it had not been flagged as critical. When we became involved, the breakdown of effective communication between the two project managers had remained unresolved for five months! The consulting project manager was determined to resolve the problem by himself; however, our conclusion was that the personality conflict was, in truth, unresolvable. To make matters worse, the contract was for a fixed price and fixed deadline, and the project's schedule had become compromised.

We passed the situation on to the CEO of the consulting company. He met with the client's CEO, and, on the following day, a more experienced and reasonable person replaced the internal project manager. Over five months of the project time frame had been lost before the executives became involved.

Great project managers ask for help and ask for it as soon as possible. This maxim is especially important for those of you in larger or more bureaucratic organizations. You will probably find that there are built-in delays in getting any information—whether good or bad—to the top. Worse, the more levels that your report passes through, the higher the probability of filtering and distortion. As the legend goes, a message from the people at the bottom may start as a statement that an executive idea stinks, but the message may be so altered by the time it reaches the CEO that it reads as a recommendation to invest in a sewage treatment plant! We may laugh, but we also recognize the painful truth.

> *Great project managers not only ask for help but also ask for it as early as possible.*

Should your project get into trouble, do everything possible to get the message to the relevant sponsor as quickly as possible. Given the issues discussed throughout this chapter, you may need to be creative in breaking through the organizational barriers that prevent you from getting to the real sponsor.

NO SPONSOR, NO START

Hell on earth is being a project manager without the bat, the bag of money, and the other executive support offered by an effective project sponsor. Professional project managers must take some responsibility in changing such a situation. Strategies include giving copies of this chapter to your senior managers, using the research of the Standish Group as a support, talking with your peers, consulting your internal audit or risk management group (if you have one), and educating yourself—then learning some more. Most likely, any organization that places you in a project without a proper sponsor will already have a history of projects that failed because of poor project sponsorship. This should give you additional ammunition in wining this battle.

Simply put, you should break this rule of requiring sponsorship only if you are a masochist. Hopefully, the ideas in this chapter will prevent you from having to decide whether you are masochistic or not.

Chapter 9

Productivity by the Numbers: What Can Speed Up or Slow Down Software Development

Capers Jones

I call it the irony of data. In a field sometimes known as data processing, we have an ironic paucity of data. We remain reluctant to commit to firm estimates, and we shy away from quantitative measurement of our work. Not knowing with any precision what we are doing, we cannot be confident about efforts to improve it. Many managers do not know, in even the simplest of terms, how much their programmers do or how fast they do it. Project costs are not estimated, they are "guesstimated." Deadlines are often the feral fantasies of inexperienced developers or naïve customers who do not know that a year is industry shorthand for anywhere between 13 and 18 months. Software metrics, the quantitative measurement of software projects and products, is considered a topic for academics.

This somewhat bitter irony is not all our fault. The academics have let us down, too. Computer science, as practiced, is often more math than science, and computer scientists have been too busy constructing theories and exotic demonstrations to take the time for real research on their subject matter.

Fortunately, a scattered group of forward-looking companies and developers has been quietly collecting data for decades. These people have compiled substantial repositories on how much it costs and how long it takes to accomplish the various tasks of software development. They know how productive their programmers are and why. They know that structured design works, but so do a lot of things. They can show that reuse pays off, but only if you do it right, and that inspections do not take time, they save it. Capers Jones is one of those who knows such things, and he has the data to prove it.

—Editor

Everybody has a theory about software development productivity. What is often missing is solid information about factors that slow down or speed up projects. Managers and developers are bombarded by ads and articles that claim ten-to-one improvements in productivity with this tool or that technique, but often there is little more than marketing hype behind the claims. In particular, vendors don't like to talk about delays and disasters, and the software literature downplays methods that lead to failure.

Software development productivity is a complex phenomenon. Software Productivity Research, Inc., has been collecting quantitative and qualitative data on about 50 to 70 software projects a month for more than a dozen years. From our knowledge base of roughly 7,000 software projects, more than 100 factors have been identified that can significantly influence the outcomes of software projects.

Productivity in software projects and software organizations varies widely. Function Points provide a standard way to estimate the size of programming problems, making it easier to compare productivity across projects and organizations. Function Points are convenient because much of the work of software development has nothing to do with coding and isn't accounted for by measuring only lines of code. (For additional information on function point metrics, point your browser to *www.IFPUG.org*.) Software development productivity can be as high as 140 Function Points per professional per month or less than 1/1,000th as much, but comparatively few projects and companies perform extremely well or extremely poorly—the distribution of productivity tends to follow relatively normal bell-shaped curves. The typical performance among some 1,500 recent software development projects (1991–1996) was around 9 Function Points per professional per month. However, the extremes at either end may have the most to teach managers about productivity.

The questions of prime interest to development managers are: What causes productivity to be significantly better or worse than average? And how can I improve my results? Many managers tend to focus on programming productivity, and measuring lines of code tends to encourage this narrow focus. However, for typical software projects, coding may constitute only a fraction of the total effort and expense. It might, for example, account for some 32% of the cost of a typical COBOL application running 1,000 Function Points and 100,000 lines of code. Taken together, design, testing, and project management typically account for a higher percentage. If managers concentrate only on coding, they may not achieve major improvements in overall productivity because coding is too small a percentage of the total effort.

FAST-TRACK DEVELOPMENT

Software development is very labor-intensive, so the major factors that speed up development substitute reuse for custom development, minimize rework, or improve the working conditions for the development team. Some of the factors with a strong positive impact on software development include

- Reuse of high-quality design, code, and test materials
- Unpaid overtime on the part of key development personnel
- Quiet, noise-free offices for key development personnel
- Use of design and code inspections before testing begins
- A powerful suite of development tools for analysis, design, and coding
- Rational scheduling and cost-estimating methods

Although it is fairly obvious why most of these factors benefit software productivity, this short list has some surprises in it, too.

> *Software development is labor-intensive, so the major factors that speed it up either substitute reuse for custom development, minimize rework, or improve working conditions for the team.*

Software reuse has the greatest impact of any technology known, but reuse also requires very high quality for the impact to be positive. Furthermore, software reuse needs to include many other deliverables besides source code. An effective software reuse program will include at a minimum:

- Reusable plans and estimates
- Reusable designs and specifications
- Reusable source code
- Reusable user documentation
- Reusable test plans and test cases

One well-known study [DeMarco and Lister, 1987] found that the size and noise level of a programmer's office had one of the strongest correlations with productivity of any factor measured. The programmers in the top quartile of productivity had more than 84 square feet of private office space, while those in the lowest had less than 44 square feet of shared office space. Programming is a task that needs quiet and solitude most of the time and interaction with colleagues and team members only every now and then. Noisy, shared offices are too distracting.

Software inspections improve productivity as well as quality. Software with many bugs in it when testing begins cannot be released. Buggy software can stretch out the testing process and raise testing costs until they account for more than half of the total project.

Pretest inspections of design and code provide a firm, high-quality basis for development and allow testing to be completed much faster with fewer problems emerging. Appropriately, IBM gave Michael Fagan, the inventor of inspections, an award for proving that inspections benefited schedules and costs as well as quality.

Good estimating and good scheduling techniques are associated with every successful software project, while bad estimating and excessive schedule pressure are attributes of major software disasters, such as the Denver Airport baggage handling system. If a project starts with a solid development plan, it has a very good chance of succeeding. If it starts with an irrational target, such as finishing three years' worth of work in 18 months, it is likely to become a disaster.

> *Good estimating and scheduling techniques are associated with every successful software project, while poor estimates and excessive schedule pressure characterize software disasters.*

Our research has yielded a useful rule of thumb for predicting the average number of calendar months from the start of requirements until the delivery of software. Raise the Function Point total of the application to the power of 0.4 and the result will be the number of calendar months needed for development. By this formula, a moderate project of 100 Function Points (equivalent to roughly 10,000 COBOL statements) is predicted to take 6.3 calendar months. For a more substantial system of 1,000 Function Points (roughly 100,000 COBOL statements), the projection is 15.8 calendar months. Step up to 10,000 Function Points or around a million lines of code, and the estimate rises to 39.8 calendar months, assuming you have adequate resources.

IN THE SLOW LANE

Factors that slow down productivity are not very well covered in the software literature. Unfortunately, it is much easier to slow down and degrade a software project than it is to speed it up and make it better [Jones, 1995a]. Factors such as these can impair productivity:

- Reuse of poor-quality materials
- Inadequate quality control
- High rate of creep in user requirements
- Excessive, irrational schedule pressure
- Random development processes
- Lack of specialization

Software reuse has the largest positive impact on software productivity but can also have the largest negative impact. How can reuse be both a good thing and a bad thing? The critical difference between the positive and negative influences of software reuse can be expressed in one word: quality. Software reuse is positive when the artifacts that are reused approach or achieve zero-defect levels. If the reused materials are filled with errors or bugs, productivity is reduced [Jones, 1995b]. Imagine, for instance, the result of reusing a software module in 50 applications only to discover that it contains a number of severe errors that trigger massive recalls of every application! To gain the greatest benefit from reuse, each major software deliverable should include at least 75% reused material, which should be virtually defect-free.

It should be apparent that quality control is a key factor in development productivity. Many managers operate under the mistaken belief that projects can be delivered sooner by skimping on quality control. This is not true for any software project that handles serious business or technical issues such as financial applications, telephone switching systems, weapons systems, and the like.

Because Function Points can be derived from requirements, one of the useful by-products of using them instead of lines of code is that it becomes possible to measure directly the rate at which requirements grow or "creep" during development. If you agree to build an application of 100 Function Points, and the customer later insists on adding features that bring the size to 125 Function Points, you know the requirements grew by 25%.

The average rate of requirements creep for software projects in the United States is about 2% per month from the time the requirements are "firm" through the design and coding phases. If the rate of creep is much higher, it can reduce the project's chances of success.

Rigor in the software development process also affects project outcomes. In one study, projects without formal process planning and process control had a very low probability of finishing on time and a very high probability of exceeding their cost estimates [Jones, 1995a]. Conversely, projects that used careful process planning had a very good chance of finishing on time and within budget. Which process was used did not seem to matter very much as long as some systematic method or development cycle was employed. Any of the formal processes, such as structured design and development, the Warnier-Orr method, information engineering, the British Jackson method, and several others, all generated results that were better than projects using no formal methods. Almost any methodology may be better than no methodology at all.

> *Without formal process planning and control, projects have a very low probability of finishing on time and within budget. Any formal process, such as structured design, information engineering, or the Jackson method, generates better results.*

In general, there is a lack of symmetry between the positive and negative influences. For example, a good development process will exert a moderately positive influence on productivity, but a bad development process—or none at all—can have a severely negative impact.

In almost every human activity, specialists can outperform generalists, and the same is true in software development. For large software projects within large companies, the use of generalists rather than specialists results in much lower productivity. The areas where specialists consistently outperform generalists include software architecture, planning and estimating, measurement and metrics, testing, quality assurance, and maintenance.

PRODUCTIVE MAINTENANCE

Maintenance is a term that commonly covers both defect repairs and enhancements in response to new requirements. Although this definition is imperfect, it will serve to show the positive and negative factors influencing productivity in the modification of existing software applications. The major factors that have been shown to improve maintenance performance include

- Maintenance specialists
- Change management tools
- Complexity analysis tools
- Code restructuring tools
- Reverse engineering tools
- Reengineering tools

Using maintenance specialists, who devote full time to defect repair and small enhancements, is at the top of the list. When generalists divide their time between maintenance and new development, it is hard for them to pay full and necessary attention to either task. Furthermore, when maintenance priorities are high, concurrent development work will be slowed.

A variety of "geriatric tools" have proved useful for dealing with aging legacy applications. Some of the more interesting tools include complexity analysis tools, which can highlight troublesome areas; code restructuring tools, which can reduce complexity and generate fresh maintenance documentation; and reverse engineering or reengineering tools for migrating legacy applications to other formats, such as converting them to client-server architecture.

Some factors exert a negative influence on the work of updating or modifying existing software, including

- The presence of error-prone modules
- High complexity of code
- Low status of maintenance specialists
- Poor or no training of maintenance personnel
- No change-control automation
- No defect-tracking automation

The factor that most reduces maintenance productivity, error-prone modules, is a one-way street. Error-prone modules slow down maintenance, but their absence does not speed it up. Typically, errors or bugs in large systems are not randomly distributed; they tend to clump in a small number of error-prone modules that cause most of the problems. Back in the 1960s, IBM discovered that 4% of the modules in an early version of the MVS operating system accounted for 38% of customer-reported errors. A similar study in the late 1970s on IBM's IMS database product revealed a more severe skew. Of 425 modules, 300 had zero defects and resulted in no customer-reported bugs, but 31 modules accounted for a full 57% of customer-reported errors.

Once such error-prone modules have been identified, they can be improved via formal inspections or removed by redevelopment. Overall maintenance productivity for an application can sometimes be raised by 50% or more.

Lower status and pay for maintenance programmers compared to developers also have been found to reduce maintenance productivity. The practice of assigning new hires directly onto maintenance tasks with little or no training is another negative factor in maintenance productivity. Besides training, good tools are also needed. Maintenance requires keeping track of numerous bug reports and many changes. Manual methods are simply not adequate for this purpose on any nontrivial applications.

PRODUCTIVITY PATTERNS

The most common pattern of factors that we have identified is where the technical work of building software in terms of design and coding is reasonably good, but project management and quality control are fairly weak. This combination is characteristic of the information systems domain, the most common form of software development, although outsourced information systems projects are somewhat more likely to use good project management methods.

Fairly good quality control as well as fairly good development skills are more likely in the domain of systems software. Here too, however, project management is often the weak link. Quality control is typically better in systems software projects because the hardware devices that the software controls (for example, switching systems, computers, aircraft) need stringent quality control in order to operate. As with systems software, military software projects are often characterized by rather good development methods and fairly good quality control but only marginal or deficient project management methods.

Large commercial software vendors tend to have better than average software development methods and much better than average maintenance methods. Once again, quality control and project management are the weaknesses noted most often in assessment and benchmark studies.

Organizations whose productivity is in the top 10% typically have better than average tools and methods for project management, quality control, maintenance, and development. Conversely, among groups that bring up the rear in terms of productivity, there is a strong tendency toward poor tools and methods for project management, poor quality control, poor maintenance, and only adequate development tools and methods. On the whole, it seems that the software development community is better trained and equipped for the technical side of development than for project management.

> *With more ways of going wrong than of getting it right, to do much better than average, development managers must pay careful attention to those factors with the greatest impact.*

Overall, the factors and patterns in software productivity suggest that there are more wrong ways to go about building and maintaining software than there are ways of getting it right. As a result, average productivity and quality levels for software projects are not particularly impressive. For software development managers to do much better than average, they will have to pay careful attention to those factors that have the greatest impact on speeding up or slowing down software development.

Chapter 10

Software Waste Management: Managing Data Migration

John Boddie

It is perhaps modern computing's most famous dictum, yet we often ignore that universal law of "garbage in, garbage out." When we do, we risk transforming well-designed software into badly behaved systems. In this chapter, John Boddie argues that controlling and cleaning up the garbage is as central to good software development as it is to modern living. We do not all have to become waste management specialists, but every manager needs a grounding in the rudiments of data migration along with an appreciation for the complexities of dealing with messy data and a respect for the work of those stalwarts who have to move it from one system to another.

—Editor

This is the day—the payoff for the technical risks, the weekends spent in front of a terminal, and the mind-numbing requirements meetings. The boss is here, along with the vice president of development and her equivalent from the user community. After a few remarks about all the hard work, you start the demo. It looks good. The user you've carefully coached is moving confidently through the screen sequences. Response time looks great. The user interface draws appreciative comments. Then someone says, "That can't be right."

"What can't be right?"

"That order. You're using real data, aren't you?"

"Yes. We wanted you to see the system in a production setting."

"Well, McDongle & Crashmore has five sites and you're only showing two."

Stay cool. You tell the user at the terminal to go to the customer profile screens, but all she can find is the two sites. The user's vice president looks at your boss's boss and says, "Are you sure this new technology is worth our giving up 60% of our customer base?"

You never planned on this, and therein lies the problem.

TRASH COMPACTORS

Software development strives for new functionality and new ways to deliver data to users. In practice, what we often do is reinvent the trash compactor. You remember—the kitchen marvel that turned a 20-pound bag of trash into 20 pounds of trash.

Alas, no level of tool or user interface sophistication can overcome the burden of bad data. Although it is one of the key determinants of development success, the process of converting data from old systems into data for new ones receives almost no attention from the development community.

Developers build trash compactors because they are focused on the processing and not the content of the data. A trash compactor doesn't care if it's crushing milk cartons or old broccoli, and our systems don't care if the telephone number for a customer is right or wrong. We conveniently overlook the fact that referential integrity rules in our databases can be satisfied with data that aren't related in the real world. Bad data, we say, are "not our problem."

> *Because they are focused on the processing and not the content of the data, developers build trash compactors, systems that don't care if the telephone number for a customer is right or wrong.*

Trash compactors can be wonderfully complex and great fun to build. Trash itself is much less interesting. Most developers would not consider "making sure the parts list is correct" a career-enhancing opportunity. Typically, such assignments fall to the most junior staff—when they can't be fobbed off on the users. But by leaving these jobs to junior programmers, what are the chances of difficulties when you attempt to deploy the system? If there are difficulties, will everyone still think you did a great job? Face it, these are jobs that nobody wants. Cleaning up legacy data is like being a referee. The best case is that nobody notices you. Any news you have is probably bad. I'm currently leading a data migration effort for a telephone company and so far we've found data for only about 70% of the routers they installed in the field. Results like these create long faces at project meetings. In fact, only the developers are pleased. They are behind schedule and will gladly embrace any outside excuse for slippage.

THE VIEW FROM THE LANDFILL

In my opinion, data migration and data quality improvement are two of the most complex and valuable data processing areas. Ask any business owner what the first priority is, accurate data or a really nice interface, and you already know the answer. Nevertheless, chances are that you will spend far more time thinking about the interface and working on it than you ever will spend dealing with the data's accuracy.

Even if you are interested in doing something about the data, you may not have the technical skills required. Java development expertise doesn't easily translate into interpreting VSAM files or using Wang utilities. Data migration work requires a renaissance person. You must understand the semantics of the data you are dealing with, the business practices that use the current systems, and the way these are expected to change, as well as the technologies that the new system, the old systems, and the migration environment use. In my current project, the data sources include Wang, Oracle, Microsoft SQL Server, Microsoft Excel spreadsheets, Microsoft Access databases, direct feeds from telephone switches in the network, direct feeds from Cisco and Newbridge routers, Lotus Notes, proprietary databases, and flat-file outputs from mainframe systems.

In data migration, you do not have the luxury of dealing with the clean abstractions that are collected into the new system requirements. No requirements document starts with the assumption that the new system will be initialized with bad data, yet this is often the case in practice. When migrating data, you must contend with idiosyncrasies from years of legacy system operation, including data elements that have been redefined, multiple codings of data fields, obsolete status values, and the like. You cannot disregard or arbitrarily correct these. If you can't find location data for a $25,000 piece of equipment, you can't leave it out of the new system just because it doesn't fit your model. Data migration can make you feel you are turning over rocks by a river after a major storm. You will start to notice odd-looking things when you start dealing with the details that have accumulated over the years.

> *No requirements document assumes that the new system will be initialized with bad data, yet this is often the case.*

PRIMARY TREATMENT

When migrating data, identify the data source for your new system first. This is not simply a matter of identifying what system will be replaced. If the system being replaced gets its data from other systems and they, in turn, get it from other ones, the chances are slim that the most accessible data is the most accurate.

Identifying data sources can be difficult. In most companies, systems environments have become so complex that data processing groups don't really understand the "big picture," and users can't identify all their data sources and data streams. In fact, one of the first things the development teams of these companies probably have to do is examine the current system and "extract the business rules." If users really understood the process details, that step would be unnecessary.

In many cases, new systems will be replacing multiple legacy systems whose data is supposed to be identical. When it isn't, you must know how the data came to be in each of the systems in order to choose which of the supposedly identical data items is correct. This involves looking at the business processes as well as the systems.

For example, my current project combines data from legacy systems for order entry and billing. Each contains customer account data, including account status, contact address, and billing address. About 20% of the records are inconsistent in at least one of these attributes. The obvious choice is to use the data from the billing system as the correct data whenever billing and order entry attributes differ. However, contact information is updated in the order entry system, and these updates are often not made in billing. Likewise, accounts are usually inactive in the billing system and are not updated in the order entry system unless the user calls and requests it. Knowing these things, we can make a rule that the data for the new system should include the billing address and status from the billing system and the contact address from the order entry system. We still need to produce reports showing the discrepancies between the order entry and billing systems. These should show all customers where the billing address differs and the account is more than 60 days overdue, which may indicate that the billing address was updated in the order entry system but not in the billing system.

Looking at the last edit date for records is not as useful as it might appear, since it's difficult to determine what changed in the record. Was it a contact name? Was it an area code in the phone number? Change dates provide collateral information, but they seldom drive adjudication in those cases where data sources contain different values.

You must map all the sources and destinations to a meta data model. To manage data migration, you have to create a meta data model and keep it current. It will be your most valuable management tool. It will track source systems and databases, the destination system and its database, and all the attributes including their formatting and coding. You will use the meta data to establish and enforce conventions, such as always using "Ave." instead of "Avenue" or "Ave" (without the period).

> ***To manage data migration, a meta data model will be your most valuable management tool.***

You can't assume that the new system is the only destination for the migrated data. If the system being replaced provided data for multiple downstream systems (not an unusual situation), then the data you are cleaning up may be a candidate for migrating to these systems as well.

All of this analysis work may sound a lot like developing software. In fact, much of it is the same, except there is more detail and more riding on understanding what all of the data really means. Since data migration always shows up early on the critical path, the work that supports it must also be accurate early.

SECONDARY TREATMENT

It doesn't make sense to scoop dead fish out of a stream unless you also block off the sewers that killed them in the first place. Data systems that include errors are likely to get new errors every day. Reducing the influx of errors means spending a lot of time dealing with users who don't have a lot of time to worry about data migration.

Downsizing of information technology personnel adds its own challenges. The people who understood the legacy systems and data have moved on, and those who are left are so overworked that they hardly have time to breathe. On the plus side, most people still working with the legacy systems are interested in doing what they can to improve the data's quality because they understand that good data makes their jobs easier. These people are also realistic enough to understand that more new systems are promised than are actually delivered and that the work you are doing with data migration may benefit them over an extended period. You need to find ways to let these people help you make the data better with as much efficiency and as little disruption to their regular work as possible.

In most cases, this work involves first generating reports that show both the current legacy data and its expected values, and then either developing code to migrate good data back into the legacy systems that should have it already or providing worksheets that let users examine the data and make the necessary changes directly. You need to coordinate the worksheets with the screens the users will be invoking to make the changes.

You also need to determine with the business owner how the errors were introduced into the system. For example, if sales representatives include dummy site address information to get sales approved faster and commissions credited earlier, it may be necessary for the process owner to curtail this practice. If not, then the data migration work needs to be conscious of orders received after a given date, knowing that the site addresses may be erroneous.

TRASH TO STEAM

In the real world, turning trash into steam sounds like a great idea. Unfortunately, it is also complex, expensive, and subject to regulations, hearings, and even public protests. Anyone involved with such projects starts to regard the simplicity of landfills with some affection and admiration. The software development equivalent of the trash-to-steam method is phased implementation. In phased implementation, data migration is no longer a simple matter of concocting files of relatively good data and loading them into a new system. It becomes a complex enterprise with transactional processing, application modification (both legacy and target), special purpose middleware, and shifting objectives. Developers who have been through the process assert that the cost and difficulty of migrating from system A to system B in phases is likely to be more costly than the development of A and B combined.

> *Phased implementation, which runs new and old systems in parallel, is the software equivalent of trash-to-steam schemes. Both sound good but are often complex and expensive.*

Typically, phased implementation requires that the new system and the old system be run in parallel, meaning that migration now becomes a two-way street. If the defined phases include both functional and organizational or geographical steps, you'll need "retrofits" to bring previously migrated data up to the current standard. You might need requirements for new data and functionality as a consequence of business process changes. If multiple systems are involved, this is a complex undertaking.

Phased implementations are often the result of mergers or acquisitions. In these situations, further complications can arise from the cultural differences between organizations and from differences in business processes, terminology, and even legal requirements. When migrating data to support a new system, none of this is an abstraction. You'll need to deal with it every day. Now ask yourself, if you are developing a new system, do you want to leave all of data migration's complexity in the hands of junior programmers and newly minted managers? Do you still believe that data migration and data quality improvement are not your problem?

Chapter 11

When in Doubt, Blame Everybody: The Responsibility for Usability

Lucy Lockwood

User interface design is but one chapter of the software design and development story, but it is often a pivotal one in the success or failure of a product. Whose fault is it when the story ends badly? Consultant and author Lucy Lockwood suggests it may be yours. Although most managers may think of user interface design as the bailiwick of professional designers, she argues that the responsibility belongs to everyone, including you. Your decisions as a manager may be the key to usability.

—Editor

The thick stack of complaints coming into your company's call center is sitting on your desk, silently mocking you. On the top of the stack is a yellow sticky note with a message from your boss: "Who is responsible for this?" The souped-up, feature-laden intranet application that you delivered to such fanfare a few months ago has turned from a technical triumph into a usability disaster. New users can't figure it out and old ones are becoming nostalgic about the good old days of simple black-and-white forms uncluttered by graphic controls that no one understands and links that lead everyone on a merry chase.

So, who is responsible for user interface design and for the ultimate usability of your products? When things go wrong, whose fault is it? Did you drop the ball as a manager? Did your programmers fail you? Or was it the crack consultant you brought in to polish up the screen designs? Should you have hired a user interface designer before the project was launched?

In software development, it is often easy to know who is responsible for a particular bit of code, but usability is a diffuse quality that may seem to be touched by everyone's work and yet be nobody's job. With usability and the quality of user interface design assuming ever greater importance in the success of software and Web-based applications, it is important to know exactly whose job these are and why.

> *Usability is a diffuse quality that may seem to be touched by everyone's work and yet be nobody's job.*

THE RIGHT WAY

As a consultant, I am often asked for answers. Whose job should it be? Who should be responsible for usability and how should the user interface design process be organized? The standard consultant's answer is, of course, "It depends." There is no one way that will maximize your chances of success. A recent sampling of some of today's best-known and most successful design and development groups [*interactions,* 2000], revealed enormous variation. No two organizations seem to be handling user interface design exactly alike. Although usability has risen in importance as a factor in product quality, user interface design has yet to find a standard home in either the software development organization or the software development process.

In many groups, the responsibility falls to a lone person, sometimes identified by an official title, such as User Interface Designer or Usability Engineer, but just as often with none. The usability specialist in such a situation may have an appropriate degree related in some way or another to human-computer interaction, but more frequently I find these are individuals who migrated into the position from earlier roles as programmers, documentation specialists, systems analysts, or quality-assurance staff. The extent to which this person has an influence on the process and the final product varies considerably. In many cases, the usability specialist kicks off the software or site design process with an overall design and broad guidance, then hopes for the best as the programming team, marketing group, management, and clients weigh in with changes.

Some organizations set up their user interface staff as internal consultants, either as a separate group to which development teams can come for help and guidance or as a pool of individuals from which a development team can select a temporary teammate to bring on board for the duration of a project.

For companies lacking internal usability resources, external consultants or design companies are often drawn upon to provide a variety of services ranging from reviews or critiques of existing designs to complete, detailed design of the entire user interface. In many cases, outsourcing portions of the user interface design process makes a great deal of sense. Formal usability testing, for example, is frequently outsourced to an independent usability lab, and such services are widely and readily available. Because most usability testing requires special equipment and facilities plus staffing by specially trained professionals, many smaller companies may be better off contracting for testing services rather than taking the private bricks-and-mortar approach.

IT'S THE PROGRAMMERS

For good or ill, in many cases there is no user interface design—or not one of sufficient quality and detail—so the responsibility and the blame devolve by default onto programmers. They are the ones dragging widgets from a toolbar onto a form; they are the ones coding the sizes and colors and labels for user interface objects; they are the ones who decide to throw up a message box and who write the text to be displayed. In the early 1990s, when Larry Constantine and I first studied the factors contributing to usability problems, we found that, regardless of who had the official responsibility, most details of design decisions affecting the usability of the end product were being made by the people writing the code.

> *Regardless of who has official responsibility, most detail decisions affecting product usability are made by the people writing the code.*

Alan Cooper, author of *The Inmates Are Running the Asylum* [Cooper, 1999] seems to agree. His solution would be to take control over user interface design away from programmers—the inmates—and put it in the hands of an elite corps of appropriately trained and highly skilled specialists. Easier said than done, I would say.

First off, there are just not enough appropriately trained and highly skilled specialists to go around. If you think it's hard hiring a good programmer in today's job market, try finding a good user interface designer. The shortfall in software engineering and computer science graduates is dwarfed by the shortfall in graduates with degrees in human-computer interaction, ergonomics, and related areas.

Second, good user interface design is closely tied to the programming that supports it. Usability is a function of both appearance and behavior, and behavior implies programming. Custom controls and custom behavior often need to be programmed. Highly usable software and Web sites reflect good user interface and information architecture, which is also tied to good architecture at the level of the code and the underlying database.

Finally, of course, the best user interface design will offer little to users if crucial details are lost in implementation or if the final product is buggy and unstable because of sloppy programming.

Just as the programmers are part of the problem, they have to be part of the solution, however much some writers might wish it otherwise. My recommendation, therefore, is to be sure your entire staff has some understanding of the basic principles of usability and user interface design. You need to provide everyone with some training in software usability, not with the idea of making them usability gurus but with the goal of establishing a common language for communication within the entire team and a foundation of knowledge about what usability is, why it matters, and how it can be achieved.

> *Training may not make everyone a usability guru, but it can establish a common language and a foundation of knowledge about what usability is, why it matters, and how it can be achieved.*

Training is the key. In my opinion, the ability to create highly usable software and site designs is something that can be learned. You do not have to be a born graphic artist to design a good graphical user interface. Far more important than artistic talent is knowing how to analyze what it is that your targeted users need and want to do with the software, how to discern the users' tasks and underlying intent. As a trainer, I have seen many programmers or other professionals with backgrounds unrelated to user interface design finish a week of training and be able to produce usable designs. Excellent designs? No, usually not, but usable designs, yes. I am far more sanguine than Cooper about programmers taking on responsibility for usability.

This does not mean you have no need for people with special talents. You may want to bring in graphic talent to polish a design and give it greater appeal. Some areas of user interface design are subspecialties in themselves, and unless your company is particularly large and resource rich, you may have to subcontract for these areas. Creating recognizable and usable icons in 32 by 32 pixels is an art form that demands special training and talent, for one example; for another, localization of user interfaces for diverse languages and cultures is a complex problem best left in the hands of experts.

For most user interface design problems, however, an advanced degree in usability engineering is not required. What is required is good management support.

MARGINALIZATION

"I'm a voice in the wilderness!" is how one usability specialist described his situation; it is a refrain I have heard in various forms again and again. Companies will hire or appoint someone to handle user interface design and be responsible for usability in a project, then effectively ignore them. This marginalization within the organization and the development process takes many forms. Where people sit, for example, has a significant impact on communication, information acquisition, and interpersonal connection. If, for example, the lone user interface designer has a cubicle on a different floor from the rest of the development team or sits off in a corner surrounded by marketing staff, that sends a powerful message to everyone about how relevant and connected the user interface design is to other development activities.

Another key issue is how much influence the user interface designers or usability group have in terms of individual projects. Is their role advisory, such that the programming team comes to them for guidance, suggestions, and feedback? Or do the usability specialists have near-absolute control over the interface design? Does the project team use or consult with the specialists on a voluntary or optional basis? Or is the involvement of specialists mandatory for all projects? What sort of mandate do the specialists have in terms of the usability of the delivered product? Can the usability group hold up release of the software because of usability problems? Does the project team have to obtain a usability sign-off as another form of quality assurance?

In general, you will be better off with more than one usability specialist on board, even if they are working on different projects. Just as two programmers will bounce ideas or problems off each other and spur each other on to produce more and better code, having more than one usability professional helps create a critical mass for usability within the organization. Because, like good code design or data architecture, user interface design is complex and detailed work, the user interface folk also benefit from having another designer with whom to share ideas or problems or from whom to get critical feedback.

On all but the simplest projects, user interface design is just too big a job for one person. Even if you have only one specialist at your disposal, you may need to draw on others within the development team—requirements engineers, quality-assurance staff, programmers, and managers—who can make key contributions to successful user interface design.

I suggest that before deciding on who and how many will do user interface design, you as a software manager need to focus on the *how*—how the development of the user interface design will fit into the whole development process and how the usability specialists will fit into the development organization.

LARGE-SCALE INTEGRATION

Once you realize that user interface design overlaps into all other areas, you realize that the job and its responsibility spread over the entire software development process. Not surprisingly, then, the best results seem to come from project teams that tightly integrate user interface design and designers with the rest of the development process. Even the best user interface designers will have little impact if they are marginalized within the day-to-day workings of the development organization. Even first-rate usability testing will be of little help if the laboratory findings are ignored in the interest of meeting an arbitrary schedule. The best graphic design will not lead to a usable application if the underlying analysis of the users' needs is inadequate or erroneous, and the cleverest icons or most elegant layout will not save software riddled with sloppy programming and bad internal architecture. It all has to work together.

I have been particularly impressed by the results achieved by pulling together a multidisciplinary team to carry out the user interface design. Such teams may involve not only user interface designers but also graphic artists, specialists in data architecture, and even programmers. The usability specialist takes the lead position, but the design emerges from a collaborative process. The developers and software architects who work on the user interface design provide continuity and a vital, irreplaceable link from design to implementation. No over-the-wall passing of design documents can substitute for personal participation. When questions inevitably arise later in the design and implementation process, those who were on the user interface team can often answer them without delay or further consultation. They were there; they know the design from the inside out, and they understand its rationale.

> *The best results emerge from a collaborative process in multidisciplinary teams involving not only user interface designers but also graphic artists, data architects, and even programmers.*

Another bonus from this approach is that programmers and software engineers begin to understand usability and to appreciate better the subtle issues in designing for usability. In one project, a programmer with Windows API experience was included in the user interface design team. By the end of several months working on user analysis and taking part in design discussions, this programmer had not only become an effective agent for carrying the message behind the design back to the rest of the software engineering staff but also had evolved into a quite credible interaction designer in his own right.

PICK ONE

Perhaps the biggest mistake you can make when it comes to managing usability is not organizing for it at all. Too many companies hire designers or usability specialists without figuring out how they are going to fit in with the rest of the team and the rest of the development process. Or they send some of the crew to a seminar or conference but then change nothing in their project planning or budgeting. The waste of training is widespread (see Chapter 3). The enthusiasm generated by a week of training in new approaches or techniques can dissipate all too quickly when there is no management follow-through. Without appropriate tools and the time and context in which to use them, the training makes no difference.

For you as a software development manager, then, the important step is to choose, to decide on some way to organize your usability efforts that fits with who and what you have and how you develop software. Then make the outcome everyone's responsibility—including yours.

Chapter 12

Creative Input: From Feature Fantasies to Practical Products

Larry Constantine

Along with the plethora of increasingly complex technical problems that permeate software and Web development today, most development projects must also cope with and manage creative input from outside sources—in particular, the great ideas that originate with marketing and top management. How do you accommodate their creative contributions without blowing out the budget or programming a bloated boondoggle? This chapter focuses on handling those visionary ideas from upper management and marketing that are supposed to define the mission for the product but often consist of wild-eyed ideas about killer apps and new paradigms and long lists of bullet points covering more features and functionality than Bill Gates ever imagined.

—Editor

Face it. If you are like most managers of software and Web applications development, you are far more comfortable dealing with "propeller heads" than with "suits" or "creatives." Programmers and other information technology professionals may have well-deserved reputations for being difficult to manage, but at least you understand them and the problems they face. Odds are, you are or once were one of them. However, the "suits" who run the business and the creative types who design graphics and ad campaigns might as well be from other planets. They speak other languages. They worry about weird things like branding and market windows or babble on about the "wow" factor and typographic integrity. Worst of all, they come into your well-understood and marginally manageable world bringing extra demands and added challenges.

Your first impulse, understandably, may be to close the door on all such strange people or to tune out their ever-so-creative ideas. This is usually not a good impulse to act upon, however, especially if the strange creature standing there rhapsodizing about artificial intelligence and speech recognition over the Web is your boss's boss. Although it's important to accept these creative inputs, it's also not in the best interests of you, your team, or the company just to blindly fulfill every management fantasy or let creative artistry ride roughshod over implementation practicalities or user experience. In the interest of project success, you have a responsibility to learn how to deal with both suits and creatives and how best to manage their inputs into the project.

FANTASY INPUT

Many software development projects and the majority of Web projects begin with fantasies and visions. Modern management practice encourages starting with an exercise in "visioning" to come up with the big picture of what a product can be and what it can do for its users and for the company.

That vision—the overall context and direction for the product, system, or site from a marketing and management perspective—constitutes what I refer to as a **Product Framework.** This is the framework within which the product will be designed and built and may include discussions of success criteria, targeted markets, the deployment environment, the grand management vision, and the overall financial and technical objectives to be achieved.

Whether based on market research, creative fabrication, or just an understanding of the people for whom a system is being built, a picture of the targeted customers and end users is also usually generated early in the product development process. This information may be compiled into a set of documents or be carried around in the heads of a few visionaries. It may include the results of interviews, findings from focus groups, or the output of executive brainstorming. In whatever form, it can be called a **User/Customer Profile**.

In addition, customers, users, and upper management often generate long wish lists of desired features and functions. In fact, especially on Web-based projects, these fantasies masquerade as requirements and are often among the first artifacts generated. In many projects, a base of genuine needs and necessities has been generously larded by creative license. Among the real requirements and a smattering of good ideas are usually more than a few features that will ultimately prove to be of limited or no value, even though they may be complex and costly to deliver.

> *Many software and Web projects begin with fantasies and visions. Real requirements and good ideas are usually larded with features that may ultimately prove to be costly but of limited value.*

The sources of such management and marketing fantasies are diverse. Some senior manager may have read an item in a business publication about the rise of WAP-enabled mobile phones and suddenly the project mandates support for mobile Web platforms, whether or not this makes technical or marketing sense. Or a group from marketing may have looked at the competition and determined that, since the leading competitor has a setup wizard, your new system must offer one, too. Or, since the Microsoft dancing paper clip is clearly the leading edge in office suite help techniques, animated agent technology gets thrown into the specifications for your next network management tool.

Such management and marketing fantasies are a fact of life. Rather than futilely resisting or buying into them without reservation, you need to see these flights of fancy not as requirements in themselves but as some of the many inputs into an orderly requirements engineering process. It then becomes a task for you and your team to separate the vital requirements from the nonsense and to close the feedback loop with marketing and management in such a way that the final requirements make sense.

The trick is to help other groups and constituents temper their unbridled enthusiasm and creative abandon with reason, realism, and pragmatism. The step toward real-world requirements starts by compiling all the sundry ideas from various sources into a single document where related ideas can be brought together to be compared and potentially combined, where conflicting desires can be sorted out, and where competing dreams can be weighed against each other.

This compilation goes by various names, but I refer to it as a **Content/ Capability Inventory**. It inventories all the proposed features, functions, facilities, content, and other suggested or demanded characteristics of a new product or product line. Many companies refer to such a document as a *product specification* or *product definition,* which may give it an undeserved air of finality and completeness. In principle, the Content/Capability Inventory is based on the Product Framework and the User/Customer Profile. In practice, it may often be pulled out of thin air.

In usage-centered design [Constantine and Lockwood, 1999] and some other model-driven approaches, a key part of the analysis and design process is identifying and characterizing something about the range of users that can and will use a system or visit a site. Often this description is a refinement of the information in the User/Customer Profile that originates with marketing and management. For instance, a user role model, which is the tool I use, is simply an inventory of the various kinds of relationships that users can assume in relation to a system or site.

Once the user roles, types, or profiles for an application have been identified, they can be prioritized. Normally, the best way to prioritize user roles is to have various stakeholders in the project sort them in terms of expected frequency and business priority, then to merge the rankings. The card-shuffling techniques described by Ron Jeffries (see Chapter 39) can be very effective. In itself, this exercise in priority setting can be a sobering process, as various groups and individuals see the results of their collective thinking and can begin to focus their attentions on specific target users and, by implication, specific features.

THE MATRIX

The next step is to cross-check the various features and functions compiled in the Content/Capability Inventory against the prioritized user roles by constructing a **Role-Support Matrix**. One version of this matrix lists proposed capabilities or contents against the user roles the system must support. Each role becomes a column in a table; proposed capabilities or contents of the software or Web site become the rows in the table and are identified by a title or short description. The table is reviewed to see which, if any, of the identified user roles are actually supported by each particular capability or content. The question is: How important is each particular feature, function, or content to the performance of a given role? In each cell of the table, a value is entered to represent the importance, based on a simple numeric scale. One possibility is a five-point scale ranging from +2 to −2.

+2 Necessary: a user cannot effectively perform the role without this content or capability.

+1 Desirable: the role is easier to perform with this content or capability.

 0 Irrelevant: the role is unaffected by this content or capability.

−1 Undesirable: the role is more difficult to perform with this content or capability.

−2 Prohibited: the role essentially can't be performed if this content or feature is present.

Features, functions, or content that end up with only zeros next to them are clearly not genuine requirements with respect to the work to be performed or the end-user population to be served. Any content or capability without a +2 in at least one column is optional and could be a candidate for being dropped from the project altogether or deferred until a later version or release. Content or capability with negative numbers, especially for more than one user role, may need to be reconsidered. Although −2s are uncommon, they occasionally arise when particular managers or groups have pushed for a pet feature that contradicts or interferes with certain work. Wizard-style interaction may be popular, for example, but wizards can slow down advanced users and actually prevent rapid performance of some sophisticated tasks.

The Role-Support Matrix may be simple in concept, but it can be a powerful management tool in two ways. First, it gives a clear and comprehensive picture of how the many possible features and functions fit with the real needs of the users the project is to serve. Second, it can be a persuasive tool for communicating with the originators of the ideas. In a sense, the matrix simply feeds back the original information in another form: This is what you want in the system; these are your stated priorities; these, then are the important features; and these are the ones that might or should be dropped.

> *The Role-Support Matrix is a powerful management tool that simply says: This is what you want; these are your stated priorities; these, then, are important; and these are things that might be dropped.*

COMMON VOCABULARY

In general, improving communication with other groups and constituencies in the product development process would seem to be a good idea, but I've found that it's possible to carry the agenda of good communication too far. After one large firm that my company has worked with began to adopt usage-centered design on a wide scale, management decided to train nearly everyone in the basic design concepts, such as user roles and use cases. The training was to include staff from the marketing and customer-contact side of the business who were involved in the initial stages of defining new products. The worthy objective was to build a common vocabulary that would enhance communication among those responsible for product definition and the designers and developers charged with building those products.

Following the training, descriptions of proposed new products started to be written in terms of use cases and the user roles they supported. Unfortunately, years of prior experience far outweighed the effects of recent training, and the newly minted lists of use cases usually turned out to be just lists of features under a new heading.

In usage-centered design, an essential use case has a fairly narrow and precise definition. It is a single case of use representing a discrete intention on the part of a user in a particular role. Features are a part of a system or even aspects of how it works that allow various use cases to be performed. Use cases are neither features nor functions but distinct things users need to accomplish with features or functions.

Problems arise because marketing people and customer engineers easily develop a sense of ownership about their mislabeled use cases and are prone to protest when the use-case models developed by the designers differ from or seem to contradict the originals, especially if the design models appear to omit cherished features or pet functionality. "Where did my 'automatic resorting on object insertion' use case go?" "Well, it's not really a use case, and it really isn't needed to support the identified user roles." "But it's in the product definition!"

We and our clients have finally concluded that the process goes more smoothly, especially in the relationships among designers and developers on the one side and managers and marketing folks on the other, when each side continues to speak in its own tongue. Tools like the Role-Support Matrix can serve as a bridge to aid in the translation. Rather than trying to get the management and marketing types to understand your language, you're better off going the extra distance in taking the responsibility for understanding theirs.

> *Rather than trying to get the management and marketing types to understand your language, you're better off taking the responsibility for understanding theirs.*

So, encourage the fantasies in terms of features and functions, but organize them and array them against the targeted users and customers. Once priorities have been set, these creative inputs can be used to construct design-oriented models, such as models of actors, user roles, task cases, and system use cases, that are needed to guide the design and development process.

Chapter 13

Software Collaborations: Managing the Complexities of Cooperation

Mary Loomis

After one industry conference, one of the leaders in object-oriented software development shared with me his fantasy of a future software development think tank. This enterprise would bring together some of the field's top innovators in practices and processes to extend the leading edge in software development. What did I think? It sounded great. But. . . .

A think tank requires thinkers: creative, energetic, and independent leaders who can push the envelope. The problem is that such innovative thinkers do not readily collaborate. Just picture what would happen if you brought together some of the top names, the top minds in the industry and put them in the same office. Managing such a collaboration could be Sisyphean. Who could lead a bunch of leaders? My colleague immediately thought of somebody—a manager for whom he himself would happily work, one with the skill and finesse to handle the position. He named Mary Loomis.

In this chapter, Loomis contributes some of her insights into managing collaborations.

—Editor

Managing the isolated software project team can be a challenge; many of us bear the battle scars we've earned in the process. Managing collaborations across multiple organizations involves further complications. Such collaborative efforts are becoming increasingly common. Quite often, your success as a manager is largely determined by the ability of people in your organization to collaborate with people in other organizations. Here are some of the guidelines that I have gathered and developed to increase the probability that a collaborative software project will be successful.

In a collaboration, diverse parties are working together for some period to achieve a common goal. "Diverse parties" means that the people involved in the project are from different organizations. Multiple management chains are involved, sometimes in different companies. Multiorganization projects are especially challenging to manage since each organization introduces into the software project soup its own motives, culture, and reward system—not to mention personalities and egos.

Working together across organizations means that real energy is needed to sustain cooperation, yet the joint effort has a finite life span. The parties will eventually return to their separate efforts. Often the parties continue to pursue other separate efforts in parallel with working on the collaboration. Depending on the circumstances, the life spans of collaborations are typically relatively short. Even when that lifetime may be measured in years rather than weeks, however, a team member should not plan to make a career out of his or her participation in the collaboration.

The goal of software collaboration is to produce some software result, ranging from a specification to a running system. There need to be valid reasons for working together toward this goal: some identifiable rationale for forming the collaboration and for management and participants to be willing to deal with its inherent complexities.

> *Working together across organizations means that real energy is needed to sustain cooperation.*

SUCCESSFUL COLLABORATIONS

Here are some of the characteristics of successful collaborations that I have observed. They are listed in no particular sequence; all seem to be important.

Leadership

A successful collaboration has a leader who is respected by the entire team. Sometimes two coleaders can work together, but they must trust each other and communicate well. Unless they agree up front on what to do to clearly resolve situations where they disagree, the collaboration will not work.

Goals

A successful collaboration has a clear goal and well-specified expectations. All the team members understand why they are working together, rather than working separately. Team members frequently assess together their progress toward the goal. The leader keeps the goal highly visible, using the team members' commitment to pursue that goal to keep the effort on track. If the goal is obscured, collaborative efforts easily get bogged down in extra work.

Roles

In successful collaborations, each team member has a well-defined role and trusts the others to accomplish their roles successfully. Without this trust, team members may encroach on each other's territory in attempts to get the overall task done. Territorial encroachment can threaten a collaboration's chances of success. If multiple team members have identical roles, then perhaps one of them is superfluous.

Buy-in

A successful collaboration has buy-in from all appropriate levels in all the participating organizations. It is important to identify not only the stakeholders who have resources invested in the effort but also the managers who can make strategic decisions that could torpedo the effort. The team should identify these people and communicate with them, asking them to state their endorsement of the work within their organizations and to the team. One technique that works well to ensure continued buy-in is to hold reviews of intermediate results, inviting the peers in the involved organizations—especially within the same company—to attend the same review. For example, instead of separate reviews for different managers and organizations, an architectural review of an effort intended to provide an integration path for multiple software product lines might include the division managers from both the affected divisions.

Schedule and Interdependencies

A successful collaboration has a clearly visible schedule, with reasonable delivery points and visible recognition of dependencies across organizations. There is a process for handling changes and for tracking status. One sign of a collaboration in trouble is the lack of a schedule reflecting the combined efforts of all the participants. The schedule is also a way to clarify the expected end of the collaboration. Successful collaborations have finite lifetimes.

Resolution Process

A successful collaboration has a well-defined process for surfacing and resolving issues. It is important to decide on such a process before the issues begin to arise. A well-defined issue-resolution process is especially important when a collaboration is being co-led by two (or more) individuals. The process must fit the cultures of the participating organizations.

Communications

A successful collaboration has a well-designed system of communications. The tools used matter less than the team decision on how the communications will take place. Typical tools include regular meetings, shared workgroup databases, e-mail and voicemail distribution lists, shared sets of presentation materials, source code control systems, and document version management systems. Meetings may take place in person or via teleconferencing or video conferencing, with notes distributed afterward to the team members. A common set of tools can make a huge difference in the operation of a collaboration. Regular communications and flexibility are especially vital in collaborations among geographically dispersed teams. When teams are many time zones apart, finding mutually acceptable meeting times can be a challenge. The team should either find an acceptable time and use it consistently or move the time around to inconvenience everybody equally. Communications meetings should be efficient, and it must be clear that participation is mandatory.

> *Regular communications are especially vital among geographically dispersed teams, but, when teams are scattered many time zones apart, merely finding acceptable meeting times can be a challenge.*

Vocabulary and Mindset

In a successful collaboration, team members understand what other members are talking about. It is worthwhile to invest the time to develop a common terminology and vocabulary. Requirements and design models are important to nearly all software projects but especially for collaborative software development. These models help clarify the semantics of the project area. They can be instrumental in helping team members understand each other. However, vocabulary is not enough. In a successful collaboration, the parties understand each other's frames of reference, personal motivations, and business reasons for being involved.

Credit

In a successful collaboration, there is plenty of credit given for everyone's efforts. Team members should openly acknowledge each other's contributions, especially across organization boundaries. Managers should give credit to the other organizations. After all, together the collaborators are expected to perform better than any of the individual organizations could alone. Extensive credit giving works best when practiced by all participating organizations. Even if you find your organization on the short end of the credit stick, I suggest you not scale back. As manager, your role is to support the entire effort and ensure overall success, not to grab the charter or to compete with your collaborators.

Force

Don't collaborate merely for the sake of collaborating. Forced situations are typically doomed. Such collaborations introduce more complexity than value. The effort might better be pursued independently by one—maybe any one—of the organizations.

COLLABORATIONS ARE DIFFERENT

The characteristics of collaborations presented so far are mostly people-related and are probably not unique to software collaborations. What makes software collaborations different, anyway? A few factors are worth noting.

First, it can be difficult to measure the progress of any software project, especially a collaborative one. Managing interorganization dependencies and risks is complicated substantially by the uncertainties seemingly inherent in accurately predicting the schedules of software projects.

Perhaps the smoothest multiorganization project I have had the pleasure to be involved in recently was not a software collaboration; it produced a software conference. I was Conference Chair for ACM's OOPSLA '97, which drew more than 2,500 participants and over 100 presenters from all over the planet. It was a complicated conference. To pull it off, four paid professionals, a dozen subcommittees, and more than two hundred volunteers from nearly as many organizations must be managed in an 18-month intensive effort. Unlike most software projects, progress is really straightforward to assess. You never hear "it's 80% done" or "I've just fixed the last bug." In contrast to software projects that often seem to start each new release *tabula rasa*, each year the new conference chair and committee build on a rich history of well-recorded experience.

Another difference inherent in software collaborations seems to be the extent of interdependencies. Much of software development tends to be rich in side effects. Unmanaged interdependencies have a way of showing up later as bugs. Management attention, careful modularization, and encapsulation can help enormously.

The software business also lacks the kinds of blueprint languages that are typically used to ensure valid communications in other kinds of collaborations, such as in designing and constructing buildings, computer hardware, airplanes, automobiles, or toasters. No matter how conscientious we are about specifying software interfaces or functionality or quality, we are hardly ever quite precise enough. Unlike in many other industries, the software business does not have large stores of tested, standardized parts to draw from when constructing new systems. Without standardization, communication of details becomes even more essential.

> *Unlike other industries, software cannot draw on large stores of tested, standardized parts, making communication of details even more essential.*

FOR EXAMPLE

Let's look at some examples of software collaborations, some more successful than others.

Next-Generation Product Architecture

Goal: specify and prototype an architecture to enable multiple successful software product lines to converge and be extensible into the future. Scope: within one company, with three major divisions involved. Time frame: 6 months. This collaboration has all the characteristics of successful projects listed above and was judged a success by the team and its management, all the way up to the point of convergence in the organization chart.

Another Next-Generation Product Architecture

Goal: same as above, but for different software products. Scope: within one division, with three geographically distant operations involved. This effort failed and was eventually abandoned. Several success factors were missing. While there was a clear leader and a specified goal, buy-in within affected parts of the organization was sorely lacking. Top-down endorsement of the effort was visible, but the team's results had no real impact. Lower-level managers did not commit to changes but continued to focus on individual success—which was how their performance was measured.

Modeling Language Standardization

Goal: reach convergence on a single specification for a language for object modeling. Scope: an industry consortium of vendors and users with vested interest in object technology (the Object Management Group, OMG). Reaching convergence required achieving buy-in from about a dozen tools vendors and methodologists, endorsement from a task force of representatives from dozens of vendor and user companies, and votes from a committee of representatives from even more companies. The success of this effort falls into the bucket I label "Minor Miracle." As cochair (with Jim Odell) of the OMG's Object Analysis and Design Task Force, I witnessed the importance of each of the characteristics listed previously.

Information System Research Pilot

Goal: develop technologies for integration of applications in a particular domain and pilot the resulting system with real users. Scope: within one company, with two major divisions involved and multiple development groups, and then deployment to a large customer. While this effort eventually produced a small-scale deployable system, it definitely did not achieve its goal. The participants learned a lot—and in that sense it was a success—but it was not the success envisioned at the outset.

There was, unfortunately, no clear leader. Sometimes the marketing group was in the lead and making commitments, and sometimes the development group was in the lead and also making commitments. The goal was really not very clear; it kept changing as the definition of the desired results evolved. Although roles were stated, they were not very clear, and some team members did not trust others to successfully execute their responsibilities. For example, one application team needed a fix to the infrastructure but did not trust the infrastructure team to be responsive, so the application team made the fix itself without communicating with the infrastructure team. Then the application team frequently complained over the next months that it was overworked, relative to the infrastructure team, which apparently had less to do!

Buy-in was also insufficient. Many levels of managers were involved. Nearly all peers communicated openly and well, except among the second-level managers. As a result, team members got mixed signals and priorities became confused. Then the torpedo arrived: a high-level manager of one of the organizations dramatically changed that division's business strategy, making the success of the collaboration essentially irrelevant to the division.

Believe it or not, this effort continued for a very long time with no real schedule. There was an official schedule, but it bore little resemblance to reality. Some of the first-level managers were quite frightened by schedules, could not seem to commit to realistic dates, and did not report slippage when it did occur. The schedule had more than one instance of that much-hoped-for event, "And then a miracle occurs!"

Although there was a defined resolution process, it lacked any effective way to identify issues. Team members were expected to surface issues by speaking up in rather large monthly status meetings. For this group, more frequent, one-on-one communication would have been much more effective, with anonymous presentations of issues for discussion at meetings.

While most participants were quite generous in giving each other credit, one manager was notably less generous. The animosity directed toward that manager did not help morale.

Need I say more?

THE CHALLENGE OF THE OBVIOUS

The characteristics of successful collaborations appear to be fairly obvious. We probably all understand their central contributions to project success. Like many principles of management, they may seem pretty obvious when captured in one place, yet we often have trouble practicing them in the real world of our daily jobs. Perhaps there are other guidelines to be added to the list. Maybe we should collaborate!

Chapter 14

Managing Outsourced Projects: Project Management Inside Out

Steve McConnell

Buy, build, or outsource? It's this decade's twist on a classic question. You may not find the word in a hardcover dictionary yet, but out-sourcing is part of the everyday vocabulary of developers around the world. Often it is intoned to make it sound like a blessing or an epi-thet, and it can be either or both. Outsourcing is looked upon with fond hope by development managers squeezed between shrinking staff and mushrooming expectations. It is eyed warily by in-house developers worried about job security. And, of course, it is the mother lode paying the salaries of the outsourcing industry.

Managing and outsourcing are not usually used in the same sentence, except by the managers at those contract development firms to which software projects are outsourced. Managers at other compa-nies, the buyers and potential buyers of outsourced development, are more likely to think that you outsource software development in part to avoid managing it yourself. Once a project is outsourced, manag-ing it is someone else's problem. After all, that is what you are paying them for, isn't it?

Steve McConnell thinks otherwise. His message is simple: out-sourced projects require the buyer to practice good management. You need to manage an outsourced project at least as well as you manage your in-house development projects, but there are some added com-plications. Fortunately, Steve has already choreographed the basic steps for you. If you follow them carefully, you and your new out-sourcing partner should both be able to finish the dance with smiles on your faces.

—Editor

Some of the greatest software project risks are associated with projects outsourced to internal or external vendors. How can you manage outsourced projects without losing control?

Consider the sad but true case of Giga-Corp. Its customers were clamoring for version 2 of its popular software product, but it didn't have sufficient technical staff to work on the upgrade, and the manager in charge of the project was already overwhelmed. Giga-Corp decided to outsource.

It created a 50-page requirements spec and sent a Request for Proposal (RFP) to a dozen vendors. The RFP did not include a budget but did indicate a strong preference for a fixed price bid with delivery within five months. After holding a meeting to answer vendors' questions, Giga-Corp received a handful of bids, all for time and materials, ranging from $300,000 to $1,200,000. The high bid came from Fledgling-Co, a start-up founded by a former Giga-Corp programmer who had worked on version 1 of the software. Giga-Corp threw it out, along with the low bid, on the assumption that those were outliers and probably the result of misunderstanding the project's technical requirements. It selected middle-of-the-pack Mega-Staff and then negotiated the estimate down to $350,000.

HEADING SOUTH

The first undeniable hint of trouble came when Mega-Staff's head recruiter called Fledgling-Co's president on a Thursday afternoon, sounding desperate. "We need three C++ programmers by Monday. Giga-Corp accepted our bid, but their senior engineer said our Visual Basic approach wasn't technically feasible and we don't have enough C++ programmers to support the project." Fledgling-Co's president said he couldn't find three C++ programmers on such short notice and wished Mega-Staff's recruiter good luck.

Somehow, when Monday rolled around, Mega-Staff showed up at Giga-Corp headquarters with three new C++ programmers. The Mega-Staff team was enthusiastic and appeared to make good progress at first, but by the five-month mark the team was nowhere close to completion. Mega-Staff promised delivery by eight months, which was acceptable to Giga-Corp because that coincided with the beginning of its next sales year. Eight months into the project, the end was still far from reach, and Giga-Corp demanded cost concessions for late delivery.

Fourteen months into the project, after more schedule slips and many painful meetings with Giga-Corp, Mega-Staff delivered about 25% of the planned functionality at a cost of approximately $1,500,000. Considering the shortfall in functionality, Mega-Staff had essentially overrun its proposed cost by 1,400% and its proposed schedule by 1,000%.

BATTENING DOWN THE HATCHES

At the turn of the millennium, many companies outsourced their Year-2000 upgrades to firms that specialized in Y2K work. Some companies outsource work to firms overseas because those firms seem to have access to more technical workers than do U.S. companies. Other companies have grown tired of software management headaches and outsource in order to get out of the software development business.

With software outsourcing on the rise, the Giga-Corp and Mega-Staff disaster is being replayed by software outsourcing buyers and vendors throughout the world. The groundwork for failure on Giga-Corp's project had probably been laid by the time Giga-Corp accepted Mega-Staff's proposal and certainly by the time they signed the contract. These problems could have been avoided if the participants had understood the basics of the software outsourcing life cycle.

Effective outsourcing consists of six steps: specifying the requirements in detail, making an explicit decision to outsource, obtaining resources, selecting a vendor, writing the contract, and building an in-house management team that will monitor the project to completion. Super-large projects—Department of Defense style—will need more steps, but most business software projects will benefit from learning the specifics of these basic steps.

1. Detail the Requirements

Because the requirements document often becomes part of the legal contract between the buyer and vendor, outsourced projects need high-quality requirements. The buyer's natural interest is to obtain the most functionality for the least cost; the vendor's is to obtain the most revenue for the least effort. If requirements aren't clearly specified at the beginning, the project can later become a battleground on which all possible ramifications of these different interests are contested. As the case study illustrated, this is a battle that both parties will lose.

If the buyer doesn't have the in-house resources to create detailed requirements, it should use a two-phase acquisition. During the first phase, the buyer outsources development of the requirements. During the second phase, the buyer puts those requirements out for bid and then outsources the development of the software. In general, if a buyer doesn't have the technical or management resources in-house to perform the tasks needed to support effective outsourcing, it should have a disinterested third party perform them.

Detailed requirements also form the basis of the buyer's effort and schedule estimates. Buyers who don't create their own detailed estimates or have them prepared by a disinterested third party won't know whether a $300,000 or a $1,200,000 bid is more believable.

> *In two-phase acquisition, the buyer outsources requirements development, then puts those requirements out for bid to outsource software development.*

2. Make an Explicit Decision

You might decide to outsource a project because you don't have sufficient technical resources in-house or in order to work with a vendor that offers specialized expertise you don't have. Or you might outsource one project because you need to keep your staff focused on a more critical project. You might decide not to outsource because you don't want to lose close management control of the project or because you don't want to put your software concept and other trade secrets into the hands of the outsourcing vendor.

The decision to outsource invariably involves weighing both costs and benefits. Because outsourcing will increase a project's risk, you should make the outsourcing decision explicitly, with full awareness of the potential problems. Don't choose to outsource because it seems to be the easiest option—it rarely seems easy by the time the project is complete!

3. Obtain Resources

The buyer must acquire sufficient resources to complete the project. These resources include budget for the proposal phase, budget to pay the vendor, and budget to manage the project on the buyer's side.

4. Select a Vendor

Choose a software outsourcing vendor carefully. Vendor selection is usually performed by creating an RFP, distributing it to potential vendors, and requesting that they submit proposals. The RFP should contain at least certain basic sections, detailed next.

Software Requirements Specification

These are the detailed requirements that were developed in step 1.

Statement of Work

The statement of work is a document containing the management requirements for the project. It specifies the demands you have about managing changes to requirements, kinds of tools and development environment to be used, technical methods and methodologies, software documentation, engineering data (design notes, diagrams, scaffolding code, build scripts, and so on), backup procedures, source code control, quality assurance procedures, and the project's management organization, especially the interaction between your organization and the vendor.

Documentation List

The RFP should specify the documents you want to have developed in conjunction with the software. You should include design documents, source code documentation, operating manuals, status reports, and any other documents you want developed.

Cost and Schedule Estimates

Include the cost and schedule estimates you prepared during requirements development. Giga-Corp didn't know how much its project should cost or how long it should take, which led it to hire a vendor incapable of performing the work. If you don't publish your cost and schedule estimates in the RFP, the proposal process becomes a game in which each vendor tries to guess your budget. If you do publish your estimates, vendors will focus on proving that they can meet or slightly exceed your cost and schedule expectations, which will give you a better basis for choosing the best vendor.

> *If you don't publish your cost and schedule estimates in the RFP, the proposal process becomes a game in which each vendor tries to guess your budget.*

The divergence among vendor estimates to Giga-Corp suggested that either the technical requirements were not developed well enough or that some or all of the vendors were poor estimators. The fact that the highest bid was submitted by the company most familiar with the software was a clear warning. If Giga-Corp didn't want to choose the highest bidder, it would have been wise to switch to a two-phase acquisition approach, using one of the vendors to develop the requirements more fully, creating new cost and schedule estimates, and then putting the project out to bid again.

Evaluation Criteria

Tell the vendors what criteria you will use to evaluate their proposals. Typical criteria include project management capability, general technical capability, technical design approach, technical methodologies, technical documentation, engineering data management, requirements management approach, configuration management approach, and quality assurance approach. Competent vendors will explain in their proposals how they plan to meet each of the evaluation criteria. By publishing evaluation criteria, you make it easier for yourself to make side-by-side comparisons among proposals, and you significantly improve the quality of information that vendors provide. If you don't publish your criteria, vendors will have to guess what is important to you, and you will be left guessing about vendors' approaches to many of your evaluation criteria.

Proposal Preparation Guidelines

Describe how you want the proposals to be organized and formatted. Include descriptions and page limits for each section, margin sizes, contents of running headers and footers, and font size. This might seem overly picky, but specifying a standard proposal format makes the job of proposal evaluation easier.

Be sure to create a sample proposal so you know the page count limits are reasonable. On larger projects, buyers distribute their proposal guidelines for review by vendors before they distribute the official RFP. That gives vendors a chance to comment on the page count, evaluation criteria, and other issues and generally helps to improve the quality of information the buyer ultimately obtains through the proposal process.

Pick the Winner

If you did your homework when you created the RFP, proposal evaluation will be nearly painless. Create a decision matrix to summarize your scoring of each proposal in terms of the evaluation criteria specified in the RFP. Be prepared to follow up with questions to cover missing or insufficient proposal responses.

You might eliminate some vendors because of low scores overall or in specific categories. For example, you might eliminate any vendor that scores less than 10 out of 15 points in project management capability. If Mega-Staff scored only 7 points in project management capability, it would have been eliminated. By publishing explicit evaluation criteria and scoring proposals based on them, Giga-Corp could have known that Mega-Staff was critically weak in project management, and Mega-Staff's eventual project overrun would have been predictable—and avoidable—at proposal time.

As the Giga-Corp case illustrates, the lowest bid and the final project price are often not related. The goal of awarding a contract is not to choose the lowest bid but to choose the vendor that will provide the best value—do the best job for the least money as judged by systematic evaluations of the proposals.

The evaluation criteria can also be used for negotiating changes to the winning vendor's proposal. Giga-Corp might have wanted to negotiate changes to requirements management and quality assurance approaches if they were the weak points in the winning bid.

5. Write the Contract

Your warm feelings about the choice of vendor will quickly evaporate if the project begins to unravel. Be sure your contract spells out the details of management requirements, technical requirements, warranties, patents and other intellectual property issues, contract termination, payment, and any other issues important to you. But don't try to draw up the contract yourself. You can lose in court if your contract doesn't mean what you think it means, so spend the money to have the contract reviewed by legal counsel before you sign it.

6. Manage and Monitor

The magnitude of Mega-Staff's overrun suggests that Giga-Corp essentially didn't monitor or control the project after the contract was awarded. Giga-Corp's managers might have voluntarily accepted a 100% or 200% cost overrun, but they would have to be trying to put themselves out of business to knowingly accept a 1,400% cost overrun.

The most common mistake I see in managing outsourced software development work is that no one on the buyer side manages the outsourced development project at all. While outsourcing can indeed reduce the amount of management needed, it increases the degree of management sophistication needed. The problems involved with managing a project across the hall are magnified when you have to manage a project across town or across the globe.

> *Outsourcing may reduce the amount of project management needed on the buyer side, but it increases the sophistication required.*

Because you can't monitor progress on an outsourced project just by walking around and talking to project team members, project tracking indicators need to be more formal. In your RFP, you should specify what management controls you want the vendor to provide so that you can track the project's progress. Such controls might include weekly status reports; weekly updates to the list of technical risks; weekly defect statistics; weekly statistics on the amount of new code added, code modified, and code deleted; weekly reports on the number of modules planned, the number coded, and the number that have passed their code reviews; weekly reports on the number of requirements specified and the number that have been fully tested; monthly status review meetings; or any of many other indicators of project health. On small projects, someone on the buyer's side needs to be put in charge of monitoring the vendor's progress and sounding an alarm when problems arise. On large projects, several people might be needed on the buyer's side.

SMOOTH SAILING

These steps might seem like a lot of work for an outsourced project. As the case study illustrated, however, the price of not doing your homework can be budget and schedule overruns of 1,000% or more. The time you spend laying the groundwork for a successful project and then steering the project to the desired conclusion is time well spent. Just ask any project manager who has been drawn by the siren's song of easy software to the rocky shores of unreliable vendors, cost and schedule overruns, functionality shortfalls, and failed projects.

Chapter 15

Tough Customers:
Toward Win-Win Solutions

Ulla Merz

Software development contracts often look good when the ink is still wet and shiny but begin to tarnish as the work progresses and the relationship regresses. What do you do when things go badly wrong between you and your customer? Trying to call Ghostbusters won't help. There is no coding cavalry to ride to your rescue. You have to work it out. In this chapter, consultant Ulla Merz continues the focus on outsourcing, collaborating, and contracting by outlining some things to keep in mind when trying to turn apparent business impasses into win-win situations.

—Editor

With outsourcing and subcontracting on the rise, the customer-vendor relationship is increasingly important to software development managers. Outsourcing brings together groups of people in a relationship that can be challenging and difficult to manage. It is a bit like a marriage. The success of the relationship depends on how much both parties trust each other and the degree to which they have each other's interests in mind. As in most relationships, customer and vendor pursue their own goals and struggle with the loss of total control.

CUSTOMER MEETS ENGINEERING PROCESS

For example, consider a large insurance company, which we will call Super Insurance. It is a real company, but the details have been disguised in order to focus on events and activities rather than the participants. Super Insurance wants to hire Omni Systems, a custom software development company, to develop a new system for their salespeople. When representatives from Omni Systems, the vendor, and Super Insurance, the customer, meet for the first time, the vendor elicits information from the customer in order to understand the customer's requirements and expectations.

This exchange of information leads Omni Systems to prepare a proposal that outlines the technical solution and provides a cost estimate. Omni Systems and Super Insurance agree to an initial six-week contract period, during which Omni Systems will define the software requirements and prepare a detailed project plan. During this period, Omni Systems' engineers are glued to the customer's words, mining every sentence for relevant information, facts, and constraints that will allow them to analyze and specify the software requirements.

The engineers discover that Super Insurance has a big vision: to leapfrog their competition with a revolutionary quoting system. Unfortunately, people at Super Insurance are busy fighting fires with their existing system and have little time to create detailed requirements for the new system. Engineers at Omni Systems complete the requirements document as best as they can. They also develop a prototype based on the requirements in the hope that it will help the customer to provide input and feedback. After demonstrating the prototype, the engineers at Omni Systems receive feedback that the prototype addresses a part of the desired new software system, but the initial rollout needs to include a handheld device using a mobile communications facility. Omni Systems prepares a detailed project plan and schedule that include the requested changes.

When the project manager at Super Insurance receives the project plan, he goes through it with a fine-toothed comb, questioning the milestones and deliverables. The project manager tells Omni Systems that he is not ready to proceed. At this point, the engineers at Omni Systems are frustrated, as they have not been able to get their heads around the requirements for the system as envisioned by the customer.

In this situation, after several months, vendor and customer reached an impasse. From their own perspectives, both parties felt that they had done everything to the best of their knowledge and ability.

DIFFERENCES, DIFFERENCES, DIFFERENCES

Reaching a common understanding of the requirements for the software system is only one of the difficulties that exist in a customer-vendor relationship. Both parties have to bridge many other differences during their journey of working together. Listed below are several typical differences. In addition to those listed here, conflicts may also arise because of differences in values, priorities, expertise, and problem-solving style.

Language

The customer is comfortable conversing in the language of its business domain, such as telecommunications, health care, or insurance, while the software vendor is trained in the language of software engineering. Words have specific meaning in each domain. Even words such as "leadership" and "process" may be interpreted differently.

Because of differences in language, a lack of agreement can go unrecognized. Being proactive can be useful. Watch for differences in interpretation. Be as specific as possible and when in doubt ask for clarification. Ask for review and feedback at frequent intervals.

> *Because customers and vendors speak different languages—the language of business domains and the language of technology—a lack of agreement can go unrecognized.*

Expectations

The customer may see the vendor not only as a contractor hired to produce a particular software system but also as a consultant available for research and advice regarding software-related questions. The vendor may expect a level of support and focus from the customer staff that is not met or a level of understanding and experience in software development that is not available.

As a result of divergent expectations, unstated expectations may not be met or, if met, are perceived as a burden for which no value or compensation is provided. To avoid this problem, you should be sure to define what success means up front and to make sure that each deliverable contributes to success. You will need to explore the meaning of success in as many aspects and levels as possible, including the organization, the groups within the organization, and the individuals within the group.

Goals

Customers typically focus on the benefits the software system provides and how it helps them to meet their business objectives. From the customer's perspective, the system needs to be available in its entirety as soon as possible. The vendor's goal is to develop and deliver a software system that will improve the customer's business operations and in turn will provide the vendor with revenue and new references for its portfolio. To best achieve this, the software vendor plans for successive deployments of well-specified functionality.

Unfortunately, the goals may be incompatible. When goals are stated and spelled out explicitly, the customer and vendor can collaborate in restructuring them toward mutual enhancement.

Decision Making

When making the trade-offs that most decisions require, the customer may emphasize speed or cost, while the vendor may emphasize technical quality, flexibility, or longevity. For example, when choosing components to integrate into the new system, the customer bases its choice on favorable financial arrangements, while the vendor focuses on the technical feasibility.

Of course, biased decisions are likely to increase the risk. Customer and vendor need to know enough about each other's domain to make informed decisions. Customer and vendor need to know how decisions are made.

Communication Style

Larger companies, those with more than 1,000 employees, may prefer to enter into customer-vendor relationships with companies of about the same size. This is not only because of the size of the work involved but also because of the similarities in communication and interaction styles. For example, information exchange may require a formal appointment, meetings may need to follow a particular protocol, or communication may need to follow the formal chain of command.

Such practices in communication can delay schedules. It is probably best to define a schedule that includes a deliverable within the first two months, at which point the customer and vendor can evaluate the effectiveness of their communication and interaction.

> *Some practices—such as formal appointments, meetings that follow a set protocol, or communication restricted to the formal chain of command— can delay schedules.*

YOU WIN, WE WIN

Of course, in the best of all possible worlds, all such differences would be ironed out early or at least planned for from the beginning. Unfortunately, it is sometimes difficult to see the issues before the business relationship is established, and the customer, the vendor, or both may realize only after several months into an engagement that many of the differences cannot be resolved within the existing framework. The result may be a complete impasse.

It is in the best interest of both parties to resolve the impasse through a win-win solution. Three approaches to creating a win-win solution are: (1) renegotiating the scope, (2) renegotiating the commitment, and (3) changing the type of work. For example, the scope can be reduced to building a proof of concept prototype, with either the customer or another vendor responsible for the pilot implementation and installation. The commitment might be adjusted to fit with the customer's urgency and availability. The work may shift from software development to consulting.

> *Win-win solutions can be achieved through renegotiating the scope, renegotiating the commitment, or changing the type of work.*

Such changes can be implemented while honoring the differences between the two parties. For example, in one particular engagement, the customer wanted to define the scope as the work progressed. The customer was also looking for a long-term engagement that involved full-time employees. The vendor's project orientation—with temporary staff, a well-defined scope, and fixed budget and time—created a conflict. For a win-win solution in this case, the vendor hired consultants near to the customer site who could serve as full-time employees. These full-time consultants took on assignments as the customer specified them. In contrast, if the customer is looking primarily for consulting, the contract might be switched from fixed time and cost to a retainer based on time and materials.

BRIDGING DIFFERENCES

In order to achieve a win-win outcome, both parties need to work together as collaborators rather than critics. Collaboration needs to occur on the business level, the process level, and the personal level.

The Business Level

As Rajiv Sabherwal points out in his article, "The Role of Trust in Outsourced IS Development Projects" [Sabherwal, 1999], a contract is a necessary but not sufficient condition for a successful outsourced project. The contract should be tailored to the customer's needs with respect to service or product development. Does the work involve research and recommendation or does it involve software development? The contract needs to be adjusted according to the expected time frame. Is this a short-term engagement (less than three months) or a long-term one? The contract should match the role the vendor is expected to play. Will the vendor be the exclusive contractor, a general contractor fulfilling the role of integrator, or a subcontractor?

The contract should spell out the structural controls that establish an element of trust between the customer and vendor. Examples are performance penalties, acceptance criteria, monitoring and reporting requirements, payment in equity and fixed bid or time and materials payment terms.

In addition, in order to achieve a win-win outcome, a psychological contract needs to be established through trust. Trust is based on knowledge, whether from previous work engagements, from social contact, or through referrals from joint acquaintances. Trust can also be built through sharing objectives. In contrast, if new objectives are discovered during the engagement that contradict those that were officially shared, caution can replace trust. Ultimately, trust is fostered by doing what you are saying, by delivering what you promise. Achieving an early success can be important to building trust.

> *In addition to a formal contract, for win-win outcomes a psychological contract needs to be established through trust.*

The Process Level

To coordinate their work, vendor and customer need to agree on a process of how to work together as well as their roles and responsibilities. If the contract involves the development of a software system, the process most likely is project oriented. For the project process to succeed, each party has roles to play and responsibilities to fulfill.

Generally, the customer is expected to provide the domain expertise. Equally important, the customer should provide information regarding existing business processes that are affected by software automation. The customer must evaluate the technical solution designed by the vendor against the customer's business objectives, otherwise, the vendor should not proceed with the development of the software system. The customer is also responsible for the final acceptance of the work product.

In case the customer cannot supply domain expertise or define acceptance of the work products, surrogates can be found. However, information about the existing business processes requires the customer's involvement. Moreover, the customer cannot delegate decisions.

The vendor is the expert on technology. The vendor is also expected to be knowledgeable about and capable of applying best practices in software engineering. The quality of the software system is in the hands of the vendor. Along with responsibility for quality comes the responsibility to review all intermediate work products with the customer. Often, the vendor is responsible for the deployment of the software system as well as the technology transfer. Only the deployment and technology transfer can be delegated to another party.

The Personal Level

In reality, the vendor organization as such does not work with the customer organization; rather, individuals from both organizations work together. Just as with any other working relationship, people have to come to know each other in order to trust in each other's abilities. It is especially important that the primary contact in the vendor organization and in the customer organization work well together. Frequent contact and open communication are helpful in building the needed trust.

In my role as customer contact with one customer, I noticed that e-mail exchanges and telephone conversations did not seem to reach closure. During my next meeting with the customer, I made it a point to focus my attention on the style of communication rather than the content. I was curious about whether differences in personality types contributed to the communication problems. I concluded that our personal preferences were quite opposite. In terms of one popular personality model, the Myers-Briggs Type Indicator, one of us preferred intuition and spontaneity while the other favored facts and planning. Neither of us recognized the value of the information the other had to share.

If personalities are incompatible, customer and vendor representatives may be able to overcome their incompatibilities by understanding the objectives of each other's roles, by listening carefully and operating on facts rather than assumptions, and by establishing common ground. Alternatively, the contact roles might need to be reassigned to people who have more compatible personalities.

> *Incompatible personalities can be overcome by understanding the objectives of roles, by listening carefully, by operating on facts rather than assumptions, and by establishing common ground.*

REVIEWING THE PROJECT

By engaging in a contract, a customer and a vendor have agreed to establish a business relationship and to bring the contract to closure. Unilateral termination is not a satisfactory outcome. When an impasse is reached, the solution requires redefining the relationship, putting a contract in place that defines the appropriate scope and commitment, and establishing trust.

To these ends, either party can conduct a project review with the goal of proposing a redefined relationship. A project review has a number of benefits. It brings the issues to the attention of a broader audience from which to solicit input and to gain support. It is also an opportunity to review the facts objectively and, above all, to identify the best options for a win-win solution.

Chapter 16

Avoiding the Iceberg: Reading the Project Warning Signs

Edward Ziv

Good management is both proactive and reactive. Software develop-
ment managers must plan and map out the strategy that will guide a
project over its course, but they must also be responsive to whatever
arises along the way. Knowing how to react neither too quickly nor
too slowly is part of the art of good management. The manager needs
to react in time to avert disaster but not so quickly as to steer an
erratic course. In this chapter, Ed Ziv suggests that you can better
strike this balance and anticipate problems by becoming familiar
with the warning signs that a project may be headed for the shoals.

—Editor

Like the captain of the ill-fated *Titanic,* project managers often keep the throttle
wide open even when danger looms ahead. Many software development disasters could be avoided if the warning signs of approaching hazards were recognized and heeded. In fifteen years of software development and project
management, I have become more familiar with some of these hazards than I
would have liked and have been able to avoid others only by following the charts
laid out by those who went before me. It would take a good-sized book to map
all the hazards, but here are five prominent warning signs that could indicate
your project is headed on a collision course.

> *Many software development disasters could be*
> *avoided if the warning signs of approaching*
> *hazards were recognized and heeded in time.*

Lack of Belief

Warning Signs

People within the company seem disinterested in the project. Resources are "borrowed" for other, allegedly higher-priority activities.

Underlying Causes

There are two common causes—either people have lost belief that the project can be finished or, just as seriously, your project is orphaned and has no sponsor.

Solution

Lack of belief is the easier of the two problems to fix. Just as skepticism builds over time due to poor or no results, confidence can be rebuilt based on achievements. First, get the project team to set and commit to short-term milestones that are concrete, achievable, and easily recognized. Avoid generalities and insist on taking the time to set measurable criteria. Next, spread the word. Let people know, one milestone at a time, what will be accomplished and how they will know it has been completed. If the team is new to you, you may want to hold back on publicizing the first milestone until you gain confidence in the team's estimation and follow-through skills.

If the issue is the lack of sponsorship, you have a bigger problem. Obviously, you need to find a sponsor. Without one, the project will be guillotined at a budget meeting, or your resources will continue to be "borrowed" for each little thing that comes along until the project eventually withers and dies unnoticed and unmourned. Your remedy starts with compiling a list of all the stakeholders—the potential sponsors—and understanding what is important to each of them.

A "godfather" or "project champion" is desirable, but a large constituency is even better. The leadership of your company has an obvious stake in the successful completion of the project, but don't overlook external stakeholders, such as customers or vendors. Keep in mind that almost any potential sponsor will want to know two things about the project: What will it cost in time, money, and people? What will be the return on investment? Be prepared to answer.

> *A "godfather" or "project champion" is desirable, but a large constituency is even better.*

Lost and Late

Warning Signs

Team members don't seem to know where to go or what to do next. Work frequently needs to be redone, and progress comes in fits and starts.

Underlying Causes

There is no project plan. There are no specifications. Without either, warnings will be going off like alarms in a burning building.

Solution

It may take managerial courage, but you must stop all work immediately! A mess of this sort typically starts because of pressure to complete the job. With any luck, by the time you call a halt, it will be clear that the "damn the torpedoes" approach is not working.

These no-spec, Web-time lunges for the finish line are a bit like driving down an uncharted road at 100 miles an hour with the windshield and windows covered in mud, while your passenger leans out the window and shouts directions. Unless you pull over and wipe off the mud, there is going to be a wreck.

Both you and the team need a road map, and you will need to be able to gauge your progress individually and as a group. Begin by facilitating a meeting with the team to set out milestones. Next, have the team members decide on and commit to delivery dates for each milestone. Ask them if they believe they can meet their objectives and time frame. The commitments must come from the team.

Studies show that projects based on the estimates of project team members have a far higher chance of coming in on time than those projects where the estimates come from above or outside. The reason why should be clear. The people who actually have to perform the work are more likely to have an idea about how long it will actually take to do the work. With a strengthened sense of ownership, they are more likely to accept accountability.

> *Projects based on the estimates of project team members have a far higher chance of coming in on time than those in which estimates come from above or outside.*

Why Are We Here?

Warning Signs

Nobody can articulate exactly why the project is being done. There is a general lack of enthusiasm for the project within the team.

Underlying Causes

Because the symptoms are general, you will need to ask some questions in order to pin down the exact cause. What are the desired results of this project? What are the project's goals? How would you know if they have been achieved? Do team members feel that they have, or have access to, all the information and resources they need? What is the balance among the constraints of cost, time, and features?

Depending on the answers, there could be several things happening. The team may be adrift because of a lack of vision or an inability to see the big picture. When developers don't know the goal, it's difficult for them to move toward it with purpose.

The team may also lack the tools, information, or infrastructure support to charge ahead. Or, the team may not fully believe in the company's commitment to the project.

Solution

Addressing each of these problems starts with one common fundamental: knowing why.

All projects have some underlying purpose in the scheme of the organization; otherwise, they never would have been started. Middle management may shrug them off as the capricious whims of the bosses, major projects may be poorly planned, and the organization may be unprepared for the full impact, but projects are never completely without purpose.

A project, whether software development, a reorganization, or a new sales initiative, is only worthwhile in terms of the value it provides. For the foundering project, you need to identify its link back to the strategy of the organization or department. If the strategy is departmental, it was designed to fulfill a larger organizational goal.

Once you know the purpose and value of your project, you can determine how "winning" will be measured. The best way to do this is with SMART (Specific, Measurable, Achievable, Related to a primary objective, and Time-bounded) goals. An effective goal focuses on the specific results that you wish to achieve rather than on the completion of a task. You should be able to measure the goal so you can be absolutely certain that it has been achieved. It should be related to the overall project in order for it to be meaningful, and it should be attached to a time constraint.

> *The best way to win is to have SMART goals, that is, ones that are Specific, Measurable, Achievable, Related to a primary objective, and Time-bounded.*

A SMART example would be "Reduce the time between order entry and customer fulfillment from three days to 18 hours by June 1." A not-so-smart one would be "Improve fulfillment."

The achievement of well-conceived goals can be measured in two ways. The first is binary, familiar to us as "Pass or Fail" or "Hit or Missed." The second is based on quantifying the success, either through a numeric scoring system—8 out of a possible 10, for instance—or by a subjective measure. In my organization, we use a system based on "Fully Meeting" expectations; overachieving is ranked as either "Exceeded Expectations" or "Far Exceeded," with underachieving ranked as either "Met Minimum Expectations" or "Unacceptable." Whatever scheme you choose, make sure all ranges of success are achievable and the criteria for each are clearly defined ahead of time.

Now that you know where you are going and why, you can start talking about how to get there. To do this, poll the stakeholders for the desired balance among cost, time, and quality or features. Although all may be valued, only one can be the primary driver, and its elevation necessarily comes at the expense of the others. Can you have two equally important drivers? The answer is "No." Only one can be primary, and it will come at the expense of the other two, regardless of their individual importance. For example, if time is the driver, accelerating delivery must increase cost as more resources are added and must reduce somewhat the opportunity for additional features. The same applies if quality is made the primary factor, as it will take more money and more time as additional features are added. A consensus must exist among the stakeholders as to the drivers, as these three factors will determine how you approach your project.

Once the goal is clear and the purpose known, the team will be able to move forward with determination. Likewise, once you can articulate the importance of your project, it will be easier to obtain any resources or information needed from those who have them.

Too Many Cooks

Warning Signs

Sponsors or other executives are micromanaging or stakeholders are intruding. There are frequent status requests, direct interventions, or well-meaning interference.

Underlying Causes

Overinvolvement is a symptom of either a current problem requiring immediate attention or the smoldering residue of someone having been burned in the past.

Solution

First, find out if there is a fire that needs to be extinguished. Talk with the concerned individuals to uncover the roots of their worries.

If the concern is not an immediate threat to the project, or is more a threat to the concerned individual than to the project, the answer is simple: communicate, communicate, communicate. Find out how often the stakeholders would like to be updated and what information is important to them. People won't worry about how the project is going if they hear from you regularly and know they can trust you to deliver both the good and bad news. The only thing worse than hearing about impending bad news is hearing about it after it's too late to do anything about it. Again, it comes down to trust, and trust comes only from communication.

On the other hand, if the issue behind the overinvolvement presents an immediate threat to the project, you should check your mitigation plan. You don't have one? Read on.

Hexed and Vexed

Warning Signs

Things keep going wrong, striking people who are unprepared. Meetings are called to evaluate the impact or to figure out how to handle the situation. It takes a long time to recover from the interruptions.

Underlying Causes

If the number of issues is really enormous or the underlying cause is either incompetence or sabotage, you have problems that go beyond the scope of this chapter.

Otherwise, remember that Murphy (of Murphy's Law) is on the roster of nearly every project team. Things happen. People get colds, vendors lose orders, and shipments get misplaced. Failing to plan for contingencies and exigencies is not optimism, it is denial. You do not need to count on bad things happening, just be prepared for them.

Solution

Define your risks and create a mitigation plan: a collection of scenarios of potential interruptions, errors, and catastrophes and how they are to be managed. To build the plan, ask the team, the stakeholders, and yourself what might go wrong at each stage of the project. For each possibility, ask yourself about the impact of the event and the likelihood of the event actually occurring. Label the likelihood and impact high, medium, or low, with the definition of each level being specific to an organization and even a project.

Volumes have been written on risk analysis, but this is where you must apply some judgment. For a project like the moon landing, NASA tried to address every foreseeable event. However, for most projects you will encounter in business, it is sufficient to address only those circumstances with a high likelihood and a high impact or a medium likelihood and a high impact.

> *For most projects, it is sufficient for risk analysis to address only those circumstances with high impact and medium to high likelihood.*

Your plan should include trigger events that will alert you that a particular problem may be occurring. The heart of the plan should consist of the steps to take in every circumstance, along with the individual(s) responsible for performing each step.

Some projects are inherently error-prone. Risks can be multiplied by overly ambitious objectives (feature loading), compressed or unrealistic delivery schedules, the presence of new team members, or the use of new development techniques or new technology. Any of these added risks should be a definite candidate for inclusion in the mitigation plan.

Better yet, avoid or reduce the risks by plotting your course through good development practices. Limit the impact of new techniques or technologies to components that are not mission-critical, and get training and practice in advance. Use pilot projects. Avoid overloading on features. Go for the modest win, and use the second release for new features when possible.

Looking for the warning signs and dealing with them appropriately may not guarantee you will not hit an iceberg, but it will improve your chances of smooth sailing.

Chapter 17

Lemonade from Lemons:
Learning from Project Failure

Norman L. Kerth

A manager who has not faced failure is still untested. Not only are project managers not always prepared for failure, they are often unprepared for the emotional fallout that failure can trigger. Emotions in the workplace? Many managers might say, "Not on my watch!" Most developers like to think of their work as rational and prefer to believe that they approach it logically. Still, when a project fails—when you fail—you can end up feeling discouraged, depressed, even degraded. But those are just feelings, you think, and this is just a job. There's more code to be cut and new projects to plan. Just get on with it!

Right. In this chapter, consultant Norm Kerth leads us in a different direction, confronting those feelings of failure head-on and suggesting that dealing with feelings may sometimes yield some unexpected payoffs for managers and developers.

—Editor

Let's admit it: too many software projects fail. When they do, the experts line up in rows to offer explanations and suggestions. They compile generic lists of reasons for failure and nod in solemn agreement about the sad state of affairs in software development. Armed with such lists, guides, and a generous dose of 20-20 hindsight, we readily second-guess the stupid or merely silly decisions that led up to the failure. We even divert attention by ridiculing someone else's project, secretly hoping we won't be next.

However, top ten lists of reasons for project failure will not help you learn the most from your experiences with failure. Every failure is an opportunity to improve the way you work. Learning and improvement require you to discuss what really happened to the people, the team, and the organization. You must

127

face not only the technical and management issues but also the people issues: what happens to self-esteem, confidence, relationships, and interactions? You must discuss how to cope with failure—and learn from it.

> *Every failure is an opportunity to improve the way you work, to face not only the technical and management issues but also the people issues of self-esteem, confidence, relationships, and interactions.*

Not long ago, I was invited to work with a software team that had experienced a project failure on a grand scale. It had spent two years and $10 million on a major new system intended to replace an aging, but still critical, system that was riddled with Year 2000 problems. After several schedule slips, cost overruns, and reorganizations, the management concluded that nothing would ever be delivered, and the project was killed.

When I began listening to and interviewing people within the organization, I discovered that they were coping with the catastrophe in a variety of ineffective ways.

Failure is Success   In this newspeak strategy, the project is simply declared a success regardless of what has been or will ever be delivered. Among those people who had declared the project a success, some were doing their best to make sure not too many questions were asked. A shroud of secrecy was being woven around the project, and developers who said too much about the project were labeled "disloyal." I was told, "We need to look positively to the future."

Saving Face   Some spin doctors said the organization's priorities had shifted due to changes in the marketplace. The project had been "put on the shelf for a while," as the company's people resources were being applied in more productive ways on more pressing matters.

Waiting for the Cavalry   Another story was that newly emerging third-party vendors were likely to provide cheaper and better solutions in the near future. Several people told me that "someone else" was investigating these possibilities. The truth was no one was actually looking at third-party options, and no one knew of any viable options. The hope that someone else was working on this problem, however, remained high.

Hunting for the Guilty   It was common to hear detailed stories about individuals who were responsible for the failure. Management pointed to the developers and developers pointed to management. The calamity was always the fault of someone else: the customer, testers, vendors, or contractors. Many team members expected someone to be fired and had their own ideas of who should be at the top of the list.

Proving the Impossibility   Another common position was, "We had the best people working on this project. We worked as hard as possible, harder than could ever be expected, and still it wasn't enough. We proved it couldn't be done. There is no shame in trying something aggressively and not making it. At least we know not to try that again."

Such coping strategies are natural ways for people to respond to failure, yet they are also ineffective in leading the organization toward learning from its failure. Each strategy prevents us from studying our mistakes and improving our abilities to manage them. These ways of coping are not unreasonable when you consider the strong push within our culture to succeed in all cases and the lack of practice within our discipline to learn systematically from our failures. Our culture often punishes failure quite harshly—so much so that many adults learn over time to only rarely take risks, if at all.

> *The coping strategies that are natural ways for people to respond to failure are also ineffective in leading an organization toward learning from its failure.*

What is it all about? It's about grief and loss. When we first join a project, hope is usually high. As we work on the project, make decisions, solve problems, and overcome challenges, we become attached to the outcome. We develop systems as well as a sense of commitment—often a moral one—to the project's success. When things start to go wrong, we work all the harder, sometimes even sacrificing weekends and evenings or skipping vacations. In the process, we become even more invested in the success of the project.

When the project is canceled, we experience grief and loss in the same way that homeowners might grieve over the loss of a home in a disaster. The magnitude of grief might be different, but the feelings are essentially the same. The difference is that grieving over a lost project is not usually accepted in the workplace. We learn to hide or ignore our feelings and to substitute various ineffective coping strategies.

One alternative is to devise a business process that recognizes the emotional component of loss and supports grieving in productive ways appropriate to the culture of the workplace. The emotions that are often ignored or inhibited can help us at this time of loss to become all the more receptive to new lessons. Working through the emotions, we become better prepared to learn from the experience.

The process of grieving the loss of a project or a professional failure has two major stages: acceptance and discovery. In the first stage, participants in the failed project need to accept that emotions of grief and loss are real, are part of the process of healing, and are appropriate for the workplace. In the second stage, once the team members have accepted their loss, they are in a better position to discover the hard lessons that can be learned.

> *Grieving over a project or professional failure has two stages: first, accepting the emotions of grief and loss as real; second, discovering the hard lessons to be learned.*

ACHIEVING ACCEPTANCE

Psychologist and grieving guru Elisabeth Kübler-Ross suggests the experience of grief and loss involves a number of common emotions—denial, anger, blame, bargaining, and depression—which eventually lead to acceptance. There is no particular order in which any person or team might experience these emotions, nor is there a certain amount of time to be spent on each.

Team members of a failed software project need to have a way to experience these emotions in a constructive manner. The workplace must be managed with an understanding that these emotions exist. Ignoring this simple reality will push the feelings underground, where they may be experienced less acutely but will continue to influence the actions of people and will be carried into later projects. Unresolved feelings can lead to counterproductive work habits and conflicted relationships among coworkers. For example, unacknowledged feelings of anger and blame can lead to chronic distrust, and depression can be transformed into habitual passiveness.

What is needed is not project psychotherapy but reasonable opportunity. I have used two simple techniques to help people through these emotions: quiet reflection, often through writing, and group discussions. The typical questions I ask include aspects of the past, the present, and the future. Following are some examples that project participants might be asked to reflect on, write about, or discuss.

Past   What did you hope would happen on this project for you? What did you sacrifice while working on it?

Present   What does it mean to you now that this system won't be finished? What did you learn about running software projects?

> *Reasonable opportunity, not project psychotherapy, is what is needed, such as quiet reflection, often through writing, and group discussions.*

Future   Where do you want to go from here professionally? What excites you about this possibility? What do you need to get there?

A sense of safety in exploring these issues is vitally important. As an operating norm, I tell all team members that I believe they did the best they could, given what they knew at the time. I urge them to write about and discuss their feelings from that position. I make clear that participation is strictly optional and no one will be pressured into sharing anything he or she prefers not to reveal. I tell them whatever they write is personal and private unless they have something they want to share with the other team members.

Depending on the magnitude of grief and loss involved in your project failure, you may want to hire a professional facilitator or a consultant who specializes in this area to help your team through this stage. For very serious failures, the recovery process could extend over months, perhaps even years, but for most situations I've seen, the process is much quicker.

With the team I mentioned earlier, I began by asking the members to send me e-mail about their feelings, after which I made a few follow-up phone calls. Then I set the stage for a team meeting during which I interviewed the president of the company and her chief information officer. The topic of the interview was the failures in each of their own careers: What was the failure about? Why was it important? What happened in the short term and over the long term? What did they learn, and how did that help them later in their careers?

In the course of about an hour, the team made some important discoveries. They found out that even the top levels of the organization knew their project failed, but no one was going to be fired. Perhaps most important, they realized that if the team did not learn how to prevent this kind of failure, it was likely to happen again. If another failure of similar magnitude were to happen in the future, a number of people would undoubtedly lose their jobs, including both the president and the chief information officer.

With these discoveries, the denial, anger, blame, bargaining, and depression finally ceased, and the team reached a state of acceptance. They were ready for the next stage.

BIG-PICTURE LEARNING

Once team members have accepted the failure of a project, having worked through their own feelings, they are ready for a project postmortem. Within the perspective that "everyone did the best they could given what they knew at the time," a postmortem can provide a productive opportunity for learning.

> *Within the perspective that "everyone did the best they could given what they knew at the time," a postmortem can provide a productive opportunity for learning.*

A postmortem can take many different forms. I usually involve the entire team, working for several days to review the project from start to end, so everyone can add his or her own piece of the story to the whole and because everyone can learn from the review. Since no one ever knows the whole story, leaving one person out of the process can create a hole.

During the postmortem, the team works together to construct the "big picture" of what happened. Members look at the project from each person's perspective and see how the same event can mean different things to different people. They discover events that were important to a few people and ignored by the rest. They study how events affected other events and learn why some events were important.

Throughout this review, we look for answers to certain questions. First, what did we do that worked well and should be kept? Second, what did we learn to do as the project proceeded? Third, what do we want to do differently next time? And fourth, what still puzzles us?

If run well, a postmortem can result in a great deal of healing and can dramatically change the energy of the community. The group I have been describing is a good example. As their review proceeded, the team discovered 23 actions they had learned that would have either prevented the failure or made apparent early there was big trouble that needed to be addressed. More important, these 23 learned actions were not yet known to the rest of the company. A similar failure was, therefore, likely to happen to any number of projects. The firm was quite vulnerable, but this team now knew how to reduce that vulnerability by leveraging off their failure. They knew changes needed to be made in their standard software development practices. Plans were made during the postmortem to organize training and take their message throughout the company.

> *Run well, a postmortem can accomplish a great deal of healing and also dramatically change the energy of the community.*

Their message was driven by the energy gained from their experience of failure. One project leader summed up the experience: "The pain and cost of failure might have been worth it if we can prevent even one more failure. The issue is not that we had a failure, but what we are going to do now that we've had one."

If you have had a software project failure, you have a choice. You can be embarrassed and try to hide the fact, but you will then learn nothing and may be condemned to repeat the experience. Or, you can embrace the failure and turn it into something even more valuable than a success.

If life gives you lemons, then make lemonade.

PART III

Under Pressure

The pressure to produce has always been a part of programming, but anyone who has been in the profession for more than a decade or two can attest that the pace has been picking up of late. The impact on developers and their managers is significant regardless of whether shortened release cycles and earlier delivery dates are truly needed or are merely the panicky response of market-driven management. On the Web, in corporate internal applications, in consumer products, and in embedded systems, project schedules are being shortened and release cycles are being compressed. Producing under pressure that may be all but relentless has become a top concern of most managers. This section offers hope for the harried and practical suggestions for the desperately driven.

Chapter 18

Death March:
Surviving a Hopeless Project

Ed Yourdon

The annual Jolt Product Excellence Awards sponsored by Software
Development *magazine are usually associated with optimism as
well as innovation. However, Ed Yourdon won the 1992 Jolt Award
for his book* Decline and Fall of the American Programmer *[Yourdon,
1992], which told us to abandon all hope for the American software
industry. True, he later softened the message when he recanted in*
Rise and Resurrection of the American Programmer *[Yourdon,
1996], but Ed is unlikely to be faulted for being a Pollyanna of the
profession.*

*As he moved from decline and fall to death marches [Yourdon,
1997], his commentaries have not flinched from the language of
drama and doom. In this chapter, he reminds us that project management under pressure too often relies on the pressure-cooker model,
in which developers are kept in "ship mode" and pushed to extremes
over extended periods until the product—in some form or other—is
finally shipped and the programmers can finally sleep.*

*Some years ago, peopleware guru Tim Lister commented on the
long-term prospects for this high-pressure model by noting the relative scarcity of workaholics older than 50 years or so. As the median
age of developers at companies like Microsoft creeps up into the mid-
30s and edges toward the 40s, perhaps we will see some more sophisticated notions of project management emerge into prominence. In
the meantime, companies will no doubt continue to pour on the
steam.*

So, everybody, ready, double time! Go, go, go!

—Editor

When was the last time you worked on a software development project that not only delivered everything the user wanted, on time and within budget, but also involved a rational, nine-to-five schedule? Most of us would consider ourselves lucky if our projects were only 10% behind schedule and 10% over budget, and we had to work only 10% overtime. Far more common is the project that's 50% to 100% over budget and behind schedule, and that operates under the gentle suggestion from management that everyone on the team should be putting in 60- or 80-hour work weeks. Such projects have earned project management's most colorful label: death-march projects. On these, the road to completion is lined with casualties and the survivors arrive exhausted.

Many of the projects in the Silicon Valley companies fall into this category; most of the Internet/Web development projects (especially those at Netscape and Microsoft!) are death marches, as were nearly all of the Year 2000 conversion projects that popped up around the country before the turn of the century. To project management, the excessive work hours seemed justified by the constraints imposed upon these projects: schedules, budgets, and staff allocation 50% to 100% more aggressive than would normally be expected. And the pressure is compounded by the unspoken realization that the risk of project failure is typically greater than 50%.

Some death-march projects involve only a handful of people and last only three to six months. For those who are young, healthy, unmarried, and uninvolved in any activities outside the workplace, these projects can actually be exhilarating—if they succeed. For the gung-ho developer, once a project is over it may take only a week or two of rest to be ready for the next one. It's usually not so pleasant when the project involves a small army of 100 to 200 people working in a state of frenzied hysteria for two to three years. That's when you start to see divorces, nervous breakdowns, and even the occasional suicide.

Though it may seem like there are more of these projects today than ever before, the phenomenon is not at all new. Arguably, much of the software developed for the NASA Apollo projects that sent astronauts to the moon in the late 1960s and early 1970s was developed through death-march projects, albeit highly successful ones. I worked on a death-march project from 1966 to 1967 that was an utter failure. In addition to the project collapse, at least one of my team members suffered a nervous collapse, and several others burned out to the point where they were never really productive again.

The reasons such projects existed in the past and will continue to occur in the future are not hard to understand. Here is a short list:

- Politics, politics, politics.
- Naïve promises made by marketing, senior executives, project managers, and others.
- Naïve optimism of youth—"We can do it over the weekend."

- Internet startup mentality.

- Marine Corps mentality—"Real programmers don't need sleep."

- Intense competition caused by globalization of markets and the appearance of new technologies.

- Intense pressures caused by unanticipated changes in government regulations.

- Unexpected or unplanned crises, such as a vendor going bankrupt or three of your best programmers leaving to form a start-up.

Similarly, it is not hard to understand why software professionals continue to sign up for such projects.

- High risks, but high rewards.

- The thrill of the challenge.

- The naïveté and optimism of youth.

- Unemployment, bankruptcy, or some other calamity as the alternative.

- Revenge.

Assuming that death-march projects will continue to be undertaken for the foreseeable future, and assuming that software professionals will continue to be asked to participate, it seems relevant to ask: How can we survive such projects, and how can we maximize the chances of success? Suppose that a good friend of yours has just been assigned the role of project manager of a high-risk, death-march project, and that he or she is seeking your advice. What is the one thing you think would be the most important advice for a project manager involved in a mission-impossible project? Similarly, what is the one thing you think would be most important for a project manager to avoid on a mission-impossible project?

I've asked these questions of hundreds of software professionals in conferences and seminars around the world, and not once has anyone recommended technology-based solutions or methodology-related answers. Faced with the reality of an unpleasant, high-risk project, no one has recommended object-oriented design, structured analysis, Java, or the latest brand-X CASE tool. Occasionally, suggestions fall within the broad category of peopleware, such as, "Hire really good people, and make sure they're fully committed." But, overwhelmingly, the advice that people offer has to do with negotiations, managing expectations, and risk management.

> *Of hundreds of software professionals, not one has recommended technology-based solutions or methodology-related answers for the challenges of death-march projects.*

In many cases, the most intelligent form of risk management is to avoid the project altogether. As a consultant, I am often asked for advice on death-march projects. Although it obviously depends on the situation, my recommendation is often: "Run! Quit now before it gets any worse! The project is doomed, and there's no reason to sacrifice your own health and sanity just because your organization has decided to embark upon a hopeless project."

Of course, different sorts of death-march projects can have varying outcomes. On the basis of the impact on participants and the chances of ultimate success, we can distinguish four types: mission impossible, kamikaze, suicide, and ugly.

> *On the basis of the impact on participants and the chances of ultimate success, we can distinguish four types of death-march projects: mission impossible, kamikaze, suicide, and ugly.*

The mission-impossible project has some chance of succeeding and making everyone happy. It ends up like an episode in the old TV series that gave us the term: because of the combination of skill, intelligence, and hard work, the project succeeds and everyone lives happily ever after. That kind of death-march project is one almost all of us would sign up for; after all, everyone likes a happy ending, and most of us are willing to put up with some stress and hard work in order to achieve success.

Other styles of death-march projects may need to be evaluated more carefully. Kamikaze projects are those in which everyone knows that failure is certain but still believes it would be a good idea to go down with the ship. Well, that may be the belief of the manager and perhaps of other team members who might be blissfully happy to sacrifice themselves for a hopeless project—but that doesn't necessarily mean that you should enlist.

In contrast, suicide projects are the ones not only doomed to fail but also guaranteed to make everyone miserable in the process. The only rational reason for participating in such a project is the conviction that no other jobs are available.

> *Suicide projects are not only doomed to fail but also guaranteed to make everyone miserable in the process.*

The ugly projects are particularly important to watch for, especially for developers whose day-to-day fate is determined by a project manager or team leader. The ugly projects are those with high chance of success, largely because the manager is willing to make any sacrifice necessary to achieve that success. This style of management is seen in certain well-known consulting firms, and while they may deliver "successful" projects, a lot of blood is usually left on the floor. Unfortunately, it is likely to be the developers' blood and unlikely to be management's.

Assuming you become the manager of a death-march project, your success or failure is likely to depend on the ability of the team to negotiate schedules, budgets, and various other aspects of the project with users, managers, and other stakeholders. Of course, the negotiations are usually carried out by the project manager, not by programmers; indeed, team members are often relegated to the position of pawns in the negotiating game. To make matters worse, project managers are rarely given any education or training in the fine arts of politics and negotiation. Most of them have a hard enough time managing a project even without the additional pressure of death-march schedules and budgets.

> *As manager of a death-march project, your success or failure depends on the ability to negotiate schedules, budgets, and other aspects of the project with users, managers, and other stakeholders.*

Even if you play no active role in the negotiations, you cannot afford to ignore them. You may be able to offer some timely and cogent advice to your manager. Perhaps you can quietly leave on his or her desk a copy of this book or the classic *The Mythical Man-Month* [Brooks, 1975] or even the wonderful article, "Double Dummy Spit, and Other Estimating Games" [Thomsett, 1996]. You might recommend the use of some estimating tools, and you should definitely urge the use of time-boxed and rapid application development (RAD) techniques in order to let everyone (including the users and senior managers) see whether or not the project constraints really are impossible.

Whatever you do, beware of the temptation to give up. Don't allow yourself the defeatist attitude of, "Well, we really have no idea how long this project will take, and it doesn't matter anyway, since they've already given us the deadline. So we'll just work 7 days a week, 24 hours a day, until we drop from exhaustion. They can whip us and beat us, but we can't do any more than that."

If you find that rational negotiations are utterly impossible, then you really should consider quitting, preferably before the project begins. An alternative is to appeal to a higher authority for more time, more money, or more people. The project manager should make the appeal because a successful appeal is extremely difficult for programmers to accomplish on their own. In the worst case, you may need to redefine the nature of the project. Instead of holding out for a mission-impossible style of success, you may need to accept the fate that you are on a kamikaze or suicide mission—or just stuck on an ugly project.

> *The project manager should make the appeal to a higher authority for more time, more money, or more people because it is extremely difficult for programmers to accomplish this on their own.*

It is very useful to see if your assessment of the situation matches those of everyone else on the team. If you're a neophyte manager, you may not know whether you can trust your instincts; you may have to trust the assessment and moral integrity of your manager. But if you have been through a few projects already, you probably should trust your instincts. Ask questions, compare notes with your fellow team members, and draw your own conclusions. If your manager has been bamboozled into accepting a suicide mission, he or she may try to convince you to go along with it. But if your manager is conning you at the beginning of the project, there's a pretty good chance that it will only get worse. My advice: run, don't walk, to the nearest exit.

Advising people to quit if they don't like the prospects of an unpleasant project may seem disloyal—not the sort of thing you would have heard when I joined the software industry in the mid-1960s. But the traditional social contract between employer and employee has been badly eroded during years of downsizing, reengineering, and corporate upheavals. The existence of a death-march project is itself evidence that the employer is ready to sacrifice its employees. Whether for a noble cause or out of desperation, programmers can still vote with their feet—at least as long as the free-market economy continues to function.

The fact of the matter, though, is that death-march projects do continue to take place, despite the fact that everyone knows in advance (whether or not they'll admit it) that the schedule, budget, and staffing assignments are crazy. Assuming that you're willing to stay in the game, several key issues will significantly influence your chances of success or failure.

The prevailing opinion throughout the industry is that new-fangled programming tools and other forms of technology will not save you. In fact, a desperate reliance on such silver-bullet technology (which may be imposed upon the project by senior management or by the Tools Police in the organization) will increase the chances of failure. Similarly, newly minted methodologies—whether unified, structured, or anything else—may turn out to be the straws that break the camel's back.

> *Silver-bullet technology will increase the chances of failure, and newly minted methodologies— whether unified, structured, or anything else— may be the straws that break the camel's back.*

However, one aspect of process is crucial. Asked what that might be, most programmers and project managers would instinctively answer, "RAD!" Rapid application development—or some other reasonable form of prototyping, spiral, or iterative development approach—is highly recommended. However, the process should be one that team members are willing to follow enthusiastically on their own, rather than one foisted upon them by the Methodology Police, whose primary concern may be achieving ISO-9001 certification. My advice is to ignore the Methodology Police; you can apologize afterwards, once you've delivered a successful product. If management doesn't like it, tell them they should save their official methodologies for projects with rational schedules and budgets; and if they don't like that, then tell them you quit.

> *Management should save the official methodologies for projects with rational schedules and budgets.*

I also advise teams on death-march projects to practice triage. Because the schedule and budget are ridiculous from the outset, you can virtually guarantee that the project team will not deliver all of the supposedly required functionality when it runs out of time and money. Thus, it is absolutely crucial to divide the work—whether expressed as features, use cases, events, or function points— into "must do," "should do," and "could do" categories. If you don't do this at the beginning of the project, you will end up doing it at the end when you've run out of time and wasted precious time and resources developing features that turned out not to be so critical after all.

Finally, what about the peopleware issues? Tom DeMarco, Larry Constantine, Fred Brooks, Watts Humphrey, and other gurus have written extensively on the subject, and I recommend that you review their advice before you embark upon a death-march project. Of course, a lowly programmer will not be making the hiring and firing decisions, and a project manager may have only a restricted scope of action, but if a project has been stuck with all the misfits and castoffs from other parts of the organization, there's a pretty good chance the

> *If you don't triage at the beginning, you will at the end when you've run out of time and wasted resources developing features that turned out not to be so critical after all.*

project is on the suicide watch. A project manager may not have *carte blanche* to choose professional staff, but on a death-march, you will need to show a little gumption and veto any attempt to assign brain-dead, mediocre staff members to the project. You should also use whatever formal and informal mechanisms are available to find out whether the other people assigned to the project intend to stay for the duration; some of them may be going through the motions of cooperation while frantically updating their résumés. If so, then perhaps you should, too.

All of this may sound rather gloomy. Yes, some death-march projects achieve glorious success, with fame, glory, and bonuses for all. However, for every mission-impossible project that achieves such wonderful results, another five or ten die a miserable death. And the crucial thing to realize is that, in almost every case, an objective observer could have predicted the failure on the first day of the project. If you are assigned to Project *Titanic,* you don't have to be a nautical engineer to figure out what your life is going to be like for the next 6 to 12 months. It's up to you to figure out what you want to do about it.

Chapter 19

Web-Time Development: High-Speed Software Engineering

Dave Thomas

If you think the product release cycle has reached a frenetic and unsustainable pace in desktop software, wait until you hear what the Web world has in store. How do you manage projects when the delivery date follows the initial budget meeting by only a dozen weeks? How do you produce reliable, usable systems when there hardly seems time for coffee or a bathroom break? Dave Thomas, one of the pioneers of object technology, knows how. Dave and his handpicked crew have learned from a long string of successes how to manage development in "Web time" and to deliver superior software on schedule.

Not everyone will like what he has to say, though. Dave is one of those no-bull working managers who tells it like it is, without so much as a nod to trends, established opinion, or the answers people want to hear. He describes a carefully crafted and streamlined engineering process that may seem to resemble such popular lightweight methods as extreme programming but with critical differences. He argues that good high-speed development needs to be model-driven development if it is to be scalable.

And he speaks from experience.

—Editor

The pace of software product development has changed dramatically over the years. The excitement of new technologies and new business opportunities has created a gold-rush culture that pulls products from development at unprecedented rates. Gone are the days of one major new release every 12 to 18 months. To be competitive, companies must deliver products in "Web time." In Web time, a year is only 3 or 4 months long!

Unfortunately, even the most advanced rapid application development (RAD) processes and tools do not stand up to the sustained demand of quarterly releases. Such schedules are achievable only through extra-human effort by talented software professionals. Coaching such a Web-time development team is an immense responsibility and undertaking. How many sports host a playoff schedule every quarter?

NO RERUNS

The process improvement literature aside, there is no repeatable software process for first-time software. For many new products, substantial portions of the product and its development are being created for the first time. You can't repeat what you have never done before. Web-time development is characterized by bootstrapping all the way to the release date. It consists of guerrilla programming in a hostile environment using unproven tools, processes, and technology, both software and hardware. It is not unusual for a Web-time project to employ new people and to have a new product requirement.

> *There is no repeatable software process for first-time software. You can't repeat what you have never done before.*

To make development even more challenging, the product typically must have an all-new user interface, which must be flashy and completely original so that it catches the attention of official surfers and editors. While their initial evaluations are often only skin deep, these are nonetheless important to the marketing department, especially when a Web-page announcement for a non-existent product can quickly yield a following of 100,000 potential customers.

ASSESSING TECHNICAL RISKS

In the fast-changing world of the Web, it is imperative to identify the technical risks and to manage them properly. Be forewarned that you may need to educate your management and customers about these risks. In the somewhat macho, Web-time world, your concern may be perceived simply as an excuse for not delivering on an aggressive schedule. Failure due to instability, reliability, or performance in a number of areas—for example platforms, middleware, tools, libraries, and integration with other products—can lead to missed promises with career-limiting results.

It is prudent to maintain a list of unknowns and monitor them carefully; seldom are these resolved without cost. The inconsistency, poor quality, and lack of documentation for existing platforms require extensive behavioral experiments and intimate systems knowledge that rival the worst days of mainframe systems programming. Don't be surprised if you must acquire and retain people with the highly specialized expertise for one or more of the platforms or tools that you are using.

DEATH BY QUALITY

The very nature of Web time, coupled with first-time software, means that whatever quality is to be injected into the product cannot be achieved through cumbersome top-down process-oriented techniques. These techniques, such as total quality management (TQM), draw their inspiration from the manufacturing of standard widgets, where repeatability is essential for continuous improvement.

> *For Web-time and first-time software, quality cannot be achieved through cumbersome top-down, process-oriented techniques that draw their inspiration from manufacturing.*

In Web time, quality must be instilled from the bottom up using talented, highly motivated, collaborative development teams—popularly referred to as *high-performance teams.* Software quality circles of small, four- to eight-person teams are a key to surviving Web-time development. The teams must stay in touch with everyone who is involved with the product: customers, software architects, product coordinators, development executives, developers, testers, technical writers, and installers.

JUST-IN-TIME SOFTWARE

Many manufacturers have responded to crises in their industries by adopting just-in-time (JIT) processes. We borrow extensively from JIT, making the necessary adjustments to continuously adapt the process to the people rather than the people to the process. We have been evolving the process for the past ten years with customers whose applications range from embedded systems to banking.

Our process is a proven, customer-driven approach for building products using high-performance teams. It uses an interactive, model-driven approach to software architecture, design, and development. The emphasis is on predictable delivery that stresses timely results over features.

> *Ours is a proven, interactive, model-driven approach to software architecture, design, and development that stresses timely results over features and provides predictable delivery in Web time.*

JIT software is a disciplined engineering approach that is based on the well-documented lessons of three decades of software development. It is architecture-driven because an architectural process defines the major subsystems and their interfaces. The process identifies components and assigns each one to a component owner, who is responsible for its design, implementation, testing, performance, and overall quality. Component ownership is a critical success factor, although the ownership may and does change during the 24-hour-a-day, 7-day-a-week cycles that are essential to develop, integrate, and test the product.

Our process is a component-based manufacturing approach to software construction [Thomas, 1995] in that we build a product from existing components (or *Beans*, as they are called in the Java world). The product evolves through a series of application models (or *prototypes*, as we constructively used to call them in engineering). Often the cycle begins with a display prototype to wow everyone with the nifty user interface. Then follows an interaction prototype, which hooks activities to the user interface to give a feel to the look. This is followed by a simulation prototype, which contains realistic models (stubs) for the product's essential behavior. And finally, the simulation prototype evolves into a design prototype for the final product.

GUIDELINES, SPECIFICATIONS, AND REVIEWS

JIT software construction may be perceived as a polite form of hacking but it is actually a disciplined process of iterative refinement. We replace the always-out-of-date software process descriptions of TQM with lightweight, mutually accepted guidelines and reviews that support high-performance teams. We use the term *guideline* to reflect the fact that guidelines are documents that record team consensus rather than standards imposed by management or the quality-assurance (QA) department. Such guidelines are essential for communication and quality and need to be maintained on the intranet. Each team develops its own guidelines, which are based on its experience in previous projects and the challenges that it faces. We also pair every team with an architect, who is both an advocate and a critic for the team.

Our primary specification tools are use cases, hypertext-based APIs, and interface descriptions. We describe class hierarchies with protocol-based interface specification and frameworks with design patterns.

It is impossible to perform in-depth reviews for all aspects of a project, so we use reviews as a method of risk reduction. Reviews can be initiated internally or externally on the basis of a perceived risk, such as complexity, vague requirements, or a developer's unknown skills or performance. We use automated QA tools to identify code that may need further review. We review the test and release plans. Finally, beta-test customers review the product before we approve it for release.

> *It is impossible to perform in-depth reviews for all aspects of a project, so reviews are a method of risk reduction.*

COMPONENT AND ASSEMBLY LIFE CYCLES

Object or component technology is a necessary, but not a sufficient, condition for success in Web-time development. To achieve high-quality software in three months, you must use components that were constructed and tested in previous time boxes. The current time box provides sufficient time only to assemble the components, update the interface, and repair major defects.

The critical success factor is the recognition that components and the product (application) have separate life cycles. Components themselves go through a life cycle from simulation to prototype, alpha testing, beta testing, and production.

In our environment-based process, all developers continuously participate in a build of the product and have instant access to all changes that are made in the development library. This access lets them incrementally roll their changes forward or backward with fine control. The process is supported by IBM's VisualAge, a proven environment for team development and configuration management. We use VisualAge to support not only our product development but also our tools and other processes such as testing and problem reporting.

MANAGING BY TIME BOXES

Time is both your friend and your enemy in Web-time software development. We manage our development using three- to four-month time boxes, so the development time within a time box is between three and six weeks. Because instability from a new tool or platform can easily consume the entire development time in a time box, management's most important decision is the decision of what to leave out.

With so little time to prepare or manage detailed development plans, we opt for a process that uses software developers and what I call *playing coaches*. Each developer has a time box and an associated deliverable for which he or she is responsible. Customers prioritize features based on the trade-offs that the engineering teams identify. As a result, choosing features is not a developer's arbitrary decision. The resulting project schedule is the sum of the component time boxes plus the system test time box.

TEST ONCE, TEST EVERYWHERE

The promise of Java is "write once, run everywhere." But for those of us who have actually lived in the multiplatform, multigeography world, we know that this really means "test once, test everywhere."

Lurking beneath the nirvana of portable APIs is the reality of trench warfare. Trying to solve insidious, undocumented problems transforms a straightforward programming assignment into an unbounded exploration of the interactions of operating systems, middleware, and tools. What is a new and exciting API for the press is a minefield of undocumented bugs and features for developers.

Most organizations simply do not provide the infrastructure that is needed to support multiplatform and multiculture development. Producing portable software requires a substantial investment in test configurations, frameworks, and tools. For various commercial reasons, from two to three releases of each operating system must be supported. In addition, it is well known that computer platforms, like pollinating trees, must be purchased in pairs so that developers can understand and test them adequately.

We have developed processes and tools for international software development so that we can support both European and Asian releases with a single release cycle. A critical success factor for Web-time global software is access to engineering experts in each geographical area, which is itself sufficient justification for hiring students from around the globe.

ABSORBING STANDARDS

We live with a plethora of standards, which can be official (such as X Window System, Motif, and POSIX) or de facto (such as Microsoft ActiveX and JavaSoft Java). Even a modest effort in tooling can provide the means to quickly absorb industry standards and reduce the error-prone manual implementation of a standard.

Our automated tools support a process to migrate standards definitions into standards-compliant object frameworks and associated test suites. The tools let us rapidly adopt a new standard for competitive advantage. Equally important, they let us track the standard and help us develop testing frameworks and platform regression testing.

RELEASE ENGINEERING

One of the most dramatic effects of Web time on our software processes has been the increased importance and technical complexity of our release engineering process. In most traditional development processes, release engineering is performed by the development team as an end-of-cycle activity or by an often-disconnected release engineering team as an independent activity.

Unlike the TQM world of controlled releases, Web-time development often consists of almost continuous releases. We have joked that we should hook our development library to our Web site so that we don't waste time baselining each release.

Release engineering is so important that we assign critical development management and software architects to the activity. We have developed special tools to build releases for multiple platforms as well as supply incremental, corrective service updates.

> *In Web-time development, which often consists of almost continuous releases, release engineering is so important that critical management and software architects are assigned to the activity.*

The team leaders' war-room meetings prioritize and ensure that all the appropriate fixes (and only the appropriate fixes) are applied to the release. While we attempted to follow a traditional freeze-fix-release approach, the instability caused by so much concurrent development has required a disciplined sequence of freeze-thaw-freeze. Two senior developers must approve any post-freeze fix.

To reduce feature creep and compress the time to integrate and manufacture, you need deep technical knowledge in order to focus on the important problems. Further, release architects and development executives must actively block feature creep, which invades through both the front and back doors as the marketing team and the developers all feel compelled to include extra fixes and enhancements.

PEOPLEWARE

Unfortunately, Web-time development is possible only if you have high-performance teams. The obvious corollary is that there is little room for the average, steady worker or a manager who needs orderly plans and working hours. As a result, we demand increasingly more of these experienced software developers, who are already so scarce. It isn't unusual for developers to work around the clock for extended periods. While the demands may be exciting for a new employee, more than ever before, they can take their toll on the relationships and families of critical, seasoned developers.

Team members must understand each other's strengths and limitations. They must measure each other by their ability to cope with and balance their personal and professional commitments rather than by the absolute hours that they may work. Team members must watch out for each other, looking for signs of depression and excess stress.

Management must understand the effect on spouses and children and offer families time out and a helping hand through special events. We encourage the visits of children and dogs to the office so that everyone can spend more time together during a hectic release schedule.

As we push the limits of Web-time software development into what resembles an extreme sport, we come close to the human limits. As development managers, however, we are far from the experience of Olympic coaches and their cadre of sports psychologists. Only by providing rest time for our teams can we help developers sustain their efforts over the long term. For those who develop software in Web time, we must seriously consider nine-month work years.

> *As we push the limits of Web-time software development into what resembles an extreme sport, we must seriously consider nine-month work years.*

Chapter 20

Taking the Crunch Out of Crunch Mode: Alternatives to Mandatory Overtime

Johanna Rothman

If the theme of this section strikes a familiar chord with you, welcome to the club. We have all been there, working under pressure, whether planned or unplanned. Caught in the maelstrom of unrealistic requirements and damnable deadlines, we grab for whatever tactic looks like it might keep us afloat. More often than not, we start putting in longer and longer hours and then expect everyone else to do so as well. As we and the programmers begin to flag, we flog them all even more, exhorting them to tough it out. "Code, code, code!" we call, like the coxswain of a desperately outclassed crew. Work harder, work smarter, work longer. More often than not, it just doesn't work. More often than not, the software is late, buggy, and inadequately documented. In this chapter, Johanna Rothman tells us that there are other ways.

—Editor

Whether you call it crunch mode, ship mode, or a death-march project (see Chapter 18), mandatory overtime is a standard practice of the industry. When a software development project begins to slip schedule or is faced with near-impossible delivery demands, the formula response is to get people to work longer hours. Soon the project is in constant crisis mode, keeping people hunched over their keyboards until all hours of the night and over the weekends.

Many arguments are used to justify mandatory overtime. Sometimes we estimate our projects incorrectly, and we rely on overtime to compensate for bad budgeting or bad planning. To try to meet unrealistic delivery dates, we exploit the people who work for us with mandatory overtime.

Managers have alternatives to mandatory overtime, however, including choosing to work differently and changing the work to be completed. Understanding the spiral that leads into constant overtime will help us clarify the alternatives.

I'M SOOO TIRED

Looking at his project schedule, a manager I'll call Peter sighed and thought, "We're not going to make it. We're supposed to freeze the code in two weeks, test for another four weeks, and then ship. We can't be late on this project or we'll all lose our bonuses. Wait, I know—I'll get everyone to work overtime! We'll bring in dinners, and maybe even breakfasts. We'll do anything, as long as we can ship this product within two months."

Peter's staff hunkered down and heroically completed the project, putting in many hours of overtime, including nights and weekends. When they finished the project, senior management requested another project with a just-maybe-possible release date. This time the project team worked three months of overtime to make the release date. By the end of that project, a couple of people quit, but Peter and the rest of the team stayed on.

Over the next year, Peter and his project team staggered from project to project, never quite doing things the way they wanted to, always in crisis mode. By the time two more versions of the product had been released, the entire original project team, including Peter, had quit. Now the company was in trouble because they had no one on staff who understood the product. Shortcuts taken by the original project team left the code and internal documentation undecipherable to the newly hired staff.

Most experienced managers have seen such a project death spiral. Some project managers believe they can achieve impossible deadlines just by getting people to work harder and longer hours. In fact, some management teams never learn how to prevent lurching from project to project. Their unending refrain is, "We're in a crunch. We need to stay focused and keep the pressure on."

SLOW SLOGGING

In reality, mandatory overtime rarely helps an organization complete its projects faster. More frequently, mandatory overtime contributes to staff burnout, turnover, and higher costs in future development.

> *Some managers believe impossible deadlines can be met just by getting people to work harder and longer hours, but this tactic contributes to burn-out, turnover, and higher costs in the future and rarely helps complete projects faster.*

You may honestly believe that mandated overtime is helping your staff get the work done. More likely, however, you are actually encountering slow progress, because your programmers are creating more defects and much of the work that was done late at night fails to stand up to the critical light of day. If you are considering imposing mandatory overtime, first observe your project, and then consider whether there are better solutions for the problem of insufficient time.

Overtime Exhaustion

Does progress sometimes seem achingly slow, despite the long hours of work? It may be that your developers are exhausted. Over time, with too much overtime, people can get too tired to think well or to do a good job.

Fatigue builds up in many ways. Some people begin to lose their social skills, becoming more irritable and difficult to work with. Some lose their problem-solving skills and start creating more problems in their code than they solve. Some people become disgusted and cynically put in their "face-time" without doing much useful work. When such telltale signs of team exhaustion appear, the overtime that people are working can be making your project even later. It may be best to give everyone some time off and to return to normal workweeks.

There are other causes of slow progress. One common contributor is that the current staff does not actually understand the product and its objectives. Overtime is unlikely to help in such cases. What will help is to get someone who understands the product to explain it to everyone else. When I suggest this to project managers, their reaction is typically, "Oh, no! Taking time for that will put us even further behind." In truth, if progress is slow and the developers do not really understand the project, the rework rate is probably increasing. Keeping the team from creating still more defects will help you achieve your goal of shipping a quality product on schedule.

As a manager, you should be measuring your rework rate: the time people spend repeating work they thought they had already completed. When the rework rate is high, no one can accurately predict when defects will be fixed.

Defects accumulate as defects in one area cause defects in other areas and the underlying product becomes progressively more unstable. Bad fixes—the kind that are dashed off in crunch mode without considering the consequences or alternatives—contribute to more instability. Tests become more difficult to conduct on the unstable software, slowing the work further and making progress less predictable.

> *Bad fixes that are dashed off in crunch mode without considering consequences or alternatives contribute to instability, thus slowing progress further.*

Dirty Work

You should also watch to see whether people are living at work. Have the cubicles degenerated into pigsties? A certain amount of mess or chaos may be the mark of healthy preoccupation, but outright filth is another matter. Workspaces with empty food boxes, soiled gym clothes, and an accumulation of grime are a sign of trouble. When people eat too many of their meals at work and fail to clean up, they are telling you something: they don't have time to take care of themselves properly.

Maybe your folks clean up their food but are too tired to clean up their brains. Watch out for whiteboards that say "DO NOT ERASE UNDER PAIN OF DEATH!" When people are too hurried to document their work properly, they are unlikely to be able to remember critical details of what they did. When people start forgetting important things, they tend to create more defects than they can fix. People may be working late only to spend much of the next day redoing the work and correcting their mistakes.

All of these factors—tiredness, lack of understanding, high rework rate, and people not taking care of themselves—are part of what can make a project seem like it is marching through molasses.

Work Differently

Even if the members of your team seem to be making good progress, are taking care of themselves, are documenting their work, and are keeping the rework rate under control, you may still think you need to get the work done faster.

As manager, you have some options for completing the work while avoiding overtime. The first step is to tell the project team about your concerns. Do not expect your programmers to be mind readers. If they don't understand your concern about release dates, they can do little to help.

Once you have explained that you want to release earlier, ask the project team for suggestions. Be open even to off-the-wall ideas; if you are late enough in the project, you may need them.

If you really want to save time on rework and fixes, institute inspections or walk-throughs for all fixes. That one step will save you more time than you can imagine.

> *If you really want to save time on rework and fixes, institute inspections or walk-throughs for all fixes.*

Changing the Work

Instead of mandating overtime in an attempt to finish on time, consider whether you really need to complete everything on the management wish list for the current release. Reassess what is truly important for this project. Do not assume that just because you have been doing something you need to keep doing it. Everything should be up for grabs. You may find that people are spending time on things that do not contribute to completion. Eliminate all the extraneous meetings, redundant reports, and make-work activities that can wait until the project is over.

Replan what you need to do based on what is most important to the project. Not everything is equally important. Rank your product requirements and see which ones truly need to be part of the coming release. Develop and get agreement on release criteria so that people know what they are working toward and when they have finished the work.

Managing the Managers

Senior management also has options when it comes to overtime, and you can influence managers away from mandatory overtime by finding out what they want and then delivering what they want. Even when a specific release date is perfectly justified, not everything may be needed by that specific date. Perhaps you can defer some requirements, some documentation, or some types of testing.

Where are the degrees of freedom in your project? If the date is truly non-negotiable, such as a major trade show or a contractual commitment, then explore the feature list and the kinds of defects customers will tolerate. Chances are good that not all features are showstoppers and that customers will tolerate particular imperfections.

If management still insists on all features and a zero-defect product by the nonnegotiable deadline, then you need to get them to see that only a superhuman manager with a staff of superhuman developers could succeed. Management cannot have everything all at once, especially if some demands arise late in the project.

> *If management insists on all features with zero defects by a nonnegotiable deadline, then you need them to understand that only a superhuman manager with superhuman developers could succeed.*

You need to find out the real objective that is driving senior management. After all, if you cannot meet the real objective, there is no point in killing yourself and your team by obeying a mandate for all-out overtime.

One way to find out what management wants is to ask the right questions. One good question is, "Who are the real clients and stakeholders?" Clients and stakeholders may be end users, another group of managers, or even middlemen if you sell to people who resell your product or service. For start-up companies, sometimes the board of directors is the driving force; sometimes the investors are calling the tune.

Another question is, "How will we recognize a successful outcome?" Move the senior managers away from defining a solution to your project management problem—mandatory overtime—to defining their problem and the results they need.

The next question is, "What is that solution worth to you?" Maybe you can get more money for subcontracting or outsourcing. Maybe you can spend money on equipment or training that will make your developers and testers more productive.

Overcoming Overtime

The best option for dealing with overtime is to prevent the need for it in the first place. If you join a project at the beginning, talk to the people who set the schedules. Find out their concerns. If, for example, senior managers are believers in Parkinson's Law, that work expands to fill the allotted time, then develop "inch-pebbles" instead of milestones. Inch-pebbles not only help you estimate the project well but also keep you aware of precisely what is happening and where to take advantage of project advances. Inch-pebbles can help you derive the shortest possible critical path and give you an early alert if you are not meeting your deadlines.

The beginning of the project is the best time to invest in tools and people. If you know of a better way to work or you know that you need more people on a project, the best time to add tools or people is in the early days. As Brooks' Law states, adding people to a late project makes it later.

Make sure your team has the needed tools and knows how to use those tools. At a minimum, every team should have a configuration management tool and a defect tracking tool. Consider early when and how your project will use the various peer-review techniques to assess and accelerate progress and to reduce defects.

Sometimes senior management wants assurance that the project team has a proper sense of urgency. I once worked with a manager who routinely took 35% off project time estimates. That quickly trained me to pad my estimates enough to account for this. I asked him why he routinely cut project estimates, and he said, "I want to make sure people have a sense of urgency. I also want them to have a stretch goal. People need to be challenged!" Unfortunately, when people are challenged with impossible objectives, they often do not take those challenges seriously and may work no harder than if they were not so challenged. Challenges that fall within the zone of the possible may actually help people improve their performance. Outside of that zone, performance declines.

> *When people are challenged with exaggerated or impossible objectives, they often do not take those challenges seriously.*

If your senior management wants assurances that the project challenges your team and that your team has a sense of urgency, ask the team. "Is the work challenging? Do you have a sense of urgency?" If the answers are "No," then ask, "What would create that challenge and urgency?"

Remember, you do not need mandatory overtime to manage projects that deliver quality software on time. There are alternatives. Renegotiating the work to be done or working differently to accomplish the critical work are ways to succeed without flogging your staff to its limits. If you create an environment that allows people to do good work speedily, they will.

Chapter 21

Reducing Cycle Time: Getting through Bottlenecks, Blocks, and Bogs

Dennis J. Frailey

Many communities work hard to increase their tax bases, but the small town in which I live once approved a whopping bond issue to take land off the tax rolls, turning a potential housing development into permanent conservation land. It turned out that the added services for new families, even after offsetting taxes, would have cost the town far more than buying the land outright. Who would have guessed?

In the real world, many things do not behave as common sense would lead us to expect. Obvious ways to make things better can actually make them worse. Widening highways can lead to greater traffic congestion. Slowing some parts of the software development process can actually speed it up. In this chapter, Dennis Frailey shows us some counterintuitive ways to avoid some of the bottlenecks in the software life cycle.

—Editor

It's crunch time! Your deadline looms and the software is far from ready. You work overtime to rush through the most important functions (see Chapter 20). You skimp on the testing, skip the quality assurance, and somehow get the product out the door. Then you resign yourself to customer complaints, frayed nerves, and a never-ending cycle that always seems to have the same pattern: there is never enough time to do it right. Still, your customers keep wanting faster service and your competitors are offering to deliver it sooner than you think possible.

Shortening your cycle time would give you a competitive edge. Deliver before your competitors do and they have to catch up while you work on the next release. The life expectancy of software products is typically short, so meeting tight schedules means your company profits more. Even if you have no competitor, the faster you develop software, the more business opportunities you can accept. Even if you have no market-driven need to develop faster, just having the ability to do so means you can start implementation later in the cycle, when requirements will be firmer and there will be less time for them to change.

CAUSES

In a cycle-time-improvement team I once worked on, we found that the causes of project delays are pretty much the same as the causes of traffic delays. In a long freeway commute, you encounter frayed nerves, plans that go awry because of unexpected delays, and an infinite supply of "other guys" who seem to move into the lane just before you do. Experts on cycle time, such as Eliyahu Goldratt, Christopher Meyer, and Michael Hammer, offer various tactics for solving these problems, but the causes all boil down to three fundamental problems: variability, overly complex processes, and bottlenecks and constraints.

> *The causes of project delays are pretty much the same as the causes of traffic delays: variability, complex processes, and bottlenecks and constraints.*

As my team implemented cycle-time improvements, we discovered that over half of the unnecessary delays were caused by innocuous things that we had not paid much attention to before, such as incompatible tools and data formats, overly complex approval processes, and a failure to plan effectively. On one maintenance project, the typical customer complaint took three months to resolve. About 40% of that delay was traced to an arcane approval process that nobody had thought to question because it had been done that way for ages.

Some delays are simply a matter of wrong priorities. I once spoke with a team whose job was to prepare the shrink-wrap packages for a popular line of software products. The packaging process added two to three months to the cycle time for delivering the software. The team knew it could reduce this to under a month by starting much sooner. But the chief programming guru, who had to approve the artwork for the boxes, would not pay attention to such "trivial" graphic decisions until the code had passed all of its final tests. As a result, the CDs sat there for months, ready to ship, while the artists prepared the final packaging. This example illustrates both a fundamental problem and a fundamental principle. The problem is that the programming guru was focused only on his part of the process, not on the big picture. The principle is that you need to optimize the entire process. This often means being suboptimal for the individual steps of the process, which is a concept that many find hard to swallow.

SYMPTOMS

Cycle-time problems are usually easy to spot, as when, for example, you see a backlog of work, such as software waiting to be tested. Such work is called *work in process* (WIP). Simple queuing theory shows that the more WIP you have, the longer your cycle time. Here's a simple equation that captures the gist of it:

$$\text{Average Cycle Time} = \text{WIP/Throughput}$$

To shorten cycle time, you must increase throughput and/or decrease WIP. However, it's hard to increase throughput without increasing WIP, so the smart approach is to reduce the WIP. What causes excess WIP? The three culprits mentioned before: variability, complexity, and barriers or bottlenecks.

A more fundamental symptom of cycle-time problems is rework. The more you do things over, the more WIP you have, which means you add cost and introduce delays. Much rework comes from simple things: rushing the work (which causes more errors), miscommunication (which may result in doing the wrong thing), and inadequate training (which means you waste time learning and making mistakes on the job).

> *A fundamental cycle-time problem is rework. The more you do things over, the more work in process you have, which means you add cost and introduce delays.*

THE VALUE STREAM

You improve cycle time by attacking the three fundamental problems, but you must pick your battles. It helps to begin by defining the *value stream,* that is, the sequence of things you do that really matter to the customer, the things you must do to deliver the product. A process called *value-added analysis* is a formal way to do this, but you can accomplish a lot by just thinking about what is really necessary and what is not. Examples of necessary, value-stream tasks include designing the software, writing the code, integrating the components, and preparing the help files. Many things you do are not in the value stream: debugging, rewriting bad modules, waiting for approvals, translating between incompatible tools, and correcting misunderstandings. By focusing on the value stream, you open your mind to the things that really matter. Everything else is ripe for streamlining or removal. Once you make a list of the tasks that waste the most time and resources, reduce or eliminate them. Then make another list and repeat. Before long, you will be pleasantly surprised at how fast your projects go.

> *By focusing on the value stream, you open your mind to the things that really matter. Everything else is ripe for streamlining or removal.*

What about testing, reviewing, and managing your projects? These are not technically in the value stream, but they are essential for getting the work done, so they are usually targets for streamlining rather than removal. Nevertheless, your customer would be just as happy if you could write perfect code with no management direction and no need for testing. Indeed, some day you may know how to do just that. After all, some Japanese cars have outstanding quality records even though they are not tested until they arrive at the dealer's lot.

You should design your process to maximize efficiency of the value stream. That is what cycle-time improvement is really all about. In most cases, there are plenty of processes that don't add value to the product.

Every method of cycle-time improvement is a way to make the value stream as optimal as possible. It's a lot like code optimization, so try thinking like a programmer. Imagine your program has one primary execution sequence that must proceed as fast as possible (the value stream). Think about how you might optimize the software to make that happen. You would design the input and output to minimize delays. You would make sure there are no empty input buffers or full output buffers. You would optimize the code in inner loops. You would match your hardware and software for maximum performance. You would evaluate your algorithms to see if there is a faster way. Every line of code you remove will speed things up, especially if you choose the ones in inner loops.

Now, stand back and imagine your software development process as a program. You are the processor and the value stream is the primary execution sequence. Where are the input/output bottlenecks? What are the repeated processes, the inner loops? Is there too much delay getting something approved or through configuration control? Is there a long wait for test resources? Do you wait and wait for requirements specifications or approvals? What steps of your process could benefit the most from better hardware? Are you taking too long to do a critical design step because the workstations are not up to the task? Is there too much paperwork to purchase needed development tools? Is your development process just too complicated? Could you simplify it? Every step you eliminate reduces variability and complexity and means fewer opportunities to introduce defects.

> *Improving cycle time is a lot like code optimization. Imagine your software development process as a program, then look for the input/output bottlenecks, the repeated processes, the inner loops.*

MEASURES

Sometimes the causes are clear but you have trouble justifying the solutions. An important step is measurement. Do you know how much time you spend doing various software development tasks? Can you measure your cycle times? If not, this may be the best place to start. My team found that by measuring and quantifying we could make things happen. For example, we convinced the company to change the approval cycle for new equipment because we were able to show how much money the delays of the former approval process were costing.

Measurement also has other benefits. When we started to measure where we actually spent our time, we were sometimes surprised. For example, the programmers typically felt they should reach agreement on the best coding conventions, but we found that the time spent reaching the best solution was much longer than the savings. A "good enough" convention would have served. (See "Problem-Soving Metarules," Chapter 6, for other ways to avoid wasting time.)

CYCLE-TIME PRINCIPLES

Sometimes the actions needed to reduce cycle time are counterintuitive. For example, consider the **Cycles of Learning Principle**, which says it is faster to do a job several times, in small increments, than to do it all at once. By attacking a job in small chunks, you make mistakes and learn from them on the early cycles but perform at top speed in later cycles, when the problems are usually more difficult. Most of us recognize this as true for software development: iterative or incremental development is often the fastest approach, provided you learn to do better each time through (see "Throwaway Software," Chapter 40).

The **Small Batch Principle** is also counterintuitive. It says economies of scale do not always work. Why? Because large-scale economies are only realized when the requirements do not change. In software development, requirements are changing all the time. Small batches reduce the amount thrown away or reworked when the rules are rewritten. Most of the time you are better off building small things and using a modular approach than trying to do everything in one large "waterfall" cycle.

The **Smooth Flow Principle** states that the optimal process is one in which each step flows at the same speed, like boxcars in a train, rather than having each step go as fast as it can, like cars on a highway. Having everyone go as fast as possible does more harm than good because people end up getting in each other's way. What does this mean for software development? It may mean you should analyze the flow through your development process, find the slowest points—the bottlenecks—and spend more of your time helping there, even if it means taking time away from design or coding tasks and helping out the people in test or configuration control.

Naïve cycle-time improvement efforts often start with the obvious approach of trying to shorten the longest step in the development process. However, rather than optimizing locally, you need to look at the whole process. Ironically, sometimes you get better results by lengthening a process step, even though this may not seem to make common sense at first. A classic example is taking longer to define requirements and to prepare an integration plan so there will be fewer problems and much less rework later. One successful project defined the integration-and-test plan first and gave control over all interface changes to the integration-and-test team. This can dramatically cut integration problems.

> *Naïve improvement efforts often start with the obvious by trying to shorten the longest steps in the process. Ironically, sometimes you get better results by lengthening a process step.*

Another cycle-time mistake is to cut out "overhead" activities, such as quality assurance and configuration control, because they seem to slow things down. If you look closely, you may find that these activities can, by cutting out rework, add more to the overall value stream than you might think. How can you tell? Measure and see. My team found that these tasks, when suitably optimized and integrated with the software engineering process, often saved many times their cost in both time and labor.

HARES, TORTOISES, AND BUREAUCRATS

Do you reward programmers who work late every night and wonder about those who leave early? This is a natural tendency. However, instead of looking at how busy developers are, maybe you ought to measure how productive they are, that is, how much value they produce. When you do, you may find that some of the busiest people are spinning their wheels a lot. Not always, of course, but we have discovered a number of cases where the real work was being cranked out by people we had once considered "too slow." Sometimes the tortoise really does beat the hare.

Overly complex processes and bottlenecks often result from precautionary measures that protect against unlikely or inexpensive problems. Company processes and procedures tend to get more and more complex as time goes by. Each time a problem arises, the bureaucratic tendency is to create a new rule. One company saved a lot of time and money by eliminating the requirement for travel authorizations. The reduction in bureaucracy saved millions of dollars each year—much more than the slightly increased cost of inappropriate travel. After all, how many employees will risk their jobs just to take an unjustified trip? Identifying and removing such obstacles is another aspect of cycle-time improvement.

> *Overly complex processes and bottlenecks often result from precautionary measures that protect against unlikely or inexpensive problems.*

YOU CAN DO IT

By attacking the root causes of cycle-time problems, you can improve your delivery schedules permanently. When you deal with causes instead of symptoms, you save money and improve product quality as well. The techniques are not hard. You just have to apply basic principles in a methodical fashion and be open to new ways of doing your work. The biggest problem often is selling your counterintuitive ideas, which is where measurement really counts. If you are not sure whether to try cycle-time improvement, remember that your competitors are constantly striving to be faster than you.

Chapter 22

Dot-Com Management: Surviving the Start-up Syndrome

Tony Wasserman

E-Business, e-commerce, e-this, and e-that: we are living and working in a B2X world. From B2B (business-to-business) to B2C (business-to-consumer) and even B2G (business-to-government), the so-called dot-coms are involved in all manner of trade and are defining a New Economy that has become everyday fodder for the mainstream press as well as for our own trade publications. Having spent five months designing user interface architecture at a dot-com start-up, I can attest to the frenetic demands of this environment (see Chapter 23). Not everybody will face the challenges of management within the fast lane of the Web world, but we can all learn from the perspective and pointers provided in this chapter by software engineering pioneer Tony Wasserman.

—Editor

Thousands of companies in the New Economy have sprung up with the goal of transforming business-to-business and business-to-consumer markets. Unlike traditional companies, where information technology is largely behind the scenes, in the dot-coms the technology is front and center. If a company's Web site is down, business stops altogether: no transactions, not even advertising revenue. If the site is slow, unstable, or difficult to use, it quickly drives customers away, never to return, with damaging results for the business. The Boo.com fashion site was but one well-publicized example of this phenomenon.

While the technology is still new and evolving, consumer expectations for e-commerce Web sites are already quite stringent. Customers expect 24-7 availability, secure and reliable end-to-end transactions, acceptable performance at modest connection speeds, and a visually attractive, easy-to-use, and easily navigable site.

Web applications must connect a wide variety of client-side browsers and devices to multiple layers of application software and databases running on the server side, potentially including an application server and middleware that provide scalability as traffic to the Web site grows. Sites often include connections to external servers, including those used for content caching, credit card verification, order fulfillment, ad serving, visitor tracking, e-mail processing, file transfer and discussion or chat forums. High availability sites also use multi-homing to increase reliability and site performance. High-volume, e-commerce Web sites are among the most complex applications to build and maintain.

MANAGEMENT CHALLENGES

The complexity and customer expectations impose stiff requirements on development, including minimal downtime, extensive attention to software and site architectures, early consideration of information design and user scenarios, careful selection of outside services, and extensive functional, performance, and usability testing.

The needed engineering activities often must take place within a start-up culture, which emphasizes time-to-market and the urgency of meeting company milestones to obtain continued funding. There isn't much leeway for error, since every company activity is strongly influenced by when sites go live and by the "burn rate" of investor capital usage. With the shift from high capital burn rates to an emphasis on traditional notions of near-term profitability, the pressure on developers and managers has increased even more. The tenet that being first to market is key to success is still widely held even though hard data don't always support it.

> *There isn't much leeway for error when every activity is strongly influenced by "go-live" dates and the "burn rate" of investor capital usage. With a shift of emphasis to more traditional notions of near-term profitability, the pressure on developers and managers increases even more.*

THE OUTSOURCING DECISION

In many dot-com start-ups, the vice president of engineering or the chief technology officer initially has responsibility for both the site infrastructure and site development, often because no one else on the management team understands any of the technology. However, that individual is unlikely to have strong knowledge in all of the different areas related to site development and deployment. In addition, there is a big difference between knowing what has to be done and actually getting it done. This difference is compounded by the difficulty of hiring the development and system administration staff to do the work. Even the best-funded and most-visible start-ups need months to build their engineering teams.

As a result, top management must strongly consider outsourcing part or all of the development and deployment work, even if the company's long-term plan involves ongoing development with an internal team. Indeed, some company founders make outsourcing decisions even before hiring their technology executive, leaving everyone to live with the consequences of those decisions, for better or worse. The dot-com economy has led to the creation of many different consulting firms that will work on all or part of site development. Of course, each of these firms has its own preferences and specializations, so that one choice may get you a "pure" Microsoft solution using Active Server Pages, IIS, and SQL Server running on Windows NT platforms, while another will get you a Java-based solution, such as Bluestone Software's Total-e-Business using an iPlanet Web server and Oracle on a Solaris machine. Clearly, these alternatives have significant implications for the ongoing development of the site, as well as for its reliability and scalability.

Other firms may focus exclusively on a site's look and feel, creating a corporate identity and blending it into a site structure based on an informal description of intended site functionality. Such design firms deliver the visual structure of the system, which may then be passed along to yet another firm responsible for the back end, putting hooks in the HTML code for invoking the various actions, ranging from scripting languages (Perl, Tcl/Tk, or Python) to JavaServer Pages with embedded scriptlets and calls to JavaBeans. Other firms may specialize in functional and/or performance testing of Web sites, using simulated system loads and automated testing tools in addition to real users performing the site functions on a variety of platforms and browsers.

Web-site hosting is also often outsourced as well. Hosting services include not only colocation but also continuous monitoring of site and server activities. New companies have been created to provide the necessary hardware and middleware, as well as the colocation services. In principle, it's now possible, though not necessarily a good idea, to have an entirely virtual organization by outsourcing all the development and site hosting.

The advantages of outsourcing are quite apparent, including delegation of tasks to service providers, access to expertise outside the company, and reduced need to hire staff to perform these functions. The potential disadvantages are equally apparent, including reduced control over technical decisions, difficulty in bringing the ongoing development in-house after initial development is completed, and higher costs, particularly when requirements are changed (a frequent occurrence in start-ups). Nonetheless, the pressures of meeting a tight schedule and building a reliable site infrastructure suggest that it is impractical to do everything internally. In particular, site colocation and visual design should almost always be outsourced. Part or all of the back-end development can be outsourced as long as the chief technologist or an expert outside consultant participates in defining some of the key technology decisions, such as Windows versus Unix systems, application architecture, and database choice.

> *You must consider outsourcing part or all of the development and deployment work, even if the long-term plan is for ongoing development with an internal team. Under the pressure of tight schedules, it is impractical to do everything internally.*

STAFFING

Hiring and retaining good technical people is hard, but it's often harder in a dot-com company. The reasons for this difficulty are numerous, including those listed next.

Need for a Broad Range of Specialized Skills   Building and maintaining a complex Web site means that you need access to people who can design Web-based user interfaces, write code in chosen languages, design and administer databases, and select and configure Web servers, application servers, firewalls, routers and load balancers. You also need people who can perform usability, functionality and performance testing. Managers must strike a balance between outsourcing this work and hiring employees and contractors.

Not for Everyone   Many people who are attracted to start-ups by dot-com success stories may not be well suited to the environment with its rapidly changing and often conflicting requirements, long hours, and uncertainty about long-term business prospects. They may also have unrealistic expectations about what it takes to create a publicly owned company. At a company with only 15 employees, minimal visible Web presence, no revenue, and only a round of seed funding, I once interviewed a candidate whose first question was, "When is the IPO?" Managers need to assess this cultural fit as part of the interview process.

> *A start-up isn't for everyone. Many who are attracted by dot-com success stories may not be well suited to the environment with its rapidly changing and often conflicting requirements, long hours, and uncertainty about long-term prospects.*

Absence of Loyalty   Within two blocks of the corner of 2nd and Folsom in San Francisco, you will find hundreds of start-ups. With such density in this and other high-tech meccas, a developer can quickly and easily hop from one company to another. A declining stock market can leave employees with "underwater" options at prices exceeding the current stock price. Signing bonuses and other incentives encourage people to switch companies at the first sign of trouble. Managers, too, are regularly approached by recruiters offering attractive opportunities elsewhere.

Competition   With far more positions than people available, candidates can be highly selective, evaluating not only the technical work and salary but also the company benefits, culture, location, and policies. Managers must not only evaluate a prospect's technical skills and cultural fit but also must quickly sell the opportunity before the best prospects go elsewhere.

Contractors   Many talented developers prefer to work as contractors, moving from one company and project to another, forgoing benefits but often obtaining small amounts of equity as well as higher take-home pay. Dot-com managers must consider judicious use of contractors, even when they might prefer full-time staff.

New Development versus Maintenance   Many developers much prefer working on new projects rather than modifying or extending existing code. If original development is outsourced, it will be harder to recruit for ongoing development when the work is eventually brought in-house. Timing is also important, since you have to start searching for potential candidates early, but hiring too soon will leave your developers with little or nothing to do.

TECHNICAL ISSUES

In dot-com start-ups, as everywhere, it's hard to create a defined, let alone repeatable, process for development. Dot-com developers have little use for formalisms or principles of software engineering but great interest in any tools or techniques that can help reach scheduled milestones. Dot-com managers joke about supplying developers with clean T-shirts, pizza, caffeinated beverages, and other amenities to encourage long hours, but this working style itself has major disadvantages, chief among them that fatigued or overstressed developers are more likely to make errors.

Steve McConnell [1996] has provided excellent guidance for dot-com organizations. He identifies 27 best practices in rapid development, many of which are particularly relevant to developers of Web applications, including evolutionary prototyping and development, staged delivery, and "signing up" for an unconditional commitment to seeing that a project succeeds.

Managers must pay careful attention to five technical areas that are particularly critical for Web applications: architecture, performance, change management, usability, and security.

Architecture

Web applications involve both site infrastructure and software architecture. Site infrastructure includes basic infrastructure, such as the machines that host the HTML code and code-generation routines, and extended infrastructure that includes servers providing additional services, such as image caching and payment fulfillment. Software architecture must be designed to accommodate frequent change and redeployment as traffic builds. For example, Web pages built with multiple levels of nested tables, carefully padded for pixel-perfect layout, can be difficult to update.

Performance

Achieving consistent, acceptable site performance is among the most difficult tasks in Web development, partly because performance is influenced by so many external factors, including Internet traffic, the performance of extended infrastructure, and connection speed. It's also difficult to predict site traffic volume, especially prior to launch. Promotions or unexpected publicity can create huge traffic spikes, sometimes crashing the site. Even without such surprises, performance degrades exponentially with more users, more contention for server resources, and larger database volumes.

Load-testing tools are needed to simulate various levels of traffic and to monitor the site after it goes live. Scalable architecture and platforms are critical when traffic builds. Food.com and iMotors.com are among dot-coms that had to redevelop sites using different technology.

Change Management

Many sites have parts that are relatively stable and others that change frequently or even continuously. Both the architecture and change management processes must support the rate of change. Traditional version control and configuration management can be transformed into content management for the various items comprising the site. It is essential to manage individual contributors and to control change authority for the various components. Change management must address which changes will be extensively tested and how updates will be uploaded to production sites. Changes to content cached by an application server from a database may necessitate restarting the application server, which may require redundancy or transaction rollback for the site.

Change management involves a trade-off between moving quickly and accepting the risks of limited testing. Some changes present very little risk, while others must be thoroughly tested. It's always essential to have a testing site apart from the production site, with at least four levels of versioning: the production site, the test site, the development site, and versions checked out from the development site by individual contributors.

Usability

No company wants its site featured in "Web Pages That Suck" (*www.webpagesthatsuck.com*), but opinions differ as to what makes a site easy to use and easy to navigate. Whatever it means, usability makes a difference, and users will quickly abandon sites that they perceive as difficult to use. Sites differ widely in the percentage of trouble-free transactions. Although live customer support may help, simple processes and fast response are better for successful transactions.

With no user interface standards for Web sites, designers often show off their creativity, sometimes at the expense of modifiability, usability, or speed. Project managers should give strong guidance to those designing the front end of the site, then invest in usability inspections, focus groups, and testing with real customers to get an accurate picture of site usability and the user experience, especially for business-to-consumer sites.

> *Web designers often show off their creativity, sometimes at the expense of modifiability, usability, or speed. They need strong guidance reinforced by usability inspections, focus groups, and testing with real customers.*

Security   Web-site security is a well-publicized problem. Protecting against such vulnerabilities as denial-of-service attacks, security holes in servers, and theft of unencrypted credit card numbers is an essential part of Web application development. Site security is such a specialized and complex domain that very few dot-coms will have all the needed expertise. It would be wise to bring in a specialist to perform a security audit prior to site launch.

Managing development in a dot-com start-up isn't for everyone, but it can be a chance to test the limits and shape the future. For someone with the right constitution in a suitable situation, dot-com management can be an intense and potentially highly rewarding experience.

Chapter 23

Cutting Corners: Shortcuts in Model-Driven Web Development

Larry Constantine

Not all desperate development is utter chaos. As other contributors to this section have highlighted, discipline and deliberateness may be precisely what is needed for speedy delivery. If, as Dave Thomas suggested in Chapter 19, you rely on models and prototypes to organize and manage the process, you may want to know which models are indispensable and which might only slow you down. Here is a fresh take on the matter.

—Editor

Readers of my writings do not have to be reminded of the benefits of working systematically. I have long been known as an advocate of systematic, model-driven design and development and have many times argued, in my columns and elsewhere, that the greater the time pressure in software development, the greater is the need for thoughtful and thorough modeling. Such advice is, of course, far easier to give than to follow.

Lucy Lockwood and I learned our lessons particularly well in one of those crunch-mode projects that tests the mettle of all involved. We were asked to design the user interface for a complex new Web-based classroom information-management system. This K–12 application was defined by ambitious but profoundly vague requirements and was to be delivered on a sanity-free schedule dictated by upper management, a timetable that seemed to leave no time for analysis, design, thinking, or sleep.

Seduced by the challenge and by the opportunities to break new ground in supporting classroom teaching, we plunged in, determined to deliver a world-class

177

design but fully realizing that there was not enough time to construct the kind of thoughtful and comprehensive design models on which we have built our reputations. Had we known the full scope of the project and the vast void in the analysis before we signed on, we might not have done it, but then we would have missed out on a lot of fun and would not have learned some new lessons in corner cutting.

We have long argued that projects of differing size developed on various time scales require different development processes. One-size-fits-all, "unified" methods are likely to fail on one end of the spectrum or the other. Large-scale projects may require elaborate models, meticulous record keeping, repeated validation and auditing, and careful tracing of information, while smaller, accelerated projects may need streamlined, low-overhead approaches. Web-based projects, in particular, may require stripped-down, speeded-up methods to keep pace with the demands of the rapidly evolving Internet world (see Chapters 19 and 22).

> *Projects of differing size and various time scales require different processes. Large-scale projects may require elaborate models, meticulous record keeping, repeated validation and auditing, and careful tracing, while smaller, accelerated ones may need streamlined, low-overhead approaches.*

Everyone who has worked on one of these exciting, sleep-depriving, mission-impossible projects has felt the need to cut corners, but how far do you go? When does paring down on process leave only a bare-boned skeleton inadequate to support the needs of the project?

As the late Robert Heinlein so aptly expressed it in the classic novel, *The Moon Is a Harsh Mistress*, "There ain't no such thing as a free lunch." Taking a shortcut always exacts a cost. Shortcutting a proven process means omitting or shortchanging some productive activities, and the piper will be paid, if not sooner, then later.

The trick is to pick the tune and the price to pay the piper. Some shortcuts save time, while others can lead into swamplands, where backtracking can be far more costly than sticking to the straight and narrow of proper analysis and design.

MODEL STILL

Despite pressure to deliver designs, we decided at the outset of this project not to abandon completely the modeling we knew would help us deliver a better product. Instead, we would simplify both the models and the modeling.

Most modern software engineering, and certainly nearly all disciplined development, is model driven to some degree. In our work as user interface designers, we use three simple models to help us understand the needs of users and to fit the design to those needs. We model user roles, user tasks, and user interface contents. Associated with each of these models is a map: a role map captures the relationships among user roles, a use-case map represents relationships among supported tasks, and a content navigation map represents how all the pieces of the user interface fit together [Constantine and Lockwood, 1999]. You may use more or fewer models in your work, but the odds are you use some kind of models.

REQUIRED REQUIREMENTS

As the user roles for this particular application appeared to be neither many nor highly varied, we radically shortened the front-end modeling by constructing only a somewhat vague and admittedly inaccurate model of user roles. We were engaging in a sort of studied sloppiness, for which we knew there would be a cost, but we had little alternative. We gathered just enough information to get a good feel for the users and their ways of working, then moved on to other matters. We never constructed a complete map of all the user roles and how they fit together.

In retrospect, this was an expensive compromise but worth the price. The heart of the matter in usage-centered design is understanding the tasks of the users. A good user-role model is a bridge to good task models and can speed up the identification of use cases in the task model, but under such tight time constraints, we concluded the payoff was not quite worth the price. Had we filled in all the blanks and crossed every *T* in the role model, we might have had fewer false starts and moments of panic, but we would not have finished the design in time.

Our advice would be to look at what models in your process serve primarily as bridges to other models rather than driving design directly. Consider cutting corners there and saving your resources for more critical steps.

> *A good user-role model is a bridge to a good task model. Consider shortcutting such models that, rather than driving design directly, serve primarily as bridges to other models.*

JUST IN CASE

Use cases are ubiquitous in software development today, and one particular form—essential use cases—plays a pivotal role in our work. Essential use cases represent the minimal core of capability that the user interface must provide to users; thus they not only capture basic functional requirements but also help structure the user interface around the core tasks.

Those of you familiar with use cases know there are two pieces to the use-case puzzle. You have to be able to list all the use cases, and you need to describe the nature of the interaction that each use case represents. In other words, to understand fully the nature of the supported tasks, you need a use-case map identifying all the use cases and their interrelationships, and you need an interaction narrative defining each use case. Or, to put it into UML-speak, the dialect of the ubiquitous Unified Modeling Language, you need a use-case diagram for the application and a flow of events for each use case.

When it came to cutting corners in the use-case modeling, we drew on our experience with larger, more disciplined projects. On one such effort, we joked that after the first hundred use cases, everyone on the team had become an expert at writing use-case narratives in their essential form. You reach the point where, once a use case is identified, you can almost instantly draft a rough outline of the essential narrative. Only for some of the more involved or exotic use cases will the interaction details not be immediately obvious to the experienced modeler.

This ability, being able to spot the occasional tough nut among the more numerous soft candies without having to bite into either, suggests one way of cutting corners in use-case modeling. If your team has enough experience in use-case modeling, then you may be able to skip writing the interaction narratives for many of the use cases. As you identify each use case, you make a quick but informed judgment about whether it represents an interesting or subtle problem in user-system interaction or just more of the same fairly obvious stuff.

> *If you can spot the occasional tough nut among the more numerous soft candies without having to bite into either, you may be able to skip over the easy use cases and concentrate on the interesting ones.*

In this way, you end up with a long list of use cases, plus narratives for some of the more interesting ones. In a pinch, this collage can pass for an understanding of the tasks to be supported by the system. In retrospect, this shortcut did not work out quite as well as it sounds because in the course of modeling the process narratives, one often discovers additional use cases. Thus, the shortcut can leave you with an incomplete list of use cases, which can mean missing functionality in the system.

Were we to start over, we probably would still hand-wave on many of the simpler narratives but would push much harder on developing a complete map of all the use cases and interrelationships. Without this comprehensive map, critical functions may be discovered only late in the process, which can cost big-time in redesign. Duh.

FACE IT

A more successful trade-off that we made was substituting "face-time" for modeling. We were lucky to be collaborating with a team of educators who combined extensive classroom experience with advanced knowledge of theory and technique. Continuous and ready access to users and domain experts can allow designers to plug holes quickly, clarify issues on the fly, and catch mistaken notions early. It is never a recommended practice to plunge into design with incomplete requirements, but inadequate requirements models are less costly if you can simply walk across the hall to check out a design idea or talk over the cubicle wall to resolve the meaning of an ambiguous term.

Both end users and domain experts are needed. Users are application ground-dwellers, intimately familiar with the ground covered in their jobs but relatively ignorant of important issues outside that scope. Domain experts are the hovering hawks of applications: they know the landscape as a whole but may see less of the practical details.

Easy access to users and domain experts allows requirements modeling to overlap parts of design and development. We call it JITR, for *just-in-time requirements*. Where and when you need the answer to a question, you get it. In one case, a ten-minute, ad hoc conversation in the hall was enough for Lucy to pin down the requirements for two incomplete screen designs.

> *With just-in-time requirements, easy and immediate face-to-face access to users and domain experts allows requirements modeling to overlap parts of design and development.*

This game can be played only if the designers, users, and domain experts are on the same playing field. If you have to play telephone tag or wait for e-mail or schedule a meeting and drive across town to a client site, you are doomed. In fact, Lucy recognized at the beginning that the only hope for success in this project was to work on-site, full-time with the client.

NAVIGATING

Normally, we prefer to build an abstract prototype before we get into the final visual and interaction design. An abstract prototype has two parts: the content model, which represents how the contents of the user interface are collected for use by users, and the navigation map, which shows how all the collections are interconnected. In our experience, abstract prototyping leads to more robust, more innovative designs [Constantine, 1998]. On this project, we chose to take the more common route and go directly from use cases into designing the layout and behavior of the user interface.

Skipping both the content model and the navigation map proved to be a mistake, and we later needed to backpedal in order to complete the navigation map before we could finish the design. The problem is that, without a navigation map showing all the screens, pages, windows, and dialogs and how they are interconnected, you have no overview of how everything fits together. Without this picture of the architecture, you make too many mistakes in placing particular features. Once we completed the navigation map and validated it with our users and domain experts, the design process got back up to speed.

> *Without a navigation map showing an overview of how everything fits together, you make too many mistakes in placing particular features within the user interface.*

PROTOTYPES

We also learned some lessons about using prototypes. Prototypes have many uses. At their best, they can serve as a proof-of-concept for a challenging approach or as the foundation for a sound architecture. At their worst, they can end up being shipped out as a hacked and patched substitute for a real product. In crunch-mode projects, prototypes can be a costly diversion of resources.

One problem is that prototypes are made to be thrown away, whether in whole or in part. There are reasonable arguments for building software to throw away (see Chapter 40), but you do not want to do so unintentionally, certainly not when there is barely time to build one system.

Prototypes can allow you to get something working quickly, but don't be seduced into thinking that building prototypes will save you time. When you are caught in a time crunch, prototypes can become a major time sink. If you know what you are doing, time spent building a prototype is far better spent building the real thing. If you do not know what you are doing, building a prototype is one of the more expensive ways to find out.

Unfortunately, prototypes often serve purposes beyond software engineering. Many companies, especially start-ups, want a prototype to show off to investors and potential customers. There are many problems with such demonstration prototypes. For one thing, the better they look, the more they risk raising expectations—from customers and from management. Cobble together a slick, working VB prototype, and people will wonder why it will take months to finish the project. You may be pressured into "just cleaning up" the prototype and turning it into a shipping product, or you may have to explain why the prototype won't work with real data or in a networked environment.

In any case, all the time you spend putting together a demo or building a prototype is time you are not building the real thing. True, some portions of well-designed, well-constructed prototypes may be recyclable into shipped versions, but any prototype built in crunch mode is probably far too messy and fragile for much to be incorporated into the end product.

In the worst scenario, which is all too common, you not only lose time creating the prototype but then are expected to baby-sit it, keeping it up-to-date and ready to demo to the next group of visitors being shown around the offices.

> *All the time you spend putting together a demo or building a prototype is time you are not building the real thing. Then you have to keep the prototype up-to-date, ready to demo to the next group of visitors.*

Even paper prototypes can carry hidden costs. We use drawing tools to mock up visual designs for review, inspection, and documentation purposes. Of course, they also make great illustrations for reports and can be turned into slides for presentations to management and. . . . The list goes on. You can find yourself providing and maintaining PR materials instead of solving design problems.

TEAMING

Our crunch-mode project also reinforced for us the value of good teamwork. On the front end, we had Chris Gentile and his brilliant team of educators. On the back end, we had Larry O'Brien and his crack engineering team responsible for the programming. We were fortunate to be working with people who could quickly spot the flaws and holes in our designs or just as quickly implement a major change. When you are five hours from deadline and up to your eyeballs in interface alligators, nothing can substitute for a few good developers and one good development manager.

PART IV

Quality Required

S oftware quality is in the eye of the beholder—or of the holder of the purse strings. It is many things to many people, but ultimately it is tied to whatever is required by the users and the purchasers of software; hence requirements and quality are treated in tandem in this section. Which of the "ilities" is required for a particular system: Reliability? Usability? Portability? Exactly what must the system do? How will we know if we have done it well? We start off with twin tirades on our manifest failures, and we end with a look beyond "good enough" software to risk taking and innovation.

Chapter 24

No More Excuses: Innovative Technology and Irrelevant Tangents

Peter Coffee

At times, it has seemed to me that the favorite words of some program-mers and their managers are "yes, but." In public seminars and private team meetings, we often hear a familiar refrain: "Yes, but that's hard to do given the current messaging structure." "Yes, but marketing wants it to work like a browser." "Yes, but we don't have time to do it right." On occasion, I have succumbed to impatience and retorted in kind, "Yes, but that is what we get paid for: solving tough problems."

Yes, we are facing escalating management challenges. Yes, the technology is changing under our very fingertips. Yes, the schedules are shrinking and the expectations are expanding. What are we going to do about it? As psychologist Sheldon Kopp expressed in his brilliant "Escha-tological Laundry List," "It is most important to run out of scapegoats."

It can be good for the management soul to listen to someone who is willing to kick butt and unwilling to listen to excuses. Peter Coffee is an incisive commentator who knows the gritty ins and outs of software development. And he is not accepting excuses.

—Editor

The manager's primary task is to eliminate people's excuses for failure. So wrote management guru Robert Townsend, who turned once-moribund Avis into a profitable company by applying this practical philosophy. Townsend's dictum gives programming managers a daunting to-do list since programmers (as a class) are often a dour and apologetic lot who are constantly explaining why things can't be done on time and up to specification.

It would seem that today's levels of CPU power, memory and storage capacity, and network bandwidth should enable developers to create applications that meet utopian levels of capability and performance. However, there still seems to be an unshrinking gap between what users expect and what, in reality, is delivered.

Is this a case of familiarity breeding contempt, with users of once inconceivable tools becoming quickly accustomed to every new miracle and soon expecting more? Or is this a case of our software development community making brilliant progress in irrelevant directions, so that our breakthroughs— though genuine and substantial—seem to be novelties that briefly impress but in the long run fail to satisfy the most crucial needs of both developers and users?

Managers must recognize the difference between meaningful progress in programming productivity and user benefit, distinguishing between useful innovations and irrelevant tangents in technology development. Armed with this skill, managers can not only be sure that scarce resources for training and technology adoption will be allocated where they'll actually do some good but can also set appropriate standards for the efforts of their teams.

> *Managers must recognize the difference between meaningful progress in programming productivity and user benefit, distinguishing between useful innovations and irrelevant tangents in technology development.*

ENVIRONMENTAL CHANGE

Part of the problem is today's dramatically different business environment compared to that of decades past. The faster tempo of today's business process makes software development less like chess or poetry and more like tennis or improvisational theater.

More than a quarter century ago, Frederick Brooks in *The Mythical Man-Month* [Brooks, 1975] was able to speak, without irony, of "the sheer joy of making things . . . useful to other people . . . in such a tractable medium." His writings imply that only a slob would fail to take the time to make code testably correct before it was deployed.

Different pressures apply today, whether we're talking about the demand to produce a compelling Web site or the need to roll out a new frequent-buyer benefits program to maintain a company's market share.

Bruce Sterling unwittingly foretold the current software development milieu in his forward to *Burning Chrome* [Gibson, 1986], alluding to "a realm of sweaty, white-knuckled survival . . . where high tech is a constant subliminal hum." Like one of Gibson's characters, today's developer may feel trapped in what Gibson called (in his novel *Neuromancer* [Gibson, 1984]) "a deranged experiment in social Darwinism, designed by a bored researcher with one finger permanently pushing the fast-forward button." Users can tell, moreover, that the people who build today's systems are not in full control of their creations. "Computers are in deep trouble . . . The promise has not been kept . . . There has been little net productivity gain," asserts cognitive psychologist Thomas Landauer [1995].

Landauer provides both anecdotal reports and formal study results that describe the incoherence of the modern computing environment, as manifest in everyday situations such as sales clerks entering the same information more than once and even doing written backups because of chronic system failures.

USERS' INCREASING DEMANDS

But that doesn't mean users want the pace of new technology to slow down. For purposes that range from pilot training to industrial equipment servicing to children's games, there's every indication that users will embrace an increasingly immersive experience.

The demands of the next generation of users can be met only by manipulating staggering volumes of data at formidable speeds. One task force has estimated the required bandwidth for an immersive (or "virtual reality") environment at 165GB per second, with roughly a petabyte (a mega-gigabyte) of state information being held by the system at any moment.

The code that animates such vast flows of data into a realistic experience will likewise pose new challenges, with user interfaces demanding the kind of floating-point computation previously associated with engineering and scientific computing. At the 1997 Microprocessor Forum, competing three-dimensional graphics extensions to the x86 instruction set took up half a day of presentations and panel discussions. No participant showed any doubt that these extensions would be needed. The controversy was solely surrounding the balance between innovation and standardization.

TODAY'S EXCUSES

We would do well to master the art of crawling at our current pace before we try to run at tomorrow's incredible speeds. Users' changing demands lead to changing requirements, yet the tools don't help developers deal with this reality of software development. Configuration management, for example, remains a brittle and unsatisfactory proposition, far too centered on source code rather than on the user's changing needs and the collaborative process of hitting that moving target.

> *We would do well to master the art of crawling at our current pace before we try to run at tomorrow's incredible speeds. Users' changing demands lead to changing requirements, yet the tools don't help developers deal with this reality.*

The average project experiences a 25% change in requirements during development, according to one massive study conducted in 1979 at IBM's Santa Theresa Laboratory. If anything, the situation is worse today, though this is likely masked in many organizations by increasing reluctance to spend the time on formal requirements definition in the first place. What can managers do to help developers meet increasing demands and simultaneously retain quality in their applications?

In one of the few systematic studies of the nature of software defects, more than half of the defects identified were disruptions to existing features caused in the process of adding new features [Collofello and Buck, 1987]. Our entire discipline of bounding the required functions of an application and continually verifying the proper execution of those functions is challenged by the incremental nature of an evolving interactive Web site or a distributed collection of network-resident objects.

This is especially true in the realm of cross-platform development. Many developers claim to embrace these new frontiers, but few are properly prepared to explore them. Too many developers are accustomed to writing and rewriting code until it behaves as they desire, rather than working from a designer's point of view based on firm understanding of language and platform specifications.

For example, a developer writing a Java application may observe a desired equal sharing of processor time between concurrent threads during development and testing on the Windows platform, not realizing that this is permitted but not required behavior. The same code will behave quite differently on Solaris, unless it is written with the Java specification in mind and the desired behaviors are made explicit.

The alternative to a formal approach is a completely unsatisfactory process that one corporate developer has nicknamed "write once, debug everywhere." The costs and the poor user satisfaction that come from this approach poison the promise of platform-neutral delivery and steer buyers in growing numbers toward the devil they know in the form of the Windows environment. Developers have only themselves to blame for the resulting narrowing of their technical options and the loss of effective competition among platform providers.

Managers can overcome these tendencies only by the difficult and unpopular means of driving projects forward from design goals, rather than letting implementation relax into the shape that seems most natural for the implementation environment. Managers must give their teams the impetus to provide what's needed, even when this isn't easy, and to refrain from incorporating "sexy" innovations that create platform dependencies unjustified by practical benefits.

CLOSING THE GAP

With Web-based applications as the focus of much new enterprise development, security issues are also coming into the picture. Taking a professional role in the area of anticipating, and if possible forestalling, the fraudulent or unethical misuse of the systems we build has become a necessity.

It is all too easy to say that commercial fraud existed before there were information systems. Development managers should recognize, however, the dramatic increases in risk that come from the quantity and anonymity of access to transactional and personal information.

Team leaders must take particular pains to become experts in the unexpected possibilities of Web-based applications. In this highly connected environment, the potential for invasion of users' privacy and for the commission of outright fraud are elevated by security loopholes in Java and ever more complex browser programs, as well as by the intrinsic power of Web-page indexing tools and facilities such as "cookies."

> *Team leaders must take particular pains to become experts in the unexpected possibilities of Web-based applications, including the potential for invasion of privacy and for outright fraud.*

Researchers have demonstrated, for example, the ability to use a Java applet to report back to its server the names of other active applets, which can then be traced through World Wide Web indexing engines to build a fairly accurate profile of Web-page-access patterns. At the same time, an applet can send a mail message that associates an e-mail address with the resulting profile. This combination of individually innocent features creates what many users would find an unacceptable loss of privacy.

TECHNOLOGY'S ROLE

As users become more realistic about these hazards, one can only become more gloomy about past hopes for technological solutions. "Intelligent agent" technology, for example, once held out as the future of productive interaction among networked users and businesses, now seems less likely to live up to its reputation.

In principle, intelligent agents could streamline what are currently time-consuming tasks, such as routine restocking of raw materials or scheduling of meetings among busy participants. In theory, this would give developers more time to deal with users' increasing demands. Research at institutions such as MIT suggests, however, that game theory quickly becomes an important discipline as soon as interacting agents represent different parties with different interests.

One possible use of agents is in negotiation among network-based components to build dynamically reconfigurable applications, in near-real time, as user needs and available resources change. Component architectures, such as JavaBeans, and network services environments, such as CORBA and Microsoft's forthcoming COM+, all contemplate this alternative to present programmer-intensive approaches such as the tedious wiring together of COM components or statically defined Java classes.

The JavaBeans architecture plays particularly well in an environment of heterogeneous, multitier systems. In this milieu, the portability of Java classes is less hampered by the quirks of graphical interfaces or other aspects of user interaction whose portability is especially tricky. Server-side Java has a strong future ahead of it—unlike client-side applets whose primary functions are likely to be served quite well by the far more approachable technology of Dynamic HTML (DHTML).

It should be no surprise that client-side Java is foundering on the shoals of the graphical user interface (GUI). GUIs have sapped other vital resources during the decade since they became the mainstream. CPU power, display size, color capabilities, network bandwidth, and other costly components of our overall architecture have all been swamped by these pesky pixels.

Graphical interfaces have also become notorious for their ability to confuse the user as application functions and interactions proliferate. Technical publisher O'Reilly and Associates built an entire series of titles around the theme of annoyances in Microsoft's Windows and Office products, which, if anything, are among the most thoroughly usability-tested products of their kind. Only their popularity makes their remaining problems worthy of such attention.

Too many graphical interfaces are built rather than designed: developers should know as much about optimizing the number of levels in a menu hierarchy as they do about optimizing loops and function calls.

A cleaner approach entirely may arise from DHTML. By organizing text into an object model that supports event-driven interaction with the user and permits programmability by scripts, this technology may do wonders for the efficiency of user interface design and implementation. DHTML makes it easy to wrap functionality around information content. All developers would do well to take the time to master DHTML.

FROM DEVELOPER TO USER

By no means, though, will DHTML or other approachable technologies close the gap between the casual user—or even the power user—and the professional application developer. User programming is a long-promised solution to the shortage of development talent, but nonprogrammers can make useful contributions only in well-bounded situations. Especially in networked environments, whose configurations vary from one moment to the next, developers will retain an edge in their ability to think in abstractions and to anticipate multi-branched situations.

Keeping your team productive in creating reliable, upgradable systems is imperative in today's environment. Since anyone with basic computer skills can build and demonstrate a system that handles one test case correctly, developing upgradable, scalable applications should be your team's distinctive competence.

> *Keeping your team productive in creating reliable, upgradable, scalable applications is imperative. Anyone with basic computer skills can build and demonstrate a system that handles one test case correctly.*

From this perspective, it's ironic that for decades the proponents of object-oriented programming have enthused about object technology's resemblance to building blocks. Were this true, users would indeed be able to take over many of the tasks that require trained developers. But the building-block metaphor, with its implications of crude and fragile approximation, sets far too low a standard for the quality and capability of applications.

Managers must be disciplined designers as much as builders and must be advocates for the user rather than defenders of the limitations of machines. Those who attend to these goals will soon define the top tier of this worthy profession.

Chapter 25

The Mess Is Your Fault: Toward the Software Guild

Michael Vizard

An outsider's view can often be helpful. Industry insiders, standing up to their eyeballs in the day-to-day doo-doo of software and Web development, are apt to lack perspective on what is really happening. On the other hand, our business is so technical and complicated that a genuine outsider is unlikely to be able to contribute much insight. An inside-outsider would be perfect—someone with access and knowledge but not caught up in the same stuff as the rest of us. With this in mind, I invited Michael Vizard, then News Editor of InfoWorld, to speak at the Software Development Management Conference. His rant on what ails us as a business and a profession was so well received that he was invited back to do it again. Here, based on his presentations, is his inside-outsider perspective.

—Editor

In software and application development, it's pretty easy to feel like everybody is out to get you. But what's most daunting about that vague sense of dread is that the paranoia is basically justified.

At its very core, the software industry consists of a small number of warring religious camps that aggressively recruit developer acolytes who can be counted upon to serve as religious zealots in the cause of the latest software jihad. In today's environment, one front in these holy wars is the battle between the adherents to Microsoft's Component Object Model for Windows and the backers of the 100% Pure Java component model. To be sure, other examples abound, but no other issue so clearly demonstrates the fundamental pressures working against the development community in its day-to-day work.

BUSINESS MODELS

To comprehend the real issues, you must first understand the business model on which companies such as Microsoft are built. For Microsoft, the single most important constituency that it needs to influence in order to be successful is the developer community. By intertwining its interests as tightly as possible with developers, it can effectively limit the number of options available to customers downstream from the development process by making sure the majority of developers see fit to tie their economic interests to developing for Windows. For this reason, we often see Microsoft chairman Bill Gates and the other high priests at Microsoft reminding the developer faithful that it is adherence to the guiding Windows principles developed by Microsoft that made them what they are today, a fact that developers would do well to remember before embracing any upstart religion called 100% Pure Java.

> *To comprehend the real issues, you must first understand the business model on which companies such as Microsoft are built.*

Of course, it is this very Microsoft dominance of the developer community that the 100% Pure Java initiative is out to usurp. After ignoring for years the crucial role that developers play, the business executives at Sun, IBM, Oracle, and Netscape have come to realize that the average computer customer could care less about Windows. All customers know is that the majority of applications run on Windows, so they buy Windows.

Fortunately for these pretenders to the religious throne, the advent of the Web and the continuing emergence of Java as a viable server-side component architecture has given them a chance to rectify the errors of their ways. In fact, it pretty much looks like the happy little homogenous world of Windows programming is coming to a close, with both sides vigorously recruiting developers to serve in their respective armies.

Just in case you've decided to program at a higher level to avoid this conflict, consider the fact that other vendors pushing programming models are just as bad. For example, database vendors, such as Oracle, invariably force you to embrace proprietary application programming interfaces to really accomplish anything. Similarly, the leading enterprise resource vendors, such as SAP, have their own proprietary development tools.

Of course, you could try to standardize on a proprietary set of middleware tools to link these environments, but then you would be locked into a set of interfaces that only the vendor really understands. Finally, you could just give up all together and outsource the project to a consulting firm, which not only will require you to adopt its methodology but will probably turn your entire company upside down in order to make the way you do business comply with its particular vision of how a business running its software should operate.

CANNON FODDER

Before you and your developers decide to risk your careers by becoming cannon fodder in someone else's war, though, the time might be at hand for you and your colleagues to consider how this state of affairs came about and whether it is really in your best interests to back any of these camps. Remember, both sides of this particular debate are pushing remarkably similar, albeit incompatible, component architectures. So, in theory, with some negotiation, it should be a mere matter of programming to make these two diverse communities cooperate for the greater good. After all, we are all part of the fellowship of developers whose primary interests lie in writing good applications. In your dreams.

The sad truth, unfortunately, is that vendors, in their heart of hearts, see developers as little more than rabble to be manipulated like the great unwashed masses. Arguably, no sight in this business is more pathetic than members of what is probably the most powerful constituency in the industry groveling like trailer-park trash for a $20 T-shirt at a trade show. When you consider that such people directly influence millions of dollars in future software and hardware acquisitions, you can't help but wonder if this situation is some sort of cosmic joke being visited on developers as we collectively enter the twenty-first century.

> *Vendors see developers as little more than rabble to be manipulated like the great unwashed masses.*

When you get right down to it, the sundry technological evils are not visited on developers through some inexplicable malevolent force; they exist because developers and their managers do not take effective actions to limit the outside influences that in so many ways undermine their best intentions and efforts.

Taken in this context, the biggest challenge facing the software and application development community today is not the pursuit of the next great technology but rather how they can effectively cooperate in the pursuit of genuine advancement. This would mean that, rather than arguing over the merits of C++ versus Java, developers would be insisting that the providers of major tools pay more than just lip service to interoperability. They would demand standards that would make it feasible on every project to use the best combination of tools, not just the ones that a single developer happens to know and, in obedience to the religious litany, has come to think will work best for every application under the setting sun.

THE STONEMASON SOLUTION

Fortunately, developers are not the first group of independent craftspeople to confront these types of issues, but with any luck they may be the last. Back in the thirteenth century, stonemasons were being economically manipulated by princes and kings who would pit them against each other. To combat this pressure, stonemasons combined their individual political weight to create the first guilds, which were really the first multinational economic organizations in the world.

What drove them to such lengths was self-preservation. The monarchies of yesteryear tried to apply economic pressure against masons by constantly hiring the lowest bidder, regardless of qualifications. Naturally, this led to a lot of shoddy work and a bad reputation for masons everywhere because major works were in constant need of repair.

For people in the software development business, this scenario is eerily familiar, with customers shaving costs by pitting teams against each other, teams that should be promoting as much cross-discipline cooperation as possible. Moreover, customers are now taking that mindset a step further by pitting low-cost offshore development teams against the home teams, a strategy that was also employed by the monarchs against masons.

> *In software development, the stonemason scenario is eerily familiar, with customers shaving costs by pitting teams against each other, teams that should be promoting as much cross-discipline cooperation as possible.*

The masons' solution to this problem was to organize across international boundaries. By doing so, they were able to maintain a sound economic foundation for their skills while at the same time creating a system in which all building was done according to a set of guidelines that ensured quality. Eventually, this allowed the masons and their freemason descendants to be a major force on the world stage during the next five centuries.

Modern organizations, such as the American Medical Association, can trace their organizational roots back to these early guilds. In fact, many of the basic ideals laid out in the United States Constitution and the Declaration of

Independence are lifted directly from democratic precepts that were first laid out in the founding charters developed by medieval guilds.

THE GUILD OF GEEKS

Unlike a union, a guild is defined as a professional and social alliance that protects the rights of its members, engages in common beneficial activities, and provides public assistance for its members. In that spirit, an effective guild in the software industry could accomplish such tasks as the those detailed next.

> *A guild is a professional and social alliance that protects the rights of its members, engages in common beneficial activities, and provides public assistance for its members.*

Set Best Practices   The truth is that a poorly written application diminishes every developer and cuts the confidence customers have in the people who build them. A guild would be an ideal format for defining and sharing those practices that represent the state of the art and craft. More importantly, a guild could effectively lobby to see that best practices are widely adopted.

Administer Certification Tests   In the same way that the major vendors gain control over third-party developers by certifying compatible applications, so too could a guild bring rogue programmers to heel. In the industry today, disciplined developers and software engineers compete with coding cowboys who are just hacking out code. Customers don't have any real way to distinguish between the amateurs writing scripts and the professionals using industrial-strength tools. There may be a role for both, but an independent certifying body could go a long way toward reducing the confusion that typically confronts customers weighing the options.

Provide Continuing Education   Despite protests to the contrary, it is not in the financial interests of most employers to pay for additional training, especially in a job market so hot that any newly acquired skills are likely to be applied elsewhere. When employers do pay for ongoing training, the conditions attached can amount to little more than indentured servitude because they want developers to stay on as long as it takes to pay off on the investment. An effective guild could easily develop its own no-strings-attached training regimen funded by the membership.

Strengthen Political Lobbying Efforts   Recently, the U.S. Congress has been debating the merits of expanding the number of visas available to bring additional developers into the country, even though thousands of middle-aged developers can't get jobs or the training they need to apply for those jobs. A guild could lobby to ensure that any legislation was balanced enough to include the perspectives and interests of developers as well as their employers. There are groups fighting valiantly today in this arena, but they are sorely outgunned by a vendor community that has substantial resources to throw around.

Enhance Public Relations   Although only a small portion of the doom and gloom associated with the Y2K crisis came to pass, many people pointed their fingers at the development community. The truth is that if anyone had listened to developers twenty years earlier, the problem wouldn't have been this costly to fix. In short, developers need not only to lobby Washington but also to speak with one voice to the media. Otherwise, the public image of the developer will remain that of the well-intentioned geek who is incapable of understanding the big picture. In reality, as the world moves increasingly toward a network economy, developers are among few people who really do understand the big picture, and they need to make their voices heard.

Create a United Front   Perhaps most importantly, developers need an organization through which they can present a united front to the vendors supplying the tools they use. Tool vendors are suppliers, yet all too often developers act as if vendors are doing them a favor by allowing them to use the tools. Then, when the vendors get into economic wars with each other, developers are expected to take sides and fill the trenches. A guild might prevent many of these wars by forcing both sides to adhere to truly interoperable industry standards that are not developed as the result of some unworkable back-room compromise among a group of vendors attending some obscure, ad hoc meetings. If we no longer accept political parties picking our candidates in smoke-filled back rooms, why should we let tool vendors pick our technology in a similar manner?

Developers have to realize that it is not what people actively do to you that really messes with your livelihood. Instead, it's the confluence of competing hidden and not so hidden agendas that conspire every day to make work life miserable. So unless you reach out to your colleagues to create a powerful organization that does more than the academically minded ACM, the systems manager–focused ITAA, or the overly broad IEEE, you will always be dependent on the mercies of strangers who do not have your best interests at heart.

LABOR–MANAGEMENT RELATIONS

For software development managers a guildlike loose alliance could be extremely beneficial because it would ultimately allow them to choose the best set of tools for the job. By leveraging the combined weight of the developer community, the number of proprietary lock-ins that could be put in place by any one vendor would be reduced. A guild would be able to devote its combined resources to ensuring interoperability and, if necessary, could advise its membership against using proprietary tool sets.

Granted, this scenario might be scary for managers because it would also put more power in the hands of the average developer. However, if sufficient care is taken to develop bylaws that prevent a guild from becoming just a trade union by another name, the benefits would far outweigh the potential drawbacks.

The need for some type of guild is a critical issue for software development managers now because demand for application development continues to grow at a double-digit pace, while the number of trained developers entering the field has been either flat or down for the past five years. No matter how you look at this trend, the bottom line is that software development managers are going to be expected to accomplish more with the same or fewer resources. Every time you have to approach a project using proprietary tool sets in a market where human capital is at a premium, management is going to be at a disadvantage. As a result, any gains made by the adoption of new component models, such as Microsoft's COM+ or Sun's Enterprise JavaBeans, are going to be only limited because the fundamental social and economic issues facing the developer community remain largely ignored.

> *Demand for application development continues to grow at a double-digit pace, while the number of trained developers entering the field is flat or down.*

At the core, the biggest issue is the total lack of respect that the developer community as a whole commands from both the people who supply them with their tools and the people who count on them to build the applications that run the world's economy.

So before you rage against the fates, in a moment of brutal honesty take a long look in the mirror and ask yourself whether you are part of the solution that can create better software and improved working conditions or just another poor, misguided soldier fighting the wrong battle in somebody else's war.

Chapter 26

Seduced by Reuse: Realizing Reusable Components

Meilir Page-Jones

Reuse is the nirvana of modern software development. Everybody wants it. Almost nobody knows what it is like. Simply put, most managers would prefer to see developers drawing on reusable code instead of reinventing the software wheel for every new project. Reuse comes with a cost, however, and Meilir Page-Jones knows well what reuse promises and what price it exacts. Arguably one of the world's leading experts on object orientation, he is author of two of the most highly respected books on the subject [Page-Jones, 1995; 2000]. In this chapter, he reveals the dark and difficult side of managing and working with reusable component libraries. If reusability is your wish, read on before you rub that lamp!

—Editor

Here's the deal. You just got e-mail from hostmaster@heaven.org that the Archangel of Reusability will visit your shop on Monday and grant you the fabled Gift of Reusable Code. When you forward the message to your managers, they almost drown in their own drool. The blessing they had dreamed of for decades—reusability—is about to be thrust upon them for free. They uncork the champagne and declare the following day a corporate holiday.

Imagine for a moment that this angel actually visited your shop. After the initial euphoria wore off, everyone would learn that reusability has an ongoing cost beyond its initial price of acquisition. Why? Because reaping the benefits of reusability makes two demands: First, you have to manage a class library (a storehouse of reusable components); second, you have to change the way you do software business, maniacally reusing what's in the library and stamping out the pestilence of nonreusable code.

CLASS CARE AND FEEDING

To make your class library viable, you must establish formal policies for storing, retrieving, entering, and removing library holdings. Let's look at the problems with each of these tasks.

> *To make a reusable class library viable, you must establish formal policies for storing, retrieving, entering, and removing library holdings.*

Storing classes in a library seems simple. But how many physical libraries should you have? The ideal answer, of course, is one. However, in a large corporation that spans many geographical locations, that answer is impractical. You can't store the library in just one location, on one physical disk. So how do you keep the libraries mutually consistent? You'll need physical configuration control.

Should there be logical levels of libraries, ranging from the small and local to the large and global, each one addressing a different scope of reuse such as department, division, or corporation? And should the same degree of formality and quality control apply to all levels of the library? What about multiple libraries, purchased from different vendors to fulfill different needs (such as graphics, finance, and statistics)? How do you keep these libraries integrated and mutually consistent? This time, the answer is logical configuration control.

Retrieving classes is also important. If programmers must spend more than two minutes finding an appropriate class in the library, they'll give up. Then they'll write the class over for themselves. Ironically, however, they may eventually enter this new class into the library alongside the similar class they never found.

How classes are entered into the library and which ones get entered is vital: what you store in the library must be worth storing. My rule of thumb for developing a class library is that it takes about 20 person-days per class to build for the here and now. It takes about 40 person-days per class to build in solid reusability for future projects. This extra effort will go into deeper design, inspections, documentation, and so on. When you're building an in-house library, don't skimp on this extra time. Don't skimp on the development budget, the documentation budget, or the maintenance budget. Deterioration will quickly set into the library if you do.

LIBRARY DECLINE

Most shops that proceed without a plan for managing their libraries wind up with a mess: classes missing vital methods, classes overlapping in functionality with other classes, classes that weren't tested adequately, several incompatible versions of the same class, obscure classes with no documentation, and so on.

If quality begins to slide downhill, everyone will cynically abandon the library. You'll hear comments like, "I'm not using the classes Genghis put into the library. His parameter sequences are nonstandard, his error handling is exceptionally poor, and his methods are restrictive. Oh, and his code is crap." Genghis will respond, "I'm not putting my classes into the library. I don't need that moron Wally calling me at 3 A.M. because he has his parameters in a twist again. Next thing I know they'll be asking me to write documentation for this stuff. Geez!"

Unlike Puff the Magic Dragon, classes don't live forever. One day, class C1 will become obsolete (perhaps because of its methods or its inheritance path) and will be replaced by C2. But if reusability has been such a hit in the shop, then C1 will be in use in 77 applications. What to do? One answer is to keep both C1 and C2 around, which makes the library messy and harder still for a newcomer to learn. Another answer is to kill off C1 immediately, which may prove awkward for the 77 applications, unless they pirate their own copies. A good compromise is to publish in a library newsletter that C1 is on its way out. Programmers will have, say, 12 months to refit applications to the new, improved, lower-calorie C2.

> *Shops that proceed without a plan wind up with a mess. If quality begins to slide downhill, everyone will cynically abandon the library.*

The best way to keep the class library under control is to appoint a librarian to oversee the activities of entering, storing, retrieving, and removing classes. The librarian may be a small team rather than a single person. The librarian's first task is to defeat the problem of unsuitable code entering the library. The librarian should let in only classes that are consistent, nonredundant, tested, and documented.

A librarian should be hard-nosed, not a passive rubber-stamper. One of our clients refers to its current incumbent as "Conan the Librarian." Within that shop, there's a dynamic tension between the librarian and the developers. Developers are rewarded for entering code into the library; Conan is rewarded for keeping it out.

> *The class librarian should be hard-nosed—"Conan the Librarian." Developers are rewarded for entering code into the library; Conan is rewarded for keeping it out.*

Learning a library takes longer than many managers expect. A developer will need 6 to 12 months to gain off-the-cuff familiarity with the soul of a 300-class library. Therefore, your shop should have a library consultant (again, perhaps a small team) to assist project teams in their reuse of classes. I think one library consultant for every four concurrent projects is a minimum. The librarian team and library consultant team may overlap.

There are numerous other tasks that librarians and library consultants must perform to keep a serious professional class library in top order. One vital example is publishing a library newsletter. The class library needs a vociferous mouthpiece. Pleistocene class librarians might publish a paper newsletter every month. Holocene librarians might try e-mail. Truly modern librarians see the component library as an excellent application for an intranet, whereby everyone can check the latest library happenings 24 hours a day.

CHANGING LIFESTYLES

Managers embarking on a technological change in the shop—such as the shift to object orientation—have to realize they must manage cultural changes, too. The three most important cultural issues in migrating to object-oriented reusability are the willpower to change emphasis from the current application to a durable library, novel organization roles for people, and a change in project work structure.

First, consider the issue of willpower. Object-oriented reusability can double project productivity. For example, let me summarize some numbers from a shop that has practiced object orientation for more than eight years and has more than a dozen object-oriented projects under its belt. An application that once took 100,000 lines of new code to develop now takes only 20,000 lines. However, each of those 20,000 new lines costs twice as much to produce as it would under traditional techniques, because requirements analysis won't go away and object orientation imposes an overhead on writing new code. This overhead includes understanding which classes you can reuse, understanding how to reuse them, and extending the library. Still, this shop is way ahead. A system that once cost 100 beans to develop now costs only 40.

So, what's the problem? The problem is commitment. Do you really want to double project productivity? If so, are you prepared to make the founding investments it takes to achieve reusability? Does everyone agree that reusability is the reason for the shop's choice of object orientation?

Let me provide an example of one company's experiences to bring home the importance of knowing your reason for getting into reuse and sticking to that reason when life gets tough. This company decided software costs would be reduced considerably if it could build systems that were at least half reused components. It also concluded that object orientation was the technique of choice for achieving reuse. So far, so good.

A task force prepared an impressive management report outlining the advantages of object orientation and emphasizing results rather than technique—clean hands rather than soap. Unfortunately, the report dwelled too much on spectacular benefits such as faster applications delivery and reduced maintenance costs. It failed to highlight the up-front investments needed, thus raising management expectations to unsustainable levels.

The shop undertook the necessary training and tooling up before putting about twenty people onto its first object-oriented project. The project was highly visible in two ways: The application was strategically important, and the project was the first to use the new, "high-productivity, rapid-delivery" object-oriented techniques.

Alas, the route to object orientation passes through a severe "technology trap." An organization's first project is unlikely to gain in productivity but will almost surely incur a huge up-front investment in tools and training and will have to buy or build a robust library of reusable classes.

> *Beware the "technology trap." The first project is unlikely to gain in productivity but will almost surely incur a huge up-front investment in tools, training, and the purchase or creation of a reusable class library.*

A year into the project, everyone knew the 18-month delivery deadline would not be met. Management traduced the project's champions of reuse and claimed they had underproduced. The champions' defense was that they'd invested the 12 months in designing a library of classes that would be robust enough to last through project after project. Upper management demanded that they abandon this time-wasting strategy and spend the remaining 6 months on the real work, coding the application itself.

I'll spare you the gory details, but 14 months later, the project was abandoned in acrimony. The coding scramble that was to last 6 months was a disaster.

Developers immediately abandoned all pretense of plans, specifications, or designs. People fell over one another in uncontrolled chaos.

The project produced two deliverables: a defect-ridden partial system that users refused to accept and a library of classes that, although good, was woefully incomplete. This last point was irrelevant, however, since the shop was forbidden to use object-oriented techniques on future projects. R.I.P., reuse.

The salutary moral of the tale is this: If you try to switch goals during a project, you may well fall between them and fail altogether. Was the real goal of the project to lay down the foundation for long-term reuse, or was it to get the current system out as fast as possible? Managers must choose their goal explicitly and then make sufficient investment to realize it. In other words, put your money where your goal is!

REAPING REWARDS

If, once they're well seasoned in object-oriented reuse, developers need to write only 20% as many new lines of code per application, then only about one-fifth of them are needed. The arithmetic may be simplistic, but the problem is real: What if reuse succeeds? What's to be done with the surplus developers? One answer is to quintuple the amount of work you do. Wonderful! But a bottleneck will show up elsewhere—in analysis of requirements, for example. If you rapidly retrain programmers to become analysts, you may only waste your time and annoy the programmers.

A better solution is to retrain and reassign some of the "extra" programmers into new roles more suited to a culture of reuse, such as librarian, library manager, or library consultant. Other possible roles include a strategic library planner who plans the future direction, structure, and contents of the library; reusable class programmers for foundation classes and business classes; application prototypers; and application designers. The surplus of talent might be turned to still other useful roles. A triage analyst might specialize in decisions such as whether to leave an existing system alone, introduce some object orientation, or completely rewrite it. And we can always use requirements analysts, implementation designers, and toolsmiths.

Massive reassignment is not trivial stuff organizationally, financially, culturally, emotionally, or intellectually. Over the long term, successful adoption of object orientation is impossible without the support and understanding of all management levels. So, if you really want reusability, be sure everybody is prepared to deal with the consequences.

The successful practice of object orientation may demand a new project development life cycle. Projects in a reuse shop begin with a mass of useful code already sitting in class libraries. This significantly affects cost and benefit analysis as well as the sequence of activities. For example, one requirement may be cheap to achieve because suitable classes are sitting in the library, ready and willing to be reused, while another requirement of comparable magnitude may need costly hand-tailored code. Such huge variations in costs may baffle clients.

Apart from any project life cycle, each class in the library has its own life cycle of immaturity, maturity, and obsolescence. Therefore, for shops that adopt object orientation, neither the traditional "waterfall" life cycle nor the more modern "whirlpool" life cycle apply completely. Perhaps object orientation requires a "Jacuzzi" model, reflecting the churning of many small whirlpools created by the intersecting life cycles of individual classes.

> *Object orientation may demand a new life cycle model. Projects in a reuse shop begin with a mass of useful code already sitting in class libraries. Perhaps this requires a "Jacuzzi" life cycle, reflecting the churning of many small intersecting life cycles of individual classes.*

LAST WISHES

Reuse is marvelous, we all agree. However, not only is it difficult to achieve, it's also difficult to manage once you have it. If you don't support the class libraries with policies for entering, storing, retrieving, and deleting classes and the people to implement those policies, the libraries won't support reuse.

Developers must also switch their focus from the application at hand to the loftier challenges of long-term reuse. This is tough, especially in a shop with a poor record of delivering even the application at hand.

If reuse is your goal, you must seriously consider the new reuse infrastructure before leaping in. Reuse will call for new roles and a whole new take on the project life cycle. It will also cost you time, money, and effort. Or perhaps I should put it another way: Be careful of wishing for reuse; you might just get it!

Chapter 27

Real-Life Requirements: Caught between Quality and Deadlines

Larry Constantine

It is one thing to pound out a column month after month with ample time for reflection and the opportunity to revise and edit your words in the bright light of the morning after. It is quite another thing to solve major problems in real time, sitting across the desk from an important client, standing at the whiteboard among members of an eager team looking to you for guidance, or amidst a panel of industry experts in front of a large audience of industry practitioners full of questions. A lively ask-the-gurus conference session before an audience of development managers led to the exchange encapsulated in this chapter.

—Editor

What are your biggest software development management problems today? We posed that question by e-mail to several hundred registered attendees for the Software Development Management Conference in 1998. Then we assembled a team of experts who had been contributors to the "Management Forum" column in *Software Development* and put them on the spot for the magazine's first Management Forum—Live! Flanked by six-foot projected "I-mag" images of themselves from two video cameras, the panelists were challenged to come up with workable solutions and usable recommendations in real time. Facing a large and largely skeptical audience of software and applications development managers, the panelists acquitted themselves remarkably well.

It helped that the panelists represented a range of backgrounds and experience. They included Peter Coffee, a well-known columnist and advanced technologies analyst whose rant (see Chapter 24) challenges developers and their

211

managers to eschew excuses. Jim Emery, associate provost and professor of sys-tems management at the U.S. Naval Post-Graduate School, offered the bifocal perspective of an academic who has studied and taught software development approaches but has also had to honcho mission-critical projects to completion (see Chapter 35). Karl Wiegers, a contributing editor to *Software Development,* was then a process improvement leader at Kodak whose thoughts on project man-agement basics appear in Chapter 7. Norm Kerth, whose own introductory remarks described him as president, founder, and head janitor of a one-man con-sulting operation, provides people-oriented guidance in object technologies for clients like Nike. His ideas on learning from project failures appear in Chapter 17.

Everyone's management problems are just a little bit different, of course, but we work under common constraints typical of the times and culture. From what attendees at the conference reported to be their biggest challenges, some broad themes emerged. As moderator of the panel, I presented these themes, along with a sampling of representative questions, then let the panelists take off at will. By the time we landed at the end of our allotted time, the panelists had filled more than an hour and a half with wit, wisdom, and solid advice.

One chapter is hardly enough to cover such a wide-ranging discussion—and only the videotape does justice to Norm Kerth's inspired, impromptu, sleight-of-hand magic trick—but here is a synopsis of the panelists' comments on one of the central topics.

DON'T SQUEEZE

If the e-mail poll was a fair indication of the general state of affairs, perhaps the leading challenge for software managers is feeling squeezed between the demands for quality and the pressure to meet tighter and tighter deadlines. The pressure is increased by the slippery slope on which so many projects seem poised, resting on requirements that are hard to identify, difficult to under-stand, and constantly expanding as the project progresses. Many development managers feel as if they're balanced on a California cliff soaked by the rains of El Niño, with muddy requirements and an uncertain foundation threatening to give way at any time to dump the project and its perpetrators over the brink.

> *The leading challenge for software managers is being squeezed between the demands for quality and the pressure to meet tighter deadlines—a pres-sure increased by requirements that are hard to identify, difficult to understand, and constantly expanding as the project progresses.*

"Our biggest problem is meeting deadlines while keeping to quality standards," responded one manager. Another complained about "coping with feature creep, ad infinitum, ad nauseum." Yet another referred to the problem of scoping requirements to fit within schedule constraints. "How," lamented another attendee, "can we build software where the only consistent rule is that all rules are subject to change?" These are not new problems, but it seems the vise grip of shortened release cycles paired with lengthening lists of requirements is felt especially acutely by many of today's development managers. Is this just the case that project reality bites or is there something we can do to cope?

Peter Coffee kicked off the discussion by pointing out that there is more than one way to fail when it comes to requirements. Many projects crash and burn because the developers fail to define requirements with sufficient care and precision. Other projects fail precisely because the developers did meticulously define precise requirements. Fixing requirements too rigidly, too early, or too thoroughly can be as much of a problem as giving them short shrift. A preoccupation with rigorous requirements can lead to "paving over the cowpath," in which new software replicates all the warts and wandering workflow of manual systems or outmoded applications being replaced. Even if delivered on time, the resulting over-specified systems will not serve the needs and interests of users well. The trick for developers is to define enough to know what to start building but not so much as to cast the code in concrete overshoes. Full specifications may take so long that user needs have changed or passed altogether by the time the requirements document is complete.

> *A preoccupation with rigorous requirements can lead to "paving over the cowpath," in which new software replicates all the warts and wandering workflow of manual systems or outmoded applications.*

CREEP SHOW

Requirements are not, as Jim Emery noted, the final word on anything. All requests and requirements from users must be examined with a critical eye. In fact, one of the best ways to meet requirements successfully is not to meet them all. Most systems are best deployed with an initial set of features that satisfies the most critical requirements first, saving additional features for future refinements that can benefit from experience and the perfect perspective of hindsight.

Users and clients are better able to accept an early but scaled-down release when they know they can count on the development team to deliver quality regularly. Norm Kerth suggested that the goal should be to establish a culture of commitment (see Chapter 36), with regular, reliable releases on a three- to six-month cycle. Not only is this model more timely, but it also gives developers a tool to manage requirements creep. Instead of expanding the scope of the current project, late-breaking requirements are deferred to the next revision cycle, which clients know will also be completed on schedule because its scope will also be actively controlled. It may require several rounds of refinement and release before client confidence is sufficient, so developers need to take the long view of educating their customers.

Of course, it is not enough just to understand requirements in a strictly technical sense. Development managers also need to understand their customers' definitions of success. A cost-conscious client on a tight budget may not be impressed when you deliver extra features that double the capability of a system but put the project 10% over budget. No client is likely to be content to take delivery today on an affordable system that meets last year's needs. Since our definitions of success are often different than the customer's, it is important to make both of these explicit when defining requirements.

DRIVERS WANTED

In understanding requirements, it is also vital to distinguish drivers from constraints, as Karl Wiegers pointed out. Drivers represent performance or functional objectives that are vital to the business success of the delivered system. Technical and resource constraints define the boundaries within which a project must be managed. Not everything can be either a driver or a constraint.

Some facets of any project must be recognized as trade-offs or options. Full features and functionality can be delivered even under highly restricted time schedules, but only at the price of quality or at added cost in development resources. Quality and reliability can almost invariably be maintained, but these may sometimes require restricting the scope or relaxing the schedule.

> *Full features and functionality can be delivered even under highly restricted time schedules, but only at the price of quality or at added cost in development resources.*

If clients don't recognize trade-offs, then there are no project management solutions and the project ends up doomed to failure. Part of establishing requirements, therefore, is educating users and clients about the intrinsic trade-offs. If we fail to inform clients of the costs, added features will appear to be free. Offered a choice between a full-featured Lexus and a stripped-down, second-hand Yugo, most of us would take the Lexus if the cost were the same. When developers do nothing but nod and take notes following every request, clients never learn they cannot have it all.

Kerth described a game that has been used to help in this educational process, a kind of hands-on metaphor for the popular technique of Quality Function Deployment. In the game, all the sundry features and functionality desired for a proposed system are marked on a collection of various wooden shapes. Users are then invited to fit the ones they want or need into a box that is too small to hold all of the shapes.

As Coffee pointed out, educating and negotiating with clients is complicated because we can never pin down the exact cost of an isolated function. What does this feature cost? It depends. Most important, it depends on the quality of the design and the robustness of the implementation. It may be possible to incorporate yet another function at a modest cost so long as we can tolerate a clumsy user interface or are willing to accept that future revisions or improvements will be expensive. A rugged, broadcast-quality video recorder can cost ten times as much as a consumer-oriented VCR, even though both may perform the same functions. Customers, users, and our own upper management can certainly understand such trade-offs, but we must take the time to make sure they understand how these apply to software. An efficient and adaptable implementation of software will cost more to program than a jury-rigged hack that will crash whenever it is modified, but how many users appreciate the difference?

> *The cost of an isolated function depends on the quality of the design and the robustness of the implementation. A function might be realizable at modest cost if we can tolerate a clumsy user interface or more costly future revisions.*

WISH LISTS

As Emery added, no matter what clients tell us, it's important for analysts and project managers to reject what we know to be wrong. Users often ask for things that are unrealistic or not in their best interests. Ultimately, we are in the business of delivering solutions to real problems, and that requires us to give clients what they need more than what they want or claim to want.

Even the way we pose our questions to users will shape what we finally face as so-called system requirements. When we simply ask users what they want, they will tell us something, whether they know what they want or not. If we ask them what else they might like, they will invariably answer again—and keep answering every single time we ask them. Unrealistic and overly ambitious requirements often arise from trying to please users too much or from inviting their requests too simplistically or too frequently. If we try to play genie and grant client wishes, we are apt to construct castles of code in the air—baroque applications, bloated with features that meet no real needs—with little hope of delivering on time or under budget.

> *If we play genie and grant client wishes, we are apt to construct castles of code in the air—baroque applications, bloated with features that meet no real needs—with little hope of delivering on time or under budget.*

USE CASES

Distinguishing needs from wants emerges as a key to managing requirements creep. Wiegers, among others, has found that use cases are a powerful technical tool that can go a long way toward drawing that distinction and offering developers some relief from the pressure to deliver everything. To be successful, a system doesn't need to satisfy every wish or fantasy of its users, but it must meet a core of critical needs. What is critical and what is merely decorative? The most important capabilities are those that let users accomplish work, making it easier, faster, and more valuable to the organization.

Analysts need to understand what users are trying to accomplish, and use cases can be a tool to aid in this task. A use case represents an external, blackbox view of the functionality delivered by a system to its users. To avoid unnecessary features, Wiegers recommends use cases that are focused on the purpose of interaction rather than the mechanics. Such use cases are known as *essential use cases* because they reduce a task to its essential core, that is, purposes freed of implementation details, technological constraints, and nonessential assumptions [Constantine and Lockwood, 1999]. Essential use cases make it easier for developers to distinguish the destination from the cowpath by which it has been reached in the past. They highlight the working goals of users, separating what users are trying to accomplish from how they might accomplish it. By building use cases based on user intentions, we can often avoid having to implement unnecessary or little-used features.

> *By separating what users are trying to accomplish from how they might accomplish it, essential use cases make it easier to distinguish the destination from the cowpath by which it has been reached in the past.*

Requirements worth defining are worth reviewing with clients and users. Not only can reviews help control requirements creep and reduce time pressure, they can also help find errors. Weigers suggested that agreed-upon requirements be reviewed for testability by developing actual test cases. Defining and walking through test cases early in the process can speed and simplify validation. This practice also highlights problematic or ambiguous requirements that may need to be altered or abandoned. Here, too, modeling with essential use cases has proved to be an advantage. Good test cases fall out of use cases like rain from a thunderhead. Tracking requirements through the entire development process is crucial for effective project management. When test cases are derived directly from the use cases that define requirements, it becomes easier to gauge progress and to recognize and avoid potential feature creep. Tying test cases to use cases also makes it less likely that important capability will be overlooked until it is too late or too expensive to implement it.

Admittedly, requirements are only part of the software development game, but if our polling of development managers is any indication, the requirements muddle is a major hole in the middle of the hand of cards that many managers are trying to play. Certainly, none of us on this panel labored under any illusion that we had solved all the problems in a single conference session. Nevertheless, in a surprisingly short time, the group offered a panoply of proven practices.

So, remember: Define requirements but don't overdefine. Educate your clients and users regarding costs and trade-offs. Concentrate on the core. Avoid scope creep by deferring requirements. Build client comfort and confidence through reliable revision and release. Learn what success means to your clients, and distinguish drivers from constraints. Understand what your users want, but meet their needs. Identify what is essential through use cases. Control and validate using test cases derived from use cases.

And never draw to an inside straight.

Chapter 28

Rules Rule:
Business Rules as Requirements

Ellen Gottesdiener

With our noses to the software development grindstone, it can be hard for us to see much of the business world around us. One way or another, the people for whom we and our developers create software are in some kind of business, a business with business rules. Just as the languages and operating systems within which we work function by a complex collection of implicit and explicit rules, so, too, do the business operations of our clients and customers. We, in turn, have our own business rules. We may expect to be told what we are building before we are prepared to supply an estimate of how long it will take to build it, and we expect our customers to understand such rules of the game. Not surprisingly, they expect something similar from us. To support them with good software, we need to understand the rules of logic behind the businesses we are serving. In this chapter, consultant Ellen Gottesdiener makes the case for business rules as requirements.

—Editor

An inept, inadequate, or inefficient requirements analysis starts a project on the wrong foot. Time is wasted at a point in development when time is of the essence, and developers will find it hard to produce a good software product based on ill-defined requirements. Capturing, validating, and verifying functional requirements are, thus, major challenges, not only for our clients and business partners but also for us as managers and software developers. We need clear and usable requirements that can guide the development of a quality software product, and a poor requirements process will not lead to a good requirements product.

The requirements process includes what techniques are used to capture the requirements (interviews, facilitated workshops, prototyping, focus groups, or the like) [Gottesdiener, 1999], what tools are used for capturing and tracing information (text, diagrams, narratives, or formal models), and how customers and users are actively involved throughout the process. When it comes to the requirements product, management concerns include the testability of functional requirements, the ability to find and resolve conflicts in requirements, the ability to link requirements back to business goals (backward traceability), and the ability to track functional requirements throughout the life cycle from design to code to test and deployment (forward traceability).

As mature managers, we no longer expect silver bullets for requirements engineering. However, in my experience there is at least one secret weapon. Whatever functional models you wish to use, whether use cases, CRC cards, or some proprietary technique championed by your boss, the important thing is to focus on the true essence of the functional requirements: the business rules.

> *Mature managers no longer expect silver bullets for requirements engineering, but business rules may still be an effective secret weapon.*

RULES RULE

Business rules are the policies and constraints of the business, whether the "business" is banking, software development, or automation engineering. The Object Management Group simply defines them as "declarations of policy or conditions that must be satisfied." They are usually expressed in ordinary, natural language and are "owned" by the business. Your business may be commercial, not-for-profit, or part of a government, but it still has business rules. These rules provide the knowledge behind any and every business structure or process. Business rules are also, therefore, at the core of functional requirements. You may use various functional requirements models—structural (data, class), control-oriented (events, state charts), object-oriented (classes/objects, object interactions), or process-oriented (functional decomposition, process threads, use cases, or the like)—but within the heart of all functional requirements are business rules.

Business rules are what a functional requirement "knows"—the decisions, guidelines, and controls that are behind that functionality. For example, functional requirements or models that include processes such as "determine product" or "offer discount" imply performance of actions, but they also embody knowledge—the underlying business rules—needed to perform those actions. An insurance claim in a "pending" stage means that certain things (variables, links to other things) must be true (invariants, or business rules). The behavior of a claim in a pending life-cycle stage is, thus, dependent upon business rules that govern and guide behaviors.

As the essential ingredient of functional requirements, business rules deserve direct, explicit attention. Since business rules lurk behind functional requirements, they are easily missed and may not be captured explicitly. Without explicit guidance, software developers will simply make whatever assumptions are needed to write the code, thus building their assumptions about conditions, policies, and constraints into the software with little regard for business consequences. Rules that are not explicit and are not encoded in software through the guesses of developers may not be discovered as missing or wrong until later phases. This results in defects in those later phases that could have been avoided if the rules had been elicited, validated, and baselined during requirements analysis. In the end, the lack of explicit focus on capturing the business rules creates rework and other inefficiencies.

> *Business rules are at the very core of functional requirements and deserve direct, explicit attention.*

Rather than just mentioning business rules as "notes" in your models, you should capture and trace them as requirements in and of themselves. Focusing on business rules as the core functional requirements not only promotes validation and verification but also can speed the requirements analysis process.

FROM THE TOP DOWN, AGAIN

In working on a business-rules approach to software development, I have come to realize that such an approach needs to be driven from the top down, like the traditional top-down methods of information engineering. Unfortunately, in the modern world, with business moving at the speed of a mouse click, a systematic, top-down analysis is often an unaffordable luxury. Consequently, I've become more practical: a business-rules approach doesn't need to be a method or methodology in and of itself. Rather it is just a necessary part of requirements engineering. It includes a process (with phases, stages, tasks, roles, and techniques), a business-rules metamodel, and business-rules templates.

> *With business moving at the speed of a mouse click, a systematic, top-down requirements analysis is often an unaffordable luxury.*

Advocates of the recently standardized Unified Modeling Language (UML) and the accompanying all-purpose "Unified Process" (UP) toss around the term *business rules* in presentations and conversations, but neither UML nor UP offers much guidance regarding business rules. UML has an elaborate meta-model and metametamodel to support its language. One of the classes at the metamodel level is called "Rules." But the UML has given business rules short shrift. The only modeling element that is practically usable is the "constraint" element, which can be attached to any modeling element. Furthermore, although the UML's Object Constraint Language (OCL) is a fine specification-level language to attach business rules to structural models, it is not a language to use during requirements analysis when working directly with business customers to elicit and validate business rules. Business rules need to be treated as first-class citizens (no pun intended), not attachments.

USE CASES AND BUSINESS RULES

At the center of the UML are use cases, which are viewed by some analysts as business requirement models while others call them user requirement models. Use cases are a functional (process) model that can be expressed as words using a natural language. Style of expression varies, and some templates include special sections, such as pre- and post-conditions, goal name, and the like [Constantine and Lockwood, 2001]. Use cases have proved themselves to be an important and useful model for capturing requirements. Due to recent work, use cases have evolved from often vague requirements deliverables into something specific, focused, and usable. The goals of use cases have received increased attention [Cockburn, 2001], and essential use cases have been developed to support usage-centered design [Constantine and Lockwood, 1999]. However, use-case narratives—the flow of events, as the UML people would say—are all too often missing the very essence of the use case, because behind every use case are business rules at work.

Failing to capture and verify the business rules that underlie the use-case models can lead to the delivery of a software product that fails to meet the business needs. Formalizing the capture of business rules concurrently with the development of the use-case model strengthens the delivered product through the synergy between use-case models and business rules.

Business rules come in many forms. I think of them as terms, facts, factor clauses, and action clauses, but there is no agreement on a standard taxonomy or set of categories for business rules nor should there be. The taxonomy should fit the problem. Some problem domains, such as underwriting, claim adjudication, financial risk analysis, and medical instruments monitoring, are more business-rule based. Other problems are more business-rule constrained, for example, payroll, expense tracking, and inventory ordering. This variability requires the selection or tailoring of a taxonomy and an accompanying business-rules template for any given business problem. The template provides a standard syntax for writing business rules in natural language. Such tailoring is beneficial since it requires us to understand the problem in greater depth by working directly with our business customers to perform this tailoring and to derive an appropriate business-rules template.

Business rules can be linked to a use case or to steps within a use case. Business rules can also be linked to other models, depending on the depth of requirements traceability and the importance of specific attributes, such as source, verification process, documents, owner, and risk. These other models can include glossaries, life-cycle models, activity models, and class models. The business rules are thus reusable across multiple types of functional requirements and can be traced along with other requirements.

> *Business rules can be linked to a use case or to steps within a use case as well as to other models, including glossaries, life-cycle models, activity models, and class models.*

Besides use cases, other models can be useful for identifying and capturing business rules. For example, life-cycle models, such as a simple state-chart diagram, can be quite usable and understandable to business analysts, especially for problems in which a core business domain has many complex states. Even object-class or data models can be excellent starting points for problems that require understanding the domain structure but do not require a lot of action to take place.

COLLABORATE WITH CUSTOMERS

Business rule discovery and validation require knowledge of the thinking processes of the business experts from whom we elicit functional requirements. Collaborative work in groups that include customers is most effective in the early life-cycle phases of planning and requirements analysis, as well as for ongoing project process improvement. Such collaborative work patterns can be effectively used to model business rules and derive higher-quality requirements, which include business-rule requirements.

In the collaborative approach to business rules that I prefer, requirements analysts and business customers collaborate to create a business-rules template that is expressed in natural language, based on common sense, and directly relevant to the business customer. In modeling use cases and user interfaces, business rules are explicitly derived and captured using this natural-language template. After all, what makes sense to our customers and users is what we express in their own language.

Collaborative modeling of business rules can be a powerful, eye-opening process. It is amazing to see customers realize that their own business rules are unclear, even to them. Often they come to realize the rules are not standardized and may, therefore, be both inefficient and even risky considering regulatory exposure and potential for lawsuits. Collaborative modeling can convincingly make the case for immediate clarification of business rules.

> *Collaborative modeling can be a powerful, eye-opening process that can help customers realize that their business rules are unclear, even to themselves.*

Eliciting business rules can be a real challenge, especially when business experts do not agree on the business rules or when the business rules are unknown or very complex. I find that facilitated requirements workshops in which business rules are explicitly discovered, captured, and tested within the context of modeling other things, such as use cases, are the most direct and productive tools for eliciting and validating the rules of the business. These workshops are planned collaborative events in which participants deliver products in a short, concentrated period of time led by a neutral facilitator, whose role is to help the group manage the process. Prior to each workshop, the participants have agreed upon what will be delivered and the ground rules for group behavior. The workshop process exploits the power of diverse people joined together for a common goal.

A successful requirements workshop requires considerable preparatory effort. Such collaborative events, when woven throughout requirements analysis, tend to increase speed, promote mutual learning, and enhance the quality of the requirements themselves. In workshops, or even in interviews with business experts, if the problem domain is very much "rule based" (versus rule constrained as mentioned earlier), using cognitive patterns is extremely helpful to accelerate the group's ability to express the rules. Such patterns, with their roots in knowledge engineering, model business experts' thinking processes and enable the rules to emerge.

Some customers may wish to take on a business-rules approach because they want to uncover the real "dirt" of the business. They are ready to ask the "why" of the business rules. Actually, the question of larger purpose should be asked of any functional requirement. If the answer does not map to a business goal, objective, or tactic, then the functional requirement is extraneous. Business rules exist only to support the goals of the business. Whereas good use cases represent the goals of external users or "actors," the business rules behind use cases are inextricably linked to the goals of the business itself. If not, the rules are extraneous and may even be in conflict with business goals. Thus, mapping business rules to business goals is a key step in validation and promotes traceability back from business-rule requirements to the business goals.

THE BUSINESS-RULE CURE

Business rules are an ounce of prevention. Unless we get them, get them right, and get them early, we are destined for problems in our projects and products. The project problems stemming from incomplete, erroneous, or missing business rules include redefining requirements and retesting results. The product problems are worse because, if the rules are wrong, in conflict, or redundant, the users of the software product suffer. Unless we get to the very heart of the business during requirements analysis with the business rule written in text by business people themselves, we are doomed to passing incomplete, inconsistent, and conflicting business-goal requirements forward into production. Thus, we must get to the very essence of requirements with business rules written by business people.

To get to the heart of the matter, active business sponsorship is absolutely required. The process can be acutely uncomfortable because the capture and validation of business rules expose the "undiscussables"—the unclear and conflicting business policies and rules. It also begs for rethinking the suboptimal rules and requires the realignment of the business rules with the business goals. To resolve such issues requires business sponsorship and leadership. To go forward with a business-rules approach in the absence of such sponsorship is treading on very thin ice. Only the collaborative efforts of information technology professionals and their business partners with the active involvement of business management can yield the benefits of a business-rules approach by quickly and succinctly cutting to the core of the functional requirements.

Chapter 29

Taming the Wild Web: Business Alignment in Web Development

Lucy Lockwood

Everybody wants to be on the Web. It is this century's Wild, Wild West, and like many past frontiers, the World Wide Web is slowly being tamed. As it becomes populated and draws more business and industry, software development moves in. Yes, software development. Web applications are applications, Web pages are user interfaces, and HTML programming is programming—which means that we had better learn from the lessons of the past if we don't want to plunge ourselves into the same chasms that we've been stuck in before. Yet every new frontier is also different. The game may not be entirely new, but some of the rules are changing.

With everyone looking to e-commerce on the Web and applications migrating to intranets and extranets, the need for clear alignment with your business takes on a new order of importance, as Lucy Lockwood argues in this chapter. Take heed: know what you are building before you build or you may get caught in a web of your own making.

—Editor

The World Wide Web has gone mainstream, and software development managers need to add an understanding of Web development issues to their management tool kit. Long gone are the days when the Web was strictly the domain of academics, researchers, marketing departments, and wild-eyed Web wonks. Applications that once were headed for client-server solutions using proprietary development tools are now likely to end up as browser-based systems on an intranet or extranet.

Creating a Web site or moving your client-server or desktop applications to the Web can look seductively easy. Browsers appear to be the long-sought "universal thin client," and the Web looks like the solution for remote computing by far-flung staff. This all seems to come at a reasonable price. No wonder, then, that the cry from both corporate management and end-user departments is "Just put it on the Web!"

In many respects, developing Web-based applications is not so different from traditional software development, but that does not mean there are no differences. Developing for the Web can mean simultaneously being on the cutting edge and taking a great leap backward. With attention focused on problems in the underlying technology, the challenge of usability is often overlooked. Building highly usable Web applications is actually more difficult than in more traditional environments. Inherent weaknesses in the underlying architecture and languages, the lack of robust tools, and the tendency to approach Web-based development as something completely new often conspire to produce ill-conceived, inefficient, awkward, and unusable results.

> *Developing for the Web can mean simultaneously being on the cutting edge and taking a great leap backward. Building highly usable Web applications is actually more difficult than in more traditional environments.*

In this chapter, I look at three issues, sometimes neglected, relating to successful software design that take on special importance in managing Web-based applications development: clarifying purposes, managing pressure, and taking control.

WEB WORK

Many organizations approach Web-site development by "doing the visioning thing." They start by identifying targeted constituencies or market segments, then brainstorm site content and quickly move into graphic design concepts. Often such sites are high on concept, color, and chaos but low on usefulness and usability. In contrast, many intranet projects start with an existing application or source material, then mindlessly port it to a browser interface. Current development tools make it easy to "browserize" almost anything. The result can be intranet applications that resemble ancient character-based programs or a text dump of the employee manual.

For truly successful Web sites and Web-based applications, you need to take a different path, one that starts with and is driven by the purposes of the site or application. Usage-centered design [Constantine and Lockwood, 1999] is such an approach. Once you clarify purposes, usage-centered design helps you understand the roles that the targeted users play relative to the application. Next, it helps you understand the tasks you need to support based on the users' intentions and purposes. You then prioritize the user roles and tasks based on expected frequency, importance to users, and importance to the business. Finally, you engineer the site's design or application to fit closely with both the users' needs and the organization's business priorities.

The end product may include creative graphics and innovative Java script use, but a usage-centered design approach avoids the pitfall of chasing style and cleverness merely for their own sakes. Although you can never optimize a system for every interaction, by prioritizing tasks you can be sure that the application readily supports the most crucial ones. Having a deeper understanding of the business and user priorities helps you determine what pieces merit extra attention and resources and which features warrant allocation to subsequent versions. You start this process by articulating a clear understanding of the application's purpose and reaching consensus on the project's business objectives.

KNOW WHY

It is most important to know why you are developing applications on the Web in the first place. In traditional applications development, the system's purpose is often well defined and tightly circumscribed. Requirements analysis and requirements engineering are well understood, but in many otherwise rational companies, this understanding goes out the window when it comes to the Web. Scoping the requirements can be even more important for the Web because, due to their nature, Web architecture and tools lend themselves to rapidly expanding scope and encourage a sort of never-ending "laundry list" approach to features and functionality. Left unbound, Web projects often lead to a mishmash of stuff that is unfocused, unsatisfying, and unusable.

> *Clear requirements are essential for the Web, where the architecture and tools lend themselves to rapidly expanding scope and encourage a sort of never-ending "laundry list" approach to features and functionality.*

Whether for an intranet application or a public Web site, you must first ask, "What is the essential purpose?" and "What is this site supposed to achieve?" Rather than approach this issue through a vague mission statement or exalted vision, you need to work with project sponsors to clarify the core business objectives. Often there is more than one objective, and so begins the process of working with clients, internal or external, to understand and examine these objectives so you can prioritize them. As in traditional applications development, different stakeholders will have different views of what is important and what must be included. A facilitated process that combines brainstorming, discussion, analysis, and various group decision-making techniques will help achieve consensus on business objectives.

Sometimes businesses approach Web development with great fantasies: "We'll just put all the repair manuals on the Web, and then we can eliminate the customer service department." Any software development manager who has been around a few years has been through such Dilbertesque scenarios before. Remember how end-user computing was going to obviate the need for MIS staff, since users would just write their own programs?

One way to introduce some reality checks is to examine the project from the user perspective. A good place to start is to ask who could or would use the site. You can group users based on shared characteristics—needs, wants, behaviors, and expectations in relationship to the site—what are commonly called *user roles*. Once identified, you need to prioritize the various user roles from the perspective of the overall business need. For example, which do you value more for the purpose of the new intranet site: the user in the role of traveling sales representative or the one in the role of warehouse shipment coordinator? Sometimes the answers are obvious, but more often they require some consideration.

Identifying potential site users helps you understand the site's purpose from a user perspective. Ask yourself, "Why would I go to the site? What would I expect to accomplish?" Whether you're a company employee or one of the random masses, you're going to use a site only if there is sufficient reason and if the gain outweighs the pain.

> *Identifying potential site users helps you understand the site's purpose from a user perspective. People will use a site only if there is sufficient reason and if the gain outweighs the pain.*

Knowing what different types of users will want to achieve by using a site, you can develop task lists. Tasks for a human-resources intranet site might include changing health insurance coverage, updating home addresses, comparing retirement plan options, and reviewing the procedures for maternity leave. Identifying user tasks and ranking them by expected frequency and importance to the users is best done as a collaborative process, such as Joint Essential Modeling (JEM) [Constantine and Lockwood, 1999], which brings together developers, clients, and user representatives to sort out user roles and tasks.

Once you understand the users, their tasks, the task priorities, and the expected frequencies, you can integrate this information with identified business objectives. Often there are notable differences between internal and external objectives or in the prioritization of tasks to be supported. An airline's primary Web objective may be "disintermediation," which, through online ticket sales, would eliminate intermediaries like travel agents or the airline's telephone representatives. In contrast, my primary objective in the FrequentFlyerFanatic role might be to find the route that gives me the most miles for the least money. Clearly, the airline is not likely to spend a lot of resources supporting my high-priority task. Nevertheless, one of the most important factors in Web success is whether users achieve their goals. If site users can't access the information they need to choose a flight or purchase a ticket online, they will go back to using their travel agents or the airline's toll-free reservation number, or worse, go to a competitor's site—the opposite of what the site was intended to accomplish. A site with insufficient user benefit or in which the frustration outweighs perceived benefit will drive away intended users.

PRESSURE

Time pressure is hardly new to software development, but we have the Internet to thank for the advent of Web-time development (see Chapter 19). In a matter of months, sometimes weeks, developers are expected to throw a Web project together, throw it out there for everyone to use, and then throw it out when everyone rejects it. You need to resist the pressure to "just get something on the Web." Doing it right always takes longer, but it also pays off.

Poorly designed and implemented Web sites deter use and can hurt a company's reputation and relationships. What kind of statement does it make, either to external or internal users, if a Web site is visually unappealing, full of typos and missing links, painfully slow, or maddening to interact with? Organizations pushing for instant presence on the Web often overlook the fact that the Internet makes it so easy to compare options. If your Web site turns users off, a better site run by one of your competitors is only a mouse click away. For intranet applications, rapid development can mean rapid mothballing for lack of use.

> *Poorly designed and implemented Web sites deter use and can hurt a company's reputation and relationships. Organizations pushing for instant presence on the Web often overlook the fact that their competitors are only a mouse click away.*

Although technology issues get most of the attention, Web applications are particularly prone to management problems. Just finding consensus on project objectives and priorities is often nontrivial because Web projects frequently cross multiple boundaries in organizational turf. Lacking experience with this type of application, many organizations do not employ established processes and roles, realistic expectations, or well-defined integration with the company's overall information technology strategy. The super-hyped, fast-changing technology of the Web encourages managers and developers alike to get caught up in the pursuit of "way cool" gimmicks while losing sight of pragmatic design considerations and solid return-on-investment rationales.

To keep a Web project from speeding its way toward the HTML junk pile, use models that help the team design the site before jumping into page layout and Java code. Use information gathered on users, tasks, and business objectives to feed the conceptual design. You can expand prioritized task lists into a task model based on essential use cases [Constantine and Lockwood, 1999]. Content models can help developers think through the site's contents, and navigation maps make it easier to work out the overall site organization in advance to be sure it supports the most important interactions. For example, frequent tasks or those with a high business priority should be highly visible and readily accessible. Less important or more infrequent uses can safely be buried farther down rather than taking up space on the home page. Simply counting the steps it takes to complete key tasks can point the way toward improvements and help avoid later rework and revision.

TAKE CHARGE

Highly usable applications on the Web are also difficult to create because developers have less control over the software's appearance and behavior in a browser environment. Development tools are gaining sophistication, however, and the underlying technologies are evolving to give developers more options. Frames, cascading style sheets, image maps, and Java applets can all be used effectively to present a more usable system to your audience. Rather than aiming for a lowest common denominator interface, it may make sense for you to limit the number of different browsers and legacy versions to support, particularly as the world seems to be converging on a couple of free, upgradable browsers.

The real challenge in Web design is neither to let your developers go wild incorporating the latest capability and every gee-whiz add-in nor to prematurely constrain the design in the face of apparent or real Web-technology limitations. Truly usable software is design-driven, not technology-driven. Rather than focusing on the inside—the HTML, Java, and the actual content—initial designs and paper prototypes should ignore technical implementation details and begin on the outside, with a focus on the users. In any case, with Web standards and technology changing so rapidly, today's technical constraints may be forgotten in six months.

> *The real challenge in Web design is neither to let your developers go wild nor to prematurely constrain the design in the face of apparent or real Web-technology limitations.*

In an atmosphere of hype and innovation, it may be easy to forget that, in many respects, Web development is not new. You need to bring to your Web projects the same discipline and good project management techniques you applied to your desktop and client-server applications: requirements engineering and tracking, project milestones and monitoring, testing and quality-assurance measures. You can readily adapt all of these to Web development.

In sum, to produce the best Web-based software, you need to know why you're on the World Wide Web in the first place. You must have a clear sense of your project's purpose and tangible objectives, and you must understand how and why you are going to use Web technology and a browser environment to enhance those objectives. Being technologically fashionable is not sufficient. You need to take the initiative as a manager and resist the pressure to just throw things together. Although dominated in some organizations by the artsy design set or by coding cowboys, Web-development efforts benefit tremendously from the use of solid requirements and software engineering techniques. Good analysis, model construction, and organized processes produce superior results. So, design to support user and business needs rather than letting technology drive the result (taking control of the interface appearance and behavior where you can), and you will deliver a more usable site that better benefits the bottom line.

Chapter 30

Calming Corporate Immune Systems: Overcoming Risk Aversion

Gifford Pinchot and Gene Callahan

When this chapter was originally going to press in the "Management Forum" column in Software Development, *I was up to my eyeballs in Internet alligators, helping a California start-up translate a visionary fantasy into a usable reality that could add a high-speed lane to the educational enterprise (see Chapter 23). This was high-risk stuff, calling for all the innovation we could muster in user interface design. There were moments when, sketching furiously on a digital whiteboard or standing dazed before a content navigation map that seemed to lead nowhere, I could feel a rising aversion to all this risky business.*

How do you find a balance between risk and security, innovation and convention? That is the question addressed in this chapter, which offers some practical pointers on overcoming risk aversion in your organization.

—Editor

Are technological gamblers endangering your enterprise? It's clear that the adventuresome programmers who set out to build a mission-critical system in an experimental language, the system administrator who is too eager to install the latest beta version of a utility, or the network engineer who enhances his résumé with a customized protocol can wreak havoc. But what about those who put their organizations at risk by avoiding uncertainty altogether? Although risk aversion can pose a real threat, it has received little attention. In a world of constantly evolving business models, the failure to innovate can slowly strangle a company just as surely as untoward technological tinkering can torpedo its mission.

> *In a world of constantly evolving business models, the failure to innovate can slowly strangle a company just as surely as untoward technological tinkering can torpedo its mission.*

Many factors can lead software developers and R&D staff to be unduly risk-averse in their decision making. Painful memories may still linger of times when previous initiatives were blocked. After putting their hearts into a project, only to have a higher-up nullify their efforts, people become reluctant to face disappointment again. Indeed, there is a prevailing frustration with the "corporate immune system" that seemingly exists to stomp out foreign bodies—new ideas. A reasonable immune system is necessary, of course, to prevent an organization from lurching in a new direction each time someone makes a suggestion. A hyperactive immune system, on the other hand, will stifle all innovation.

A common problem with new technology initiatives is a staff fear that, along with the new technology, there will come a separate set of experts and star performers. For instance, a company's C++ guru may worry she'll lose status in the move to Web applications requiring Java and Perl skills.

Employees also often don't understand the far-reaching goals of the organization, making it difficult for them to see how their project may be necessary or helpful. Another common attitude among technical personnel is a lurking suspicion that the risks of failure to their career far outweigh the rewards of success.

Managers can also contribute to a culture of excessive risk aversion. If there is a lack of active management sponsorship for new technology initiatives, backing them may appear too risky. Managers also might not recognize, or might even feel threatened by, "intrapreneurs," those who are as key to inspiring internal creativity as entrepreneurs are to launching a start-up. Finally, managers are in charge of team formation, which, if poorly done, can cripple innovation.

> *Managers can contribute to a culture of excessive risk aversion through lack of active management sponsorship for new technology initiatives or by failing to recognize and support "intrapreneurs."*

STIFLING CHANGE: A CASE STUDY

We became intensely aware of these problems while watching some middle managers destroy an exciting project at a client company. The CEO was spearheading the effort, which he felt was critical to the success of his organization. The project would have moved critical data exchange onto the Internet, automating and streamlining an expensive, time-consuming manual process, saving money, boosting customer satisfaction, and positioning the company as a technical leader in the industry. The project flew along at a tremendous clip through several rounds of initial prototypes, with a small group working on the effort. Then the process was opened to input from others, and the CEO stopped directly managing the process.

What happened next is all too common. Two of the new team members, a security expert and a technical manager, placed so many roadblocks in the project's path that, with potential costs spiraling out of control, it was eventually shelved. First, the security expert raised many concerns about compromised data. Most of these issues involved a one-in-a-million chance of a security violation. The solutions he suggested for these "problems," such as security cards for every user, would have quadrupled the cost of the application. Meanwhile, rather than moving to a quick market test, the technical manager continually insisted on generating reams of cost-benefit analysis. Not only did the analysis itself drive up costs, it was performed against the mushrooming costs of the security expert's Byzantine solutions. And though the analysis counted all possible costs, it tallied only those benefits that could be absolutely quantified (mostly staff reductions), while ignoring many less quantifiable benefits, such as vastly increased customer satisfaction and, consequently, increased sales.

The result of killing the project was the death of the company as an independent entity. It didn't have to happen. What went wrong here?

First of all, there were perverse incentives. While the shareholders, the clients, most of the employees of the company, the suppliers, and the customers all would have benefited from this system, for the two employees mentioned above, the potential risks outweighed the potential benefits. If the project succeeded, they could expect little credit. On the other hand, if, for example, a security breach were to have occurred, the security expert would have been held directly responsible and perhaps even fired. By contrast, the ultimate failure of the project or company (which continued to lose money and was ultimately absorbed by a competitor), would matter very little to his résumé—after all, who could hold a security expert responsible for the profitability of a large corporation?

INTREPID INTRAPRENEURS

The project also suffered because it wasn't supported by a hands-on intrapreneur, only by an enthusiastic CEO. Intrapreneurs are the dedicated drivers of a specific innovation. They are the visionaries who act to make dreams a reality. The CEO, in his enthusiasm, tried to manage the project without finding a team leader with enough intrapreneurial spirit to push through the detailed resistance that was slowing progress to a crawl. This is a good recipe for failure—a highly innovative project managed by a part-time leader from far above the level of the doers. The secret to success is empowering a passionate hands-on intrapreneur whose every day is immersed in achieving the dream.

> *A highly innovative project managed by a part-time leader from far above the level of the doers is a good recipe for failure.*

This is also an example of a botched team formation. Rather than being a group of enthusiastic volunteers, the appointed team included members who were not committed to the project's success. This is like launching a start-up organization in which only half the partners really want the venture to succeed. No banker would invest in such a flawed team. Getting the incentives right is one way to sort out those who truly want the project to succeed.

Finally, the project lost its sponsor in the middle of development. An effective sponsor supports an intrapreneurial group's ideas by protecting it from the corporate immune system and by helping it acquire the resources for implementation. The CEO was the original sponsor. When he backed off, no lower-level manager was left to protect the project and support those on the team who wanted it to succeed. The CEO, unfortunately, was not close enough to the action to see what was really going on with the staff members who were blocking innovation.

GETTING THE INCENTIVES RIGHT

What, then, is a more effective way of managing innovative projects? First of all, create a system in which managers are rewarded for being courageous sponsors of innovation. Don't promote naysayers—keep them as critics if they are good—but do promote people who are willing to back good projects. To find the best sponsors, ask the intrapreneurs who have succeeded at an important innovation, "In your darkest hour with this project, who defended you and helped you through it?"

Organizations should always approach innovative projects with a dedicated core team of intrapreneurial volunteers. If there are no intrapreneurs and team members who are motivated to join the project, don't do it. As the venture capitalists say, "Better to have a class A entrepreneur with a class B idea than a class A idea with a class B entrepreneur." Bet on a good team of people and let them find ways to address the problems. For example, if you are worried about security issues, raise the question, but let the team find the answers. Don't select an inner enemy as part of the team.

> *Better to have a class A entrepreneur with a class B idea than a class A idea with a class B entrepreneur. Bet on a good team of people and let them find ways to address the problems.*

Another key to successful innovation is a well-designed incentive system for team members. If the company is small, stock options, employee ownership, and profit sharing work well, especially if the staff is empowered to make a difference. If the company is large, one scheme that has proved successful is creating a team reward system that gives all members a share in the success in exchange for a tiny salary reduction to buy the "shares." Asking team members to take this risk lets those who don't want to join say so. Or an organization can go all the way and establish a free "intraprise" system, where internal departments compete with external vendors for the business of other departments. In a corporation employing this paradigm, the information technology department will not have captive users in accounting, marketing, and sales but will have to compete with other internal development groups, as well as outside consulting firms, for their business.

THE VIEW FROM BELOW

What if, as a first-level manager or an individual contributor, you don't have the power to change the way the company is run? Pay attention to the care and feeding of your sponsors. Recruit sponsors by asking for advice rather than asking right away for budget or people. While it's easy to turn down a request for a quarter of a million dollars for an experimental project, almost everyone will respond immediately to a request for advice. Once potential sponsors start helping you, they will begin to see your project as partly theirs since they have already invested some time in it. Now they have an interest in seeing that the time was spent wisely, on an ultimately successful undertaking. Take their best advice, put it in practice, and thank them for it when it appears to be working.

Even if you aren't the team leader, you can contribute to a common vision of success. Get together frequently over pizza and beer. Write a business plan together, even if you don't know how to do it. You also should try to get assigned to projects that turn you on. Then move from the role of technical contributor to one of the intrapreneurs who care about the overall success of the project.

You do this by broadening your interests, joining discussions outside your technical expertise, and learning to do financials.

Once you are on a project that excites you, try to promise less than you can deliver—too much advance publicity draws unwanted attention to your project and triggers the corporate immune system. Be willing to do any job needed to make the project succeed, regardless of your job description. And work to keep costs low. There is nothing like a huge budget request to alert the corporate antibodies to your presence. The best innovative teams are the ones that learn the most at the lowest cost. Don't buy fancy equipment if you can get going on what you can scrounge up. One of us once midwifed the birth of a successful corporate intranet by bringing it up on an old NeXT workstation, which our client had been ready to sell for $25 [Callahan, 1997].

> *There is nothing like a huge budget request to alert the corporate antibodies to your presence. The best innovative teams are the ones that learn the most at the lowest cost.*

Lastly, realize that barriers are inevitable. Rather than resenting them or considering them a reason to stop, skirt or dissolve them with the help of your sponsors. Bureaucracy believes there is only one right way to move forward, only one place to go for help. If that were true, as soon as you ran into a nonbeliever with a monopoly on some form of approval or resources, you would fail. Fortunately, in most organizations, there are many places to go for resources, assistance, and feedback. Develop these options. Be committed to the good of the company and your project's success, but be cunning about how to achieve those goals. And always remember that it is easier to ask for forgiveness than for permission.

Chapter 31

Inventing Software: Breakthroughs on Demand

Larry Constantine

Continuing on the theme of risk and innovation introduced in Chapter 30, this chapter presents some techniques for breaking new ground that have proved themselves in numerous projects. While developed in the course of work on user interface design, these ideas are sufficiently broad and soundly based in the nature of software problems and problem solving as to invite wide application.

—Editor

All software companies want to break new ground, they just do not want to be the first to do it. In an era when innovation appears to reign and "first to market" seems to be the rallying cry of every new dot-com, it can be surprising that so many software developers and their managers actively subvert their own creative potential for leading the way. In truth, it often seems that some companies would rather claim to be innovators than actually do innovative things.

Hollywood and TV scenarios notwithstanding, innovation is no accident. Inventors rarely stumble by blind luck onto their best ideas. Prolific inventors of useful products know that creative breakthroughs emerge from specific contexts and grow out of particular practices. Useful inventions are more likely to come from the periphery than from the center of the corporate scene. Innovation thrives in garage laboratories, at corporate "skunk works," and within freewheeling teams of bright nonconformists. Within certain limits, practicable innovations can be generated on demand, and such success can be repeated again and yet again. The secret, known in one form or another by all the most innovative groups in our industry, is to recognize that innovation is a process, not a product.

> *Useful inventions are more likely to come from the periphery than from the center of the corporate scene. Innovation thrives in garage laboratories, at corporate "skunk works," and within freewheeling teams of bright nonconformists.*

For years, my company and its clients have been using this "secret" to create user interface breakthroughs on a schedule. Of late, some of the client teams that we have trained, coached, or collaborated with have generated a string of software patent applications, one or two of which could well revolutionize graphical user interfaces (GUIs).

We do not have the hubris to believe that we are the only ones who can get this kind of result. In fact, we are so convinced that the creative engineering process we employ is learnable—and teachable—that we recently created an all-day workshop called "Inventing Interfaces." It was an experiment. To our surprise and delight the class maxed out the occupancy limit for the room where it was held and received rave reviews. However, it was the marginal notes and added comments on the evaluation forms that really highlighted for me some of the problems facing the software industry today. In this chapter I want to take a look at a few of the more insidious blocks preventing true invention in software.

LOOKING FOR ANSWERS

Our class on inventing interfaces had been promoted as a hands-on experiential workshop focused on the process of innovation, yet a vocal group afterward complained about the time spent learning, practicing, and applying creative engineering techniques. They wanted to see more examples of the innovative user interface designs that others had created.

The artist learns how to paint by painting. Creative engineering is learned by engineering creatively. It seems obvious, but imitation is the opposite of innovation. I could show you dozens of innovative user interface designs, but you would still not know how it was that the designers arrived at those innovations. Reviewing the innovations created by others is important if you want to buy a solution off the shelf. If you want to create something yourself, something that is both new and really works, you need to know how to do it yourself.

I think of it in terms of the old saw about fish. Give people fish and they are fed for a day; teach them how to fish and they are fed for a lifetime. The problem with our class was simply that we were being teachers, not fishmongers, and some of the participants just wanted to take home some fish.

> *The artist learns how to paint by painting. Creative engineering is learned by engineering creatively. Examples of innovations do not help because imitation is the opposite of innovation.*

It has always struck me as ironic that the really fun part of programming—what got most of us into this business in the first place—is solving problems and puzzling things out, yet so many programmers keep looking for easy answers. Managers compound the error when they keep looking to see what their competition is doing rather than figuring out what they themselves should be doing.

If you look for answers, especially if you go for the easy answers, often the best you can hope for is me-too design derived from warmed-over solutions to other people's problems. In fact, doing your homework well and thoroughly researching what has gone before may even sometimes work against you, particularly if what you want to do is explore new ground.

I have a lifelong habit of trying to work out problems for myself before looking to see what others have done. After I have struggled with a problem on my own and worked out some solution—or at least established a direction—I will then go back and check my thinking against the established canon and the received view. Not having immersed myself in prior work, I often find that what seemed obvious to me had actually escaped many others. Bingo. Another breakthrough. Extensive research and background reading may be a sound formula for writing an academic paper or preparing a thesis, but in the real world it can mire your thinking in the well-worn and muddy ruts already traveled by everyone else.

Of course, there can be good reasons for looking to what others have done. Good reasons for review include comparing notes after the fact, checking your thinking against others, and looking for useful additions or potential enhancements to a solution you have already devised. Before the fact, you might look at the work of other creative designers working on similar problems to find inspiration rather than to find answers.

ONE-WAY STREET

A third reason to look to the work of others is to help break out of the numbing mindset that there is only one way or one right way to solve a given problem. Development managers, in particular, need to learn never to accept certain phrases or stock answers from their programmers. "It may be clumsy (or inefficient or a resource hog or inelegant), but that's the *only* way you can do it in Java (or HTML or C++ or the Windows API or using MFC)," says the programmer.

"Bunkum!" says the savvy manager. "Go back to the drawing board and figure out another way."

Still worse is the programmer who says, "There is no way! You can't do that in Windows." In programming, there is no such thing as "can't." In software, all things are possible; it is only a matter of how long and how hard you want to work at it. An acceptable answer is, "Given the current delivery schedule, I don't see a way to solve it." Such an answer puts the spotlight on the real problem: not seeing a way.

The categorical thinking of "only one way" or "no way" can lock you into one view and prevent you from seeing workable and innovative ways out of a dilemma. A talented programmer at one client site was recently working on some custom Windows controls for an innovative industrial automation tool. Unfortunately, his tabbed dialogues did not behave the way they needed to for use in the new application. When this was pointed out, he asserted categorically that it was impossible. It has been more than a few years since I spent my days cutting code, but I knew, equally categorically, that this could not be the case. In fact, not knowing the details of VB, MFC, and COM but understanding the broad concepts and intrinsic logic of user interface programming gave me a distinct advantage. On the spot, I "invented" a work-around that logic told me ought to work. After a last round of token protests, the programmer agreed to try the approach, which he did. Within weeks I got an e-mail saying the suggested trick had worked.

> *Never accept stock excuses; in software, there is no such thing as "can't"—all things are possible. Categorical thinking can lock you into one view and prevent you from seeing workable and innovative ways out of a dilemma.*

THE LEGACY LOCK

Further fueling the can't-be-done mentality of many developers is the looming shadow of "The Legacy." Legacy users, legacy techniques, and legacy features often stand in the way of progress. Because that is the way Microsoft does it in Windows or because the previous version of your product got it wrong, you justify not doing it better on the next release.

Nearly every step of real progress throughout human history has been met with initial resistance from people firmly entrenched in the legacy, people who thought the old ways were just fine—or even better. I am not referring to the dubious sort of "progress" that our industry hails as a new paradigm every six months or so. I am thinking of real progress that genuinely makes new things possible or old things easier.

> *Legacy users, legacy techniques, and legacy features often stand in the way of innovation. Real progress is invariably met with initial resistance from people firmly entrenched in the legacy.*

The so-called "voice of the customer" has, for many software developers, progressed from a novel source of inspiration to just another excuse for same-old-same-old software. If you make the mistake of asking your users or customers whether they want a user interface just like the old one, almost invariably the majority will answer in the affirmative. Many will prefer known and familiar pain to unfamiliar uncertainty. "At least I know the quirks of the current system." Ask them, and they may steer you toward a ponderous Windows rendition of some outmoded green-screen application. Don't listen. If we always listened to such voices of the customers, we would all still be using line-at-a-time, text-based terminals capable of little more than emulating the paper-roll teletypes they replaced.

The installed-base legacy is a reality that must be taken into account in making design decisions and planning business strategy, but it has been enlarged by the anxious fantasies of timid managers and designers into a looming behemoth casting its shadow over the entire software horizon. With few exceptions, most legacy practices eventually give way to something better. The tiller bars and ropes that steered some early "horseless carriages," familiar though they were to legacy users, eventually gave way to steering wheels that offered superior control to the driver. Given enough time, most of the current abominations and annoyances of Windows can also be expected to pass into history.

The rule regarding legacy features and legacy interface techniques is actually relatively simple. Managers should approach the issue not as a question of whether to continue supporting the legacy users but as a strategic business decision of *when* to stop supporting them. Only in this way can you both innovate and plan for the transition effectively.

> *The rule regarding legacy features and legacy interface techniques is not a question of whether to continue supporting legacy users but a strategic business decision of when to stop supporting them.*

Closely related to the leg irons of The Legacy is the myth of perfection. Things are the way they are on conventional user interfaces because, so the argument goes, market forces, continuously growing user sophistication, and technological evolution have winnowed the wheat from the Windows chaff. This argument wrongly equates state of the art with best of breed. Defenders of this status quo usually overlook the premises from which they argue. Evolution has not stopped, market forces have not ceased to grind, and users have not frozen into some GUI mass. There is still ample room for improvement and innovation, and if your brilliant new widget works well enough and is sold appropriately, the market will accept it.

The way will be led by those developers with the courage and the creativity to innovate. If you honestly believe that current state-of-the-art technology is a given that will always be, just compare Windows 3.1 to Windows 2000. Microsoft learns; so can you, and so can your users.

GIVING UP

In my own experience as a user interface designer and collaborator on design teams, very few really good ideas spring fully formed from some fertile brain. Even the most fertile fields may need to be plowed and replanted more than once to yield the best crop.

In software, the innovations that are not merely different but actually make a difference are almost always the result of worrying away at a problem. Many potential innovators begin on the right track but then get nowhere because they are all too ready to abandon their bright ideas at the least criticism or the first sign of trouble. The innovative teams that have generated software patent after patent know enough not to give up too soon on a promising direction. They treat the limitations, shortcomings, or hidden defects that emerge on closer inspection as new problems to be solved creatively.

If necessity is the mother of invention, dogged persistence is the midwife. On the other hand, if you want to give birth to software innovations, you also have to learn when to change tactics. With practice, you will recognize when to back up and back off in order to get a fresh perspective on the problem before pushing away at it again.

> *If necessity is the mother of invention, dogged persistence is the midwife. Innovative teams know enough not to give up too soon. They treat emerging limitations, shortcomings, or defects as new problems to be solved creatively.*

UNDEFINED PROBLEMS

To solve a problem, you have to know what problem you are solving. Innovation hinges on defining the problem in the right way. For one example, everyone knows that tabbed dialogues using several rows of tabs are hard to use. Even Microsoft, with its fancy usability labs staffed by highly trained specialists, keeps turning out multirow tabs that are clumsy and confusing to users. Usability guru Jared Spool has concluded that no solution exists; he says simply not to use them.

But what is the problem? The real problem is not with multiple rows of tabs in themselves but with their behavior, which is difficult for users to interpret. Programmers will protest that the algorithm for what happens when you click on a tab in a back row is both simple and logical, but to the eye it looks like a random reshuffling rather than a straightforward interchange of rows and tabs.

Defining the problem as one of visual perception—the inability of the user to follow and make sense of what is happening—establishes a direction for seeking a workable solution. Animation solves the problem neatly and cleanly. Make the selected row appear to pop to the front, slide down, and then have the remaining rows slide back up behind it, and you have a multirow tabbed dialogue that seems completely understandable, even "intuitive." (A complete description of this solution is found in Constantine and Lockwood [1999].)

That one is solved, but there is no shortage of other software problems out there still waiting for someone with the persistence and vision to invent a good solution. It could be you and your team. Why not?

PART V

Processes and Practices

This section explores the processes and practices by which software and Web applications are developed. It begins with a plunge into some of the fundamental organizational and professional assumptions on which modern practices are based. Is the much-lauded Capability Maturity Model obsolete? Is optimization an inappropriate or unattainable goal? From the somewhat philosophical starting point, we move into case studies and experience reports, then specific practices that can improve processes. The section finishes off with a critical look into "unified" processes and modeling languages.

Chapter 32

Order for Free:
An Organic Model for Adaptation

Jim Highsmith

The whole is greater than the sum of its parts. The founder of general systems theory, Ludwig von Bertalanffy, first propounded that fundamental principle of systems back in the 1940s. When a collection of parts is organized into a system, such as a software development group formed out of a bunch of programmers, the whole will exhibit qualities and behaviors that are not properties of any of its parts. To understand the system—a company, an industry, a nation, an ecosystem—one must understand these emergents that arise not from the pieces themselves but from the interrelationships among them.

Complexity combined with energy generates order. Nobel Laureate Ilya Prigogine anticipated later discoveries in chemistry and biology with the mathematics of nonequilibrium thermodynamics. Any system that is sufficiently complex and far from equilibrium will evolve to higher and higher levels of order and organization as long as it continues to import free energy. He is talking about us, about corporations, about dogs, toads, and forests.

I cut my intellectual eyeteeth on general systems theory at MIT Under that heading, the subject matter may have fallen out of fashion, but the principles of systems theory and systems thinking— refined by decades of research and another generation of revision— apply no less today than in those heady days of my undergraduate years. Software development managers owe it to themselves to understand some of the basic tenets of a theory that at once describes the software systems being constructed and the human systems doing the construction. Here, Jim Highsmith offers his take on modern systems thinking applied to the software development enterprise.

—Editor

On the desk in my office sits EEK, an entirely self-contained, enclosed, living ecosystem (*www.eco-sphere.com*). Five inches high, EEK contains algae, very small shrimp and snails, and multitudes of microscopic bacteria. They all live by exchanging stuff with each other or converting light to biochemical energy. Meanwhile, on the monitor beside EEK, a forest of digital beings (Biots) exchange digital stuff. They live, eat (each other, of course), mate, give birth, evolve into new organisms, and die—a sea of artificial life created in silicon by one of the available artificial life programs.

I use these two visions of life, the real and the artificial, as constant reminders of a new way of thinking about complex systems and about how complex software products come into being. In the last ten years, software has entered a new frontier: a place where the frequency of change and the speed of the market have created a raw, hostile environment for software development, one where the basic tenets of process improvement, software engineering, and command and control management are insufficient for success. It is a frontier, I believe, where we can learn something by studying life and its mechanisms for adaptation and evolution.

> *The frequency of change and the speed of the market have created a raw, hostile environment, one where the basic tenets of process improvement, software engineering, and command and control management are insufficient for success.*

Within recent decades, the study of complexity and complex adaptive systems in fields such as evolutionary biology, ecology, and physics has begun to spill over into the management of organizations. Some of these concepts help explain why leading-edge, high-tech companies have succeeded by breaking historic patterns of behavior and also give us some insight into how organizations may operate more effectively in the future.

In this chapter, I'll introduce some fundamental concepts about how adaptation through spontaneous self-organization may help us work in this world of rapid change and high speed. Then I'll describe how organizations existing in this era of the Internet and massive connectivity might take advantage of these concepts. In essence, I want to explore two questions: What is spontaneous, emergent order, and how do we get it?

ADAPTATION, NOT OPTIMIZATION

In a slower-paced, less-complex world, the remnants of the Newtonian age work to perfection. Optimization has been enormously successful through rigorous process improvement, detailed task control based on predicted outcomes, and hierarchical management. In our industry, the pinnacle of optimization may be the Software Engineering Institute's Capability Maturity Model (CMM) Level 5 organizations—optimized to produce known quantities at a high level of efficiency. But if CMM Level 5 is the pinnacle, why are there so many successful software companies that can't even spell CMM? Are they just lucky, or is something else at work?

What about the unknown? What if we don't know exactly what product the market wants? What if competitors' products disrupt our carefully laid plans? What if a new technology makes our product development efforts obsolete? What if our general sense of direction is fogged? What if we are facing an impossible delivery schedule? Optimization has limited application in these situations.

Companies and software development groups in fast-moving markets need a different approach. In these environments, adaptation is significantly more important than optimization. Further, in this context, adaptation is more than just another word for change management.

> *In fast-moving markets, adaptation is significantly more important than optimization.*

WHAT IS SELF-ORGANIZATION?

As software engineers, we tend to approach the problem of building complex software products from the perspective of engineers. Engineering is largely based on predictable events, deterministic patterns, and linear construction—overall, by an attitude of "I can make it happen." We believe larger, more complex problems need a rigorous engineering discipline—an imposed order.

What if there is another source of order? What if there is both imposed order and a second, spontaneously arising order?

Biologist Stuart Kauffman, author of *At Home in the Universe: The Search for the Laws of Self-Organization and Complexity* [Kauffman, 1995], has spent more than thirty years trying to answer this question using genetic (Boolean) network simulations to study the complexities of biological evolution. His basic premise is that natural selection is a necessary but not sufficient condition to have evolved complex organisms. Natural selection, by itself, faces awesome mathematical odds. In a 100,000-node genetic simulation (the approximate number of human genes), the potential set of states is 1,030,000. However, in certain situations, Kauffman found the model would settle down and cycle through a set of only 317 states, a kind of "order for free." Natural selection is important, but self-organization is the root source of order.

Self-organization is a property of complex adaptive systems analogous to a collective "Aha!"—that moment of creative energy when the solution to some nagging problem emerges. Self-organization arises when individual, independent agents (cells in a body, species in an ecosystem, developers in a software team) cooperate to create emergent outcomes. An emergent outcome is a property beyond the capability of any individual agent. For example, individual neurons in the brain do not possess consciousness but, when they're combined, consciousness emerges. We tend to view this phenomenon of collective emergence as accidental, or at least unruly and undependable. The study of self-organization is disproving that view.

> *Self-organization arises when individual, independent agents (cells in a body, species in an ecosystem, developers in a software team) cooperate to create emergent outcomes.*

Kauffman's investigations into biological complexity offer insight into managing organizational complexity. There are those who, like Kevin Kelly, executive editor of *Wired* magazine, think the insights are far reaching [Kelly, 1995].

HOW DO WE GET IT?

As natural selection is necessary but insufficient to create biological complexity, optimization is also necessary but insufficient to create products in complex environments. Achieving emergent results in an organizational context requires

- Creating an adaptive mindset and accepting the limits of imposed order
- Revising development practices to support self-organization through an adaptive life cycle
- Rethinking management, especially how we create collaborative environments

Collaboration may be even more important than we realize. Can it really be as much a source of order as discipline and engineering are within our complex interactions? If so, are the resources we are spending on our collaboration networks nearly enough?

Many software developers feel "un-alone" time is mostly wasted. To their way of thinking, collaboration is little more than the following:

- Overpowering others in meetings through their own towering intellects
- Wasting time spent in meetings when they could be back in their cubes coding, testing, and so forth
- Attaching an alias to every e-mail
- Something for others who don't have a clue about what is going on
- Touchy-feely, time-wasting meetings cooked up by the bozos in human resources
- Creating a project intranet page

In *No More Teams: Mastering the Dynamics of Creative Collaboration*, Michael Schrage [1989] offers my favorite definition of collaboration: "The act of collaboration is an act of shared creation and/or discovery." Communication is passive—I send you something. Collaboration is active—we jointly create something. At its best, collaboration produces more than the sum of the parts. For nontrivial products, collaboration is not an option. How well we collaborate is the variable.

> *Communication is passive—I send you something. Collaboration is active—we jointly create something.*

This raises a variety of interesting questions about collaboration. The initial questions are important. First, how can we improve the collaborative efforts of single, colocated feature teams? Second, how can we improve the collaborative efforts of multiple, virtual feature teams? Answers to these questions involve both interpersonal and informational dimensions.

But complex systems research is pointing us toward even more fundamental issues. Is an organization's ability to adapt quickly a direct function of its ability to collaborate? And, more pointedly, is that ability to adapt a function of an organization's collaborative structure?

The process approach (change management, change agents, and changing an organization's culture) has gained immense popularity in recent years as companies try to keep up with rapid change. Small companies in rapidly changing markets seem to evolve quickly, without much ado about formal change processes. The more interesting phenomena are larger organizations, such as Microsoft, that operate in rugged market landscapes and exhibit adaptability without extensive formal change process efforts. Why? A first response may be that the market demands nimbleness to survive. But that doesn't explain why certain companies are better at adapting than others.

One implication to be drawn from both theory and experience: the structure of an organization's collaboration network has significant impact on its ability to produce emergent results and, ultimately, on its very ability to adapt.

Companies establish so-called "skunk works" to foster innovation because the structure of the larger organization is too rigid. Netscape, however, doesn't have a skunk works; it *is* one. Could it be that much of the effort applied to change processes in larger organizations is wasted because their collaboration structure is not conducive to adaptation? Should these firms be spending at least as much time experimenting with their collaboration network structure as the latest change-management technique? Many firms are spending millions trying to promote change when their collaboration structure is solidly locked into stability.

> *Companies establish so-called "skunk works" to foster innovation because the structure of the larger organization is too rigid.*

TUNING COLLABORATIVE NETWORKS

We've had hundreds of years to perfect hierarchical management structures, but less than twenty to deal with networked organizations. The movement in many of today's companies toward a flattened hierarchy to deal with administrative issues and networked teams to actually produce products is being done with little data about how to tune those networks for effectiveness. This is one area where a better understanding of complex adaptive systems may provide significant payback. Complexity research and my own experiences with software development teams provide several ideas for tuning collaboration networks.

First, it appears that above a certain point, the number of connections decreases adaptation. While the absolute number of connections is the key parameter in Boolean networks, organizational connections would include characteristics such as flow, diversity, and richness of the connection. Complexity studies also indicate that adaptation occurs at the edge of chaos, a transition zone between confusion and stagnation. Kauffman's work shows that this edge of chaos isn't only real but appears to be a fairly sharp edge. The optimal number of connections for balance is relatively small.

This relatively low number of connections per node does not seem to vary much with network size. As networks get larger and more nodes are added, the connections to each node must remain relatively constant. In today's networked companies where a "hook 'em up, link 'em up, ride 'em out" mentality prevails, we may be unwittingly pushing ourselves into the chaotic zone, where emergent results are lost in the noise.

> *In today's networked companies, we may be unwittingly pushing ourselves into the chaotic zone, where emergent results are lost in the noise.*

Kauffman's work also analyzes the complexity of the rule base within a node. If the goal is to balance at the creative edge, it appears overly complex rules override the benefits conveyed by connectivity. Although we know overly rigorous rules stifle creativity, we must have a better understanding of how rules and connections interact to keep organizations poised at the edge.

Finally, there is a clear link between organisms and the ruggedness of the competitive landscapes in which they adapt. As markets stabilize and companies settle into the ordered realm, they move away from the edge and become resistant to change. When the market changes suddenly, these companies cannot catch up—their control hierarchies have ousted their collaborative networks in the power struggle. Bringing in the local culture change guru will not be enough to overcome their structural deficiencies.

BALANCING ACT

As I continue to sit at my desk, one of the shrimp in my ecosystem swims madly around in circles. I wonder if the link between biology, complex adaptive systems, organizations, and collaborative networks is caught up in the same kind of meaningless swirl. But I am heartened by Kauffman's comment: "There are times in any science when one senses that a transformation to deeper understanding is pressing upward, in some as yet poorly articulated form. We may be in such a period in biology."

I submit we may be in the same position with respect to organizations in the networked era. The link between complex adaptive systems concepts and organizational performance still lies in the area of poorly articulated form. But our needs will not always wait for the well-articulated and the proven; it is part of surfing on the leading wave.

Adaptation does not replace optimization; they are complementary. It is not either/or but a balance, a teetering on the edge to gain the best of both. However, most organizations understand optimization but confuse adaptation with ad hocracy. As complexity increases, the failure of optimization is met with a fervent call for greater optimization, for more imposed order—exactly the wrong strategy. A better understanding of adaptation as a key to combating complexity, and a new perspective on collaboration as an activating mechanism, should help restore a balance—both to produce order for free and to create more agile companies.

Chapter 33

Beyond Level Five:
From Optimization to Adaptation

Jim Highsmith

The beat goes on. So does the debate. Structure or subversion. Control or creativity. Engineering or art. Software developers, consultants, and managers have been arguing the sundry sides of this apparent dichotomy for decades. To many, the rigid progression of successive levels of maturity so lauded today represents the ultimate surrender of creative programming to procedural bean-counting. For my part, I have always taken the sonnet view of poetic license. Every sonnet is exactly 14 lines long, yet are Shakespeare's Elizabethan nuggets degraded by this discipline? Is haiku any less an art for its rigorous 3 lines of 17 syllables? Does the syntactic rigidity of programming languages enable or constrict inventiveness? I would argue that the very best structures create a framework for creative processes and products. In this chapter, writer and consultant Jim Highsmith returns to make an impassioned plea for passion and argues that a philosophical model of organic adaptation best yields that elusive balance at the boundary between order and chaos—the fabled borderlands where you can find both manageability and flexibility in the same place.

—Editor

According to the Software Engineering Institute (SEI), the optimizing organization is the epitome of software development practices. Today it seems that every development group wants to earn that coveted accolade of SEI Level 5. "Successful companies," states Bill Roetzheim [1999], "standardize every business process to the point where an average employee can be successful simply by following the outlined process." Yuk. Will all you average employees out there who want to spend your careers following a collection of regulated, simplistic rules please raise your hands?

Repeatable, standardized processes reflect the attitude of software development traditionalists who believe in optimizing management practices characterized by rigorous rules and tight control. Optimization solved yesterday's software delivery problems. However, today's software project managers must deliver concrete results in shorter time frames while being constantly bombarded with myriad changes and risk-laden decisions. On complex, e-business-like projects—those defined by high speed and uncertainty—it is my contention that while some optimizing practices are necessary, they are also insufficient. It is adaptation practices that are essential. This issue of adaptation versus optimization changes the perspective of project managers from a mechanical view that lets you predict the future, follow a plan with minimal deviation, and drive out ugly process variations to an organic view in which the determinants of success are creativity, innovation, fast learning, skilled problem solving, and effective decision making.

The transition from an optimizing to an adaptive perspective involves defining an organic organizational model to replace our mechanistic one; describing a new adaptive management style, one I've labeled *Leadership-Collaboration*, to replace the command-and-control style that permeates optimizing organizations; and finally, examining the role of rigor in adaptive organizations.

THE BIOLOGY OF ORGANIZATIONS

Biological metaphors are hot, mechanical metaphors are not—at least in recent management literature. Kevin Kelly [1995] characterizes newer organizational systems as having lack of central control, autonomous subunits, high connectivity, and nonlinear causality. These systems are said to be more adaptable, evolvable, and resilient. Arie De Geus [1997] wrote that the machine metaphor has long shaped management thinking, our notions of control, and our approach to people. De Geus describes how viewing companies as a collection of living beings shapes management thinking in distinctly different ways.

Mechanical thinking results in process thinking. Organic thinking results in pattern thinking. The difference between processes and patterns is key to understanding the organic nature of organizations. Visualize the traditional input-process-output diagram with a feedback loop that includes a control block. This picture has dominated our view of mechanical and electronic control systems and, unfortunately, our view of organizational systems. The process is known—step, step, step—and the control block is likened to a thermostat in a heating system, adjusting temperature based on measurements and a plan (the set temperature). All mechanical, rule-based, predictable, and controllable.

> *Mechanical thinking results in process thinking.*
> *Organic thinking results in pattern thinking. The*
> *difference between processes and patterns is key to*
> *understanding the organic nature of organizations.*

The SEI's Capability Maturity Model (CMM) is the pinnacle of the optimizing viewpoint. The CMM and its highly structured, process-centered managerial cousins, such as business process reengineering, attempt to counteract uncertainty by admonishing people to be more certain. It is about as effective as telling a raging Mt. Everest storm to desist.

If the SEI were a business selling five products—from the basic Level 1 model to the luxury Level 5 model—why would selling fewer than ten luxury models in 15 years be considered successful? Software development is characterized by the SEI and strict process adherents as being undisciplined and remaining in a state of immaturity. But maybe, just maybe, the software development community isn't undisciplined or immature after all. Another explanation for the handful of Level 5 organizations is that there are only a half-dozen environments in the world that are stable and predictable enough for the "optimizing" approach to work.

In reality, solutions to complex problems are highly dependent on initial conditions and variable inputs, and the rules are either heuristic or nonexistent. Complex systems give rise to perpetual novelty that, in turn, resists canned solutions. For example, great chess players don't follow rules; they understand "patterns" of past play that indicate what future moves may be beneficial. Following the 14 recommended steps in a requirements definition process does not guarantee success—it is not a process in the sense of an algorithm. The 14 steps define a pattern that increases the odds of a favorable outcome, but they are in no way a guarantee. Requirements definition is not a repeatable process that you can measure and refine to the point of statistical control. It is a pattern that you must continuously adapt as you learn from your environment.

> *Solutions to complex problems are highly dependent on initial conditions and variable inputs, and the rules are either heuristic or nonexistent. Complex systems give rise to perpetual novelty that, in turn, resists canned solutions.*

Processes are limited to a discrete set of acceptable inputs; patterns can deal with variety and ambiguity. Processes imply you don't have to think; patterns challenge your creativity and problem-solving abilities. Processes are measured; patterns are assessed. Processes are controlled; patterns are learned from, adapted, and influenced. Processes are mechanical; patterns are organic.

THE LEADERSHIP-COLLABORATION MANAGEMENT MODEL

Saying, "We are an adaptable organization!" doesn't make it so—even if you are Jean-Luc Picard. Adaptability involves profound cultural changes. Dee Hock coined the word *chaordic* to describe adaptable organizations, those balanced on the edge between order and chaos. Hock, the former CEO of Visa International who presided over Visa's growth to 7.2 billion transactions and $650 billion in revenues annually, says simply and effectively, "Simple, clear purpose and principles give rise to complex, intelligent behavior. Complex rules and regulations give rise to simple, stupid behavior" [Hock, 1999].

The Leadership-Collaboration model embraces Hock's chaordic idea. In this model, leadership replaces command and collaboration replaces control. Managers who embrace the Leadership-Collaboration model understand their primary role is to set direction, provide guidance, facilitate the decision-making process, and expedite connecting people and teams.

Adaptive organizations are messy, anxiety-ridden, exciting, exuberant, bubbling, and redundant. They are just this side of chaotic, but not quite there. Adaptive organizations listen to the world around them—their customers, suppliers, employees, competitors—and respond to what they learn, not to what some process rule told them. Control-oriented managers revel in structure; collaborative managers revel in connectivity and real-world ambiguity.

> *In the Leadership-Collaboration model, leadership replaces command and collaboration replaces control. Control-oriented managers revel in structure; collaborative managers revel in connectivity and real-world ambiguity.*

Leadership-Collaboration style managers believe in people and passion. Ardent structure proponents confuse structure and skill—they deem unstructured to be unskilled. Dave Thielen (see Chapter 37) may have fallen into this trap when he argued that "average" programmers need more structure than "above-average" ones. First, I abhor the concept of an "average" person. If you create the right environment and align capabilities and roles, everyone can be the best they can be, to paraphrase the Army slogan. Second, while structure can support and leverage skill, I don't think increasing structure makes up for skill deficiency. For example, if I have trouble articulating good questions, no amount of structure will turn me into a good systems analyst—it will merely leave me a poor and grouchy systems analyst. There is a place for structure, but substituting it for skill isn't that place.

Another underappreciated aspect of skill arises from knowledge management: the concepts of tacit and explicit knowledge. At a simple level, explicit knowledge is codified, or documented, and tacit knowledge is that still in your head. Best practices may be written down, but it takes tacit knowledge—from experience, know-how, thought, judgment, and more—to bring them to fruition. Explicit knowledge provides you with the rules; tacit knowledge provides you with the deeper understanding that tells you when to break or bend the rules. You can no more become a good programmer from reading a C++ book than you can become a golfer by reading a treatise by Tiger Woods.

Proponents of process and structure assume that knowledge can be written down, encapsulated in little "knowledge objects" (called *best practices*), and plunked into people's brains much as reusable code is plunked into the next application. But whether you are a professional golfer or a professional software developer, the essence of your skill is tacit—it can't be written down and plunked into the next recruit. The essence of skill isn't what we record on paper; it's defined by proficiency, mastery, virtuosity, savvy, and artistry. Tacit knowledge transfer takes time, energy, and face-to-face apprenticeship. Structure is not a substitute for skill.

> *Proponents of process and structure assume that knowledge can be written down, encapsulated in best practices, and plunked into people's brains much as reusable code is plunked into the next application.*

RIGOR IN AN ADAPTIVE ORGANIZATION

In the twenty-first century, we will need to move beyond arguments about unstructured versus disciplined approaches to software development. We need a new framework. The science of complex adaptive systems (whether the components are neural networks in the brain or team members in a project) provide a clue to the role of rigor in an adaptive organization. Complex adaptive systems generate emergent (creative and innovative) results while teetering at the edge of chaos. This phenomenon, this tiny edge hovering between the twin abysses of stability and chaos, is driven from connectivity and information flow, not isolation and rules. "When systems of any kind (for example, beehives, businesses, economies) are poised on the edge of chaos between too much structure and too little structure, they 'self-organize' to produce complex adaptive behavior," write Shona Brown and Kathleen Eisenhardt [1998] in *Competing on the Edge*. Too much structure reduces problem solving and innovation, too little creates chaos and ineffectiveness.

In an optimizing organization, the role of rigor is to control, raising predictability to a statistical plateau. In an adaptive organization, the role of rigor is to provide just enough structure to prevent chaos but not enough to dampen the creativity of our collaborative networks. "A little bit less than just enough" is my guideline for implementing rigor. If people and their passions are the true core of any development effort, then rigor must be wielded with a deft touch, not with brute force. As one manager put it, "We need rules to keep our rules under control. Anything that smacks of rigidity makes me nervous" [Petzinger, 2000].

> *In an adaptive organization, the role of rigor is to provide just enough structure to prevent chaos but not enough to dampen creativity.*

In our turbulent world, brimming with both remarkable opportunity and frightening uncertainty, we need an adaptive model of project and organizational management, a model that views rigor as a balancing mechanism rather than an end goal. We need a model that draws creativity and innovation out of people's passions, because when structure drives out passion we have failed as leaders. It is not the individual practices of the CMM, such as requirements management and configuration control, that are obsolete but the framework of maturity levels and the philosophy of predictability and control that are outdated. What we need is a new framework—patterns and connectivity—and a new philosophy—organic and adaptive—that sustain developers and their passion in our quest to tilt at the windmills of complexity.

Chapter 34

Optimization or Adaptation: In Pursuit of a Paradigm

Sylvain Hamel and Jim Highsmith

Discipline and structure—how much, when, how? These questions preoccupy not only the parents of toddlers; they are, as this section attests, perennially vexing matters for software developers and managers. We explored such questions on more than one occasion in the "Management Forum" column in Software Development. *When Jim Highsmith (see Chapter 33) took on the industry's best-known model of structure and discipline, the Software Engineering Institute's Capability Maturity Model, he proposed replacing the storied Level 5 and its attempts at optimizing the development process with a more organic model based on adaptive control. One of the Forum's readers, software engineer Sylvain Hamel, took such energetic exception to Highsmith's critique that we decided to continue the dialogue. Here is the sum and substance of their exchange.*

—Editor

HAMEL DEFENDS

As a developer working in an organization that abides by a software process, I take exception to Jim Highsmith's characterization of software processes in general and their relationship with creativity in particular. The Software Engineering Institute's (SEI's) Capability Maturity Model (CMM) is not, as Jim Highsmith proclaims, "a collection of regulated, simplistic rules" meant to strangle an organization's creativity, but a powerful tool that enables an organization to produce better products while providing its employees with an improved working environment.

In fact, Highsmith's own solution to the chaos of software development—adaptive patterns—is diminished by his inaccurate portrayal of what constitutes a software process. Highsmith writes, for example, "Following the 14 recommended steps in a requirements definition process does not guarantee success." The CMM Level 2 requirements management process, however, does not define 14 steps. There are two goals, one commitment, four abilities, three activities, one measurement, and three verifications. Nowhere in the CMM process is a particular methodology for requirements management imposed. There aren't 14 steps in the CMM that must be used to do requirements management—or any other software development life-cycle activities, for that matter.

The CMM and other prominent software development processes, such as the Rational Unified Process (RUP) [Kruchten, 1999] and the Australian-developed OPEN process [Henderson-Sellers and Unhelkar, 2000], are not about "rigorous rules and tight control" as Highsmith writes. These process models emphasize that an organization should first observe the model and then adapt the process to its needs. In fact, a key SEI document is entitled "Process Tailoring and the Software Capability Maturity Model" (CMU/SEI-94-TR-024). The CMM process is not applied as-is on all the projects of the organization; it must first be tailored for the organization and then tailored for each project [Constantine and Lockwood, 1994; Mogilensky and Deimel, 1994].

> *The CMM and other prominent software development processes are not about "rigorous rules and tight control"; rather, they emphasize that an organization should first observe the model and then adapt the process to its needs.*

Highsmith argues that while optimization solved yesterday's software delivery problems, today's accelerated market requires an organization to focus on adaptation. However, Highsmith overlooks the fact that optimization implies adaptation. The SEI describes Level 5 as the level at which "the entire organization is focused on continuous process improvement." Process improvement suggests that the organization takes into account changes in its environment, new tools and problems with the process identified in previous projects. Process optimization only means that the organization tries to improve, adapt, and correct its software process—using past project information—before problems escalate out of control.

Granted, very few organizations are at Level 5 because it takes tremendous commitment from upper management to allocate the time, people, and money needed for continuous software process improvement. Additionally, there is a lack of commitment for software process improvement in most organizations because upper management does not appreciate the long-term benefits. Highsmith only adds to the problem by creating a false impression of what is a software process and why it is used. Highsmith tells us that the CMM and other such processes "attempt to counteract uncertainty by admonishing people to be more certain." But what is the main part of the CMM? It is the key process goals for each level. And what are these goals? The industry's best practices and common sense. To reach a particular CMM level, an organization does not have to do everything described in the key process areas (KPAs) for that level; however, the goals of the KPAs must be satisfied. There is no admonition there as Highsmith argues, but there is a reduction of the uncertainties (and risks) because the organization documents and verifies what is done during the software development cycle. If something goes wrong for a project, the information will be used on the next one to avoid making the same mistakes.

> *Uncertainties and risks are reduced when an organization documents and verifies what is done during development. If something goes wrong, the information can be used to avoid making the same mistakes again.*

A colleague of mine once worked in a systems engineering department that didn't follow a software process. When a project ended, the design documentation didn't correspond to the equipment in production, and there wasn't any time or money to document or correct any of the found problems. When a new project began, the new team used the old documentation as a design reference and, therefore, repeated many mistakes from the previous project. Without a formal process to verify and validate the design, do configuration management, or manage requirements, the same mistakes continued to be made on each and every project.

These errors ultimately created delays and cost each project more money than it would have cost to simply update the design documentation. The systems created did increase in complexity from one project to the next, so upper management has finally decided to implement a process. This organization wants to move from chaos (which does not work) to structure because a process helps reduce (not eliminate) many problems by establishing verification and validation, configuration and requirements management activities, and so on.

A software process, when well implemented, also reduces the stress placed on the software development team. I have been developing embedded-system software for 15 years and hadn't worked in an organization with a software process until 4 years ago. The main activities of the first software process in which I worked were verification and validation of the design to ensure that the proper software was being built, and those two activities greatly reduced the amount of stress I experienced. During the previous 11 years, there was no formal verification (walk-through or review) of my design whenever I developed a software component. Consequently, the verification was done only when my software component was integrated into the product, and errors (some small, some big) were common because I had misinterpreted some requirements and no one had checked my design.

> *A well-implemented software process reduces the stress placed on the software development team.*

Today, I work in an organization where formal verification and validation begin with the system requirements down and extends to the detailed design and unit test planning. This means that, if I misinterpret a requirement, two or three of my colleagues are there to catch my error. This doesn't mean that I do a sloppy job because somebody else will correct it; rather, I know that a huge mistake, one that will require weeks of work to correct, won't be found four months later during integration. In another organization that is currently at CMM Level 3 and progressing toward Level 4, a colleague has also confirmed this benefit of a systematic software process: all the software development team members experience less stress.

Highsmith also writes that "processes imply you don't have to think." I am happy to report that I do not think less now that I work within a software process. In fact, we have more time to think about software design with a process, and we may even be more creative because we do not have to spend as much time and energy to organize our work. I see no link between a software process and limited creativity.

Software processes and methodologies are often compared with the construction of a building. Is the architect's creativity limited by mechanical engineering rules and building code regulations? Perhaps a little because he has to comply with a minimum ceiling height, provide emergency exits, consider the characteristics of the materials used, be concerned with aesthetics, and so on. However, the architect's own creativity and skills are the principal limiting factors in the building's design.

> *Is an architect's creativity limited by mechanical engineering rules and building code regulations?*

Creativity, knowledge, and skills are personal attributes. I agree with Highsmith that structure does not substitute for skills, but do people lose their skills because they are using a software process? I think not. A process doesn't dictate how a person thinks. The CMM doesn't try to prescribe the skills of a person to be "plunked into the next recruit," but it does try to establish a predictable result from the person's skills and creativity—namely, the resulting system and software design. Once written, these results may be used by the "next recruit" to improve her skills and enhance her knowledge.

The CMM does not specify a methodology, although some other processes, such as the RUP, do suggest particular methods, such as object-oriented programming. The CMM does not dictate what method to use to analyze client needs, to find system requirements, or to allocate requirements to subsystems. Each organization must define its own method. What the CMM implies is that the organization will define a method that is documented in writing. In fact, the organization should probably have more than one method to modify the process to each type of project. In fact, the CMM doesn't even define a software development life cycle (SDLC); the organization must decide which SDLC to use.

Software process models, such as the CMM, are much more helpful than Highsmith would have us believe. Some organizations may misuse them, but the goals of these models are hardly overly restrictive. Software processes are frameworks to organize our work. And because software development techniques evolve, the process must be improved to follow the organization environment changes. As Larry Constantine writes in his introduction to Highsmith's piece (Chapter 33), "the very best structures create a framework for creative processes and products."

HIGHSMITH RESPONDS

Mr. Hamel's lament contains two main themes, both ever-present in debates with CMM proponents: first, that I don't understand the CMM, particularly that it espouses continuous improvement and adjustable processes; and second, that I advocate process-less hacking, caring naught for quality. Wrong on both counts.

Let's take the second point first. A mountain of documentation, processes, forms, model diagrams, repository entries, procedures, and checklists have been foisted upon the development community in the name of quality. None of these things ensure high quality, just as the lack does not ensure poor quality. According to CMM proponents, anyone who doesn't toe the party line is automatically branded as a hacker, and I for one am acutely weary of that argument. A similar debate now rages over Extreme Programming (XP). Critics say XP is an excuse for hacking, but one doesn't have to talk to XP practitioners for long to know that this is a bum rap. Mr. Hamel writes about the "lack of commitment for software process improvement in most organizations." After 20 years of trying, maybe it's not the lack of commitment but the lack of results that has earned management's attention.

> *A mountain of documentation, processes, forms, model diagrams, repository entries, procedures, and checklists have been foisted upon the development community in the name of quality, yet none of these things ensure high quality.*

High-quality results are critical. However, there are legitimate differences of opinion over how to achieve them. I think high quality in turbulent environments is derived from a mix of rigorous (optimizing) processes and innovative (adaptive) patterns. It's my belief that rigorous processes are necessary but insufficient—and they need to be kept to a minimum. The CMM and "Methodologies" (with a capital *M*) may have some continuous improvement practices, but the ones I've seen have been primarily optimizing in nature. However, before we get too mired in the debate about process, another issue here is the definition of quality. Quality, for me, implies more than freedom from defects. Quality relates to value, a multidimensional array of scope, schedule, defects, and cost. Every project or product has a value profile, and that profile should drive the balance between optimizing and adapting practices—not some arbitrary maturity-level designation.

Much of Mr. Hamel's critique tries to explain why the CMM is so wonderful and that if we would all just read past the cover pages of CMU/SEI-93-TR-025, CMU-SEI-93-TR-024, and CMU/SEI-94-TR-024, we (or I) would see the light. Having spent the better part of three decades developing, consulting, teaching, and implementing CMM-like and non-CMM approaches to software development, I have some ideas about what works, what doesn't, and why. Mr. Hamel writes that "optimization implies adaptation." Words are tricky things; one person's interpretation of either "optimization" or "adaptation" may be very different from another's. For me, there is a big difference—as more than a dozen management books published during the last couple of years have explained. Adaptation implies far more than adjusting processes. It means exploring into an unpredictable future; it means implementing practices that encourage intense collaboration; it means nurturing improvisation; it means leading rather than managing; and it means instituting learning practices (yes, even including processes like software inspections). I won't be so presumptuous as to list these books on adaptation, but I can assure Mr. Hamel they don't have titles like CMU/SEI-94-TR-024.

> *Adaptation implies far more than adjusting processes. It means exploring into an unpredictable future; it means implementing practices that encourage intense collaboration; it means nurturing improvisation; it means leading rather than managing; and it means instituting learning practices.*

In the final analysis, however, I'm really not anti-CMM. I've spent a 30-year career advocating good software engineering practices, and I agree completely with Mr. Hamel's points about problems with chaotic environments—if that is what he thinks I am advocating, then he has misread my argument. I just don't think the CMM is the right model for every software project or every software development organization. The CMM contains useful practices, but in our turbulent, fast-moving, unpredictable, e-business world, the CMM often has the wrong structure and philosophy for the products we need to deliver.

Chapter 35

Adaptive Software Development: An Experience Report

James Emery

The pull between thinking and doing is one that most of us have experienced at one time or another. Practicing managers and developers seldom have much time for deep thought about the processes and methods by which they accomplish their deeds. Academics, by contrast, may have the time and the mandate to think about these matters but can suffer from a paucity of practical experience on which to reflect. The case study from James Emery in this chapter continues the theme of adaptive development raised in the preceding chapters by turning to real-world experience.

When it comes to applications development, Emery is that rare breed who can both do it and teach it. Over his long career combining a commitment to academe with hands-on experience in applications development projects, he has made useful contributions on both sides of the ivied wall. In fact, in the early 1960s he devised the first practical notation for representing program modules, inspiring my own work on structured design and ultimately laying the groundwork for modern structure charts and even today's Unified Modeling Language.

—Editor

After four decades of trying to get it right, software applications developers still experience an embarrassing number of outright failures or, more commonly, projects that take too long, cost too much, and deliver crummy systems. All of us pay a heavy price for this. Even the most imaginative information technology vision will come to naught if an organization cannot ultimately deploy adequate application software. By that test, many organizations have not done very well.

Over the years, I have been closely involved in a number of software development projects based on an adaptive software development process. All followed a common formula: Use a small team, work about a year in a relatively informal environment, and develop a series of prototype applications that eventually lead to an acceptable production system. Although it is not always easy to pull off and carries some definite risks, I believe adaptive development is the preferred way to proceed for most development projects.

The largest project with which I have been involved was a transfer agency application for a medium-sized mutual funds company. The application was a mission-critical mainframe program that handled all of the accounting functions associated with purchases, sales, and reporting for all shareholder accounts. Comparable systems developed for other mutual funds companies typically consist of several million lines of COBOL reflecting years of work by hordes of programmers. We developed our system in just 14 months with a team that never grew beyond four persons.

An adaptive approach offers a widely applicable recipe for success, although it is not without risk and does not scale indefinitely to larger and larger projects. As an application's requirements grow in expanded functionality and increased reliability, developers must eventually resort to a formal, disciplined process appropriate for managing dozens of analysts and programmers. If I find myself flying as a jet passenger at 35,000 feet, I would like to believe that the air traffic control system has been subject to a highly disciplined development and quality assurance process. But I would be quite content to have my mail-order invoice generated by an application created through a less rigorous process. Such applications are far more common than air traffic control systems.

> *An adaptive approach offers a widely applicable recipe for success, although it is not without risk and does not scale indefinitely. As an application's requirements grow, developers must eventually resort to a formal, disciplined process.*

A CASE FOR ADAPTIVENESS

One particular project provides a good illustration of both the power and pitfalls of an adaptive approach. It involves the development of a comprehensive accounting system for the Naval Postgraduate School, where I serve as CIO. The School offers fully accredited graduate programs in science, engineering, management, and security affairs. Its 1,400 students come from the Navy and other

U.S. military branches, as well as from allied nations around the globe. The staff includes over 300 faculty members and 500 support personnel. The campus network connects a midsized mainframe, numerous servers, and about 3,000 PCs and workstations.

The accounting system will eventually have over 100 direct users. The complexity and functionality of the system are representative of medium-sized, state-of-the-art applications. It presently consists of about 120,000 lines of code, 75 tables, 40 screens, and 70 reports. It has the demanding reliability requirements typically associated with an accounting and timekeeping system.

The existing official accounting systems were designed to meet the School's statutory requirements for financial management, but they offer precious little decision-making information or operational support. To meet these needs, each academic and support department has had to cope on its own. This led to the independent development of a variety of incompatible systems, each with unique data and functionality. Lacking a standard system at the department level, staff in the comptroller's office have had to manually reenter departmental data into its central system, with all of the extra cost and inconsistencies that this entails.

About a year and a half ago the superintendent of the School set a high priority on developing a contemporary system. The goals established for the system were: to eliminate duplicate data entry and storage; to allow School-wide access to common financial data; to provide a friendly and productive human interface; and to be flexible and adaptable enough to meet a variety of needs within the academic departments, staff support groups, and top management.

POTENTIAL SOLUTIONS

We considered adapting the best of the existing departmental systems for School-wide use, employing a government-developed program, or adapting a commercial accounting package. We concluded that none of these alternatives met the School's unique requirements. No departmental system was extendible to the School as a whole, accounting packages targeted at the commercial market did not handle arcane Navy accounting regulations, and government-supplied software or commercial packages designed for the government market did not deal with the special complexities of an educational institution that has a large variety of activities supported from numerous funding sources. Reluctantly, we set out to develop our own tailor-made system. The superintendent set a seemingly impossible goal for installing the system by the beginning of fiscal year 1998, giving us less than nine months to do the job. The formal project schedule revealed that we had almost no slack.

Nevertheless, adaptive development is not an excuse for proceeding precipitously without adequate analysis and a full understanding of requirements.

The development team initially spent about a month interviewing selected users. Existing homegrown departmental systems were also reviewed to identify features that should be included in the new system.

> *Adaptive development is not an excuse for proceeding precipitously without adequate analysis and a full understanding of requirements.*

DEVELOPMENT APPROACH

The process we used rests on three essential ingredients: (1) an adaptive methodology that can take advantage of organizational learning that takes place during development, (2) a productive set of software tools that makes it feasible to respond quickly to user feedback, and (3) a small team of highly competent developers. These components are mutually dependent—shortcomings in any one of them can destroy the effectiveness of the entire approach.

Adaptive Methodology

With an adaptive methodology, a project proceeds through an iterative process that eventually converges to an acceptable design. Each iteration is manifested in a working prototype that demonstrates exactly how the designers have interpreted user specifications. This provides a very effective means of communication with users because they can gain concrete, hands-on understanding of the application instead of relying on abstract written documents that are difficult to impossible for most users to comprehend. Eventually the evolving prototype becomes functional and robust enough to deploy as a production system. Once in production, the application can be expected to undergo periodic revisions throughout its life.

An effective iterative process should start with a prototype design that matches as closely as possible the eventual production system. The process of generating initial requirements is similar to that used in a more traditional project except that analysts do not harbor the illusion that the up-front specifications will remain stable throughout implementation. This realism enables the analysts to generate good initial specifications while avoiding a fruitless quest to get everything exactly right the first time.

> *An effective iterative process starts with a prototype design that matches as closely as possible the eventual production system.*

An adaptive process does not imply an unplanned one. The project should be planned in detail, with frequent updates as the project evolves. Early attention should also be given to the design of a sound data model. Although a number of changes in the data model may take place during the implementation, its design generally remains relatively stable compared to the human interface and business rules.

Adaptive development conflicts with the school of software engineers who prize fully defined initial requirements and a disciplined, reproducible implementation process. With an adaptive process, one does not know up front all the details of what the end result will be; instead, one arrives at the end result through a process of organizational learning and discovery. It is intrinsically a somewhat uncertain and ambiguous venture. Nevertheless, it may often be the best way to produce a successful end product.

Truly effective systems are rarely developed from a stable and comprehensive up-front statement of requirements. Any system that meets real organizational needs must evolve through a series of changes. It is far better to encourage and plan for these changes than it is to view them as anomalies in an otherwise immaculate process.

> *Any system that meets real organizational needs must evolve through a series of changes. Better to encourage and plan for these changes than to view them as anomalies in an otherwise immaculate process.*

Productive Development Tools

Quick response to user-driven changes requires an exceedingly productive development environment. This can be achieved only with a powerful set of development tools. Substantial changes to the current prototype should generally be possible in no more than a day, with minor changes made in a couple of hours or less. Essential to the approach, tools must allow a seamless migration through a series of prototypes to the eventual production system—without transliteration to a different production language.

A productive development environment generally consists of several complementary tools. It is difficult to select and master the right tools from among the huge proliferation of products available in the market, but the resulting enhanced productivity can easily be worth the effort. A typical tool set should include a database designer, a generalized report writer, and a project scheduler. The principal development language for our system was Visual Basic augmented by Acuity

Visual Tools, a comprehensive set of Visual Basic components closely integrated with Microsoft SQL Server.

Team Organization and Composition

It is well known that some of the best software is written by small teams of very competent individuals. To tackle a sizable project with a small team, the productivity per team member must be very high—as much as an order of magnitude greater than industry averages. To achieve this, the team must combine strong technical abilities with sound application knowledge and good human relations skills. By avoiding most of the management and coordination overhead required of a large project, a small team can devote its efforts to getting the job done.

> *By avoiding most of the management and coordination overhead required of a large project, a small team can devote its efforts to getting the job done.*

The development team leader for the School project, a mid-level Navy officer, had considerable management experience and an excellent formal education in information technology (IT), but he lacked hands-on IT experience. All of the actual coding of the application was done by a single programmer with a strong background in development of commercial (but not government) accounting applications. He proved adept at understanding our special requirements and responding to requests for changes in the prototype design. The final member of the team joined on a half-time basis from one of the academic departments. She had extensive accounting experience along with considerable writing and end-user computer skills.

Using a small development team greatly facilitates informal coordination. Communication should not be limited by hierarchical reporting relationships; each member should feel free to contribute ideas in open dialogue. Everyone needs to be motivated to get the job done with little central direction. This kind of informal but highly effective team cohesion is one of the greatest strengths of a small team.

Various user groups were also essential contributors to the project, principally through an advisory board consisting of members drawn from departmental administrative personnel, the comptroller's office, and the central academic planning and budgeting office. Meeting once a week, the board reviewed each prototype and provided critical feedback.

LESSONS LEARNED

By the fourth quarter of 1997, we had already celebrated with a victory party, but it was a bit premature. The timekeeping portion of the system was completed in time and was run in parallel with the old system for two months in all of the academic departments. People were quite happy with the new system, judging it to be a distinct improvement over the existing system. However, we did not meet the ambitious original schedule. The nonlabor portion of the system (such as accounting for purchases) was only partially finished, and the completion date had to be pushed back to the first quarter of 1998.

Among the difficulties we encountered was the political challenge of getting final approval and acceptance of the new system. The new timekeeping system feeds data into the official Department of Defense payroll system; before the new system can replace the old, the comptroller's office must certify that it is accurate and meets statutory requirements. Prior to recent changes in the financial management of the School, we did not have enthusiastic buy-in from some key accounting staff members, who may have viewed the new system as a rival to their own system. The delay added extra costs, which put the project up against the local contracting authority. Clearly, we should have done a better job of anticipating these problems.

> *Political challenges involved in getting final approval and acceptance of a new system can cause delays.*

This project effectively illustrates the promise and perils of an adaptive development process. What general lessons might be gained from our experience?

1. An adaptive approach can provide a very effective development process. Despite the delays we encountered, I believe we have made substantially more progress than if we had followed a more conventional approach.

2. Success requires that all of the right pieces be put in place—methodology, tools, and team. This is not at all easy to do.

3. A new team faces a significant learning curve to build team cohesion and master the tool set adopted for a project. The investment can pay huge dividends, however, in the form of greatly increased productivity.

4. An ambitious schedule always runs the risk of missing its deadline. If the penalty for delay is high, some slack must be built into the schedule.

5. For an adaptive process to work, incentives must be in place so that stakeholders have a real stake in the project's success. Without this, it is too likely that

the process will not converge on an acceptable solution within an acceptable time period.

6. It is essential to maintain communication with all stakeholders, emphasizing the goals and general principles that guide the effort. Stakeholders often have little knowledge about a contemporary information system and even less about how it might be implemented through an adaptive process. Some will be bothered by the seemingly unplanned and ambiguous nature of the process. Others may find it difficult to believe that early prototypes are not cast in concrete, because their past experience has taught them that computer systems cannot be modified. Still others may err in the opposite direction, insisting that the design be endlessly modified to accommodate their ever-changing whims.

Finally, and perhaps most importantly, any project that can potentially bring about substantial organizational change must have unreserved top-management support. Even with such endorsement, a new application may be doomed unless it gets genuine buy-in from the functional managers and users most involved in its operation.

Chapter 36

Creating a Culture of Commitment: Of Deadlines, Discipline, and Management Maturity

Larry Constantine

Nobody believes programmers or their managers anymore. The distrust has grown through decades of broken promises, of bargaining in bad faith, of slipped schedules and blown budgets. When I speak on this subject, I often ask members of the audience to raise their hands if they have ever participated in a project that delivered what it promised on schedule and within budget. Never have more than a scattered few hands gone up, and often some of those are withdrawn after a few moments' reflection.

How did we get to this sorry state? We say we will do something and then fail to keep our words. We agree to deals with the devil, committing to delivery dates that we know are ridiculous and impossible. Knowing that we will fail to meet expectations, upper management, marketing staff, and our customers and clients escalate the stakes, hoping that by insistence on even earlier delivery we will somehow be driven to deliver later but still soon enough. The never-ending games of mistrust continue as the bar is raised higher and higher in the accelerating pace of Web-time, crunch-mode development rampant in the dot-com world described in Part III. How do we ever get out of this mess?

—Editor

Deadlines. We all face them repeatedly in our professional and personal lives. We dread them and we are driven by them, but we cannot avoid deadlines. Commerce and technology run by the calendar, and the most significant entries in many calendars are those red-circled delivery dates when a project is due. Without deadlines, many projects might never finish, yet they can also become tyrants that make us slaves to success or mock our failures.

Most software development deadlines are soft. The difference between delivery tomorrow and delivery next week may be small and hard to determine. In truth, most software projects are delivered late, in part because announced delivery dates are often regarded as arbitrary, capricious, or unrealistic—as, indeed, they frequently are. There are exceptions, of course. Developers working on Year 2000 remediation faced a particularly firm deadline. When the clock struck midnight, the calendar clicked over and the systems went live. The demonstration for a product launch at COMDEX must be run when scheduled— bugs, botched interfaces, and all—or the vendor may take an even bigger beating in the trade press or on the NASDAQ.

> *Most software development deadlines are soft. The difference between delivery tomorrow and delivery next week may be small and hard to determine.*

As a writer and educator, many of the deadlines I face are rigid and immutable. The magazine for which I write a regular column goes to press on a certain day each month. Any copy that fails to arrive by the deadline will not be seen in that month's issue. The twice-annual Software Development Management Conference that I organized for many years was held on specific dates fixed far in advance. Speakers could not postpone their conference presentations because their material wasn't ready or they hadn't worked out all the bugs in their code examples. When 10 o'clock on the appointed day rolled around, a room full of people was waiting for them to start the class.

Of course, some people do not take even such absolute deadlines seriously. At a conference on Web design and development, one of the scheduled presenters telephoned the conference organizers less than an hour before his all-day tutorial was to begin. He claimed he had been working too hard and felt too tired to teach!

I suppose it is also possible to take such commitments too seriously. The audience was unaware at the time, but I once presented an early-morning keynote speech while still feverish from a stomach virus that had kept me awake all night with my head in the sink. Nevertheless, I also confess to giving magazine editors the heebie-jeebies with my late-but-still-in-time copy e-mailed at the last possible second.

Not long ago, as I scrambled to deal with the crisis precipitated when none of the five pending contributions to my monthly column were delivered when promised, I started thinking about deadlines and discipline, about maturity and the culture of commitment.

Whether praised and promoted or criticized and condemned, the notion of process maturity has become part of the lexicon of modern technical management. Most readers will be familiar with the Capability Maturity Model (CMM) developed by Watts Humphrey of the Software Engineering Institute at Carnegie Mellon University. The CMM recognizes five levels of maturity in organizations, ranging from "initial" to "optimizing." Many software development managers long to reach Level 5, but their organizations are stuck at Level 1.

Although it is easy to focus on the numbers and on the specific practices that contribute to those numbers, the CMM is about more than just what you do and how you document it. As organizations change their practices and processes—as they become better organized and more effective—their cultures change.

HEROIC MODELS

At the lowest level, which characterizes most development organizations and has sometimes been called "chaotic," we find a culture of heroic creativity. Great programmers and project leaders are respected, even idolized for their creative skills and knowledge. Success is linked to heroic efforts and extraordinary individual achievement. To many people, this sounds like a good thing, but such cultures become dependent on heroes and heroism. Often they are marked by spectacular successes and equally spectacular disasters. Because they depend on extraordinary effort, you can't depend on them under ordinary circumstances.

A drawback of the heroism culture is that individuals not only get the credit for success—they also are blamed for failure. If a project is late or a system is unreliable, it must be someone's fault. When a project comes in late, as it most often does, the finger-pointing begins. In a witch hunt for scapegoats, the trick is to cover your behind by deflecting attention onto others. Since individuals are looked to for solving problems, they are also blamed for problems not solved. The processes by which the product was built or the project was managed are seldom subject to close scrutiny. It can be difficult in such an organization to discover that problems might lie in how deadlines are determined or how project milestones are defined—rather than in the people trying vainly to meet them or reach them.

> *A drawback of a culture based on heroic effort is that individuals not only get the credit for success—they also are blamed for failure.*

In a culture of heroism, deadlines, indeed commitments of many kinds, are not taken seriously. Programmers scoff at delivery schedules promised by sales staff members. Managers who learn not to trust estimates from developers pad budgets, add slack to schedules, and double or even triple estimated development times. Customers and upper management, hardened by past failures and expecting schedule slippage, will squeeze for tighter budgets and earlier delivery. It's all a game. Everybody plays it and nobody takes the numbers or dates too seriously. Promises become empty. "We'll have the beta version to you by the first of the month," comes to mean "We'll do our best to have it done sometime next month, but don't count on it." Who believes Microsoft when it announces a product release date? Who believes your department when it says a project will be finished at a certain time? Who believes developers when they say a system is "90% complete"?

COMMITTED CULTURE

A culture of commitment, by contrast, is based on trust—trust that promises will predictably be kept. Within such a culture, projects are completed not through heroic and exceptional efforts but through competent and consistent application of efficient techniques. Schedules are kept because they *can* be kept and have been negotiated on the basis of realism and honesty. All the parties to the development process—management, developers, and customers—understand what they can reasonably achieve, at what cost, and on what schedule.

Within a culture of commitment, promises are kept, in part, because the promises that are made are realistic and achievable. To know that a development schedule is achievable, you must know how big a project is and how much can be accomplished with the resources at hand. This is not a matter of heroics but of measured performance. Instead of chaotic extremes, development becomes marked by predictable, professional results.

> *Within a culture of commitment, promises are kept, in part, because the promises that are made are realistic and achievable.*

How do you create a culture of commitment?

To begin with, be careful what you promise. After a triumph in battle, the biblical Jephtha promised to sacrifice the first thing he saw when he returned home. When he arrived, he was greeted by his only daughter. By becoming more careful about your commitments, you are less likely to find yourself caught in a trap of your own making.

Don't make promises you know you can't keep. Keeping to schedules and budgets is far easier when you don't commit to the impossible in the first place.

This means that you must know what you and your developers can and can't do. That, in turn, is based on keeping careful records that are systematically and repeatedly reviewed. Software metrics can help, but even just being more mindful of the level of effort expended and the sources of delays and pitfalls can improve your projections.

As a manager or project leader, you need to start with yourself and work outward. In dealing with those above you, you must be prepared to stand your ground in negotiating achievable agreements, then do whatever is necessary to make it possible for your team to achieve them. This means refusing to play the popular management game of "delegated delusion," in which unrealistic expectations are simply passed down to would-be heroes or losers, who are given pep talks and are told, "We know you will come through for us."

> *Managers must learn not to accept commitments they know are unreasonable. They must be prepared to stand firm in negotiating achievable agreements, then do whatever is necessary to make it possible to deliver as agreed.*

Managers must learn not to accept commitments they know are unreasonable. By building a reputation for consistently meeting commitments, development managers will increase their power to negotiate. By demonstrating dependability and predictable performance over time, they improve their credibility.

Managers should not expect developers to commit to and keep schedules in which they have had no say. All too often, features and delivery dates are set by marketing departments or by internal customers without consultation or input from the very people who might know what can be done and how long it will take.

Developers who are realistic about contracts and progress are often derided for not being "team players" or criticized for "negative thinking." Realism and skepticism should not be confused with pessimism. Development teams need skeptics and critical thinkers who are willing to question risky commitments. Such people should be recognized and rewarded for their potential contributions to a culture of commitment.

> *Realism and skepticism should not be confused with pessimism or negative thinking. Development teams need skeptics and critical thinkers who are willing to question risky commitments.*

RIGHT QUESTIONS, RIGHT ANSWERS

What do you do when your developers tell you the schedule set by management is impossible? The typical tactic is to say, "Wrong answer!" and tell them to go back and find a way. In a culture of heroism, the assumption is that they are not trying hard enough. In a culture of commitment, managers, project leaders, and developers learn to trust one another's judgments. In such a culture, the manager would ask, "What schedule is possible? What date can you commit to? What resources do you need to make it possible?"

Over the long run, managers and developers interested in contributing to a culture of commitment must learn to blame the process, not the people. When schedules slip or budgets are exceeded, you should question what went wrong rather than who screwed up. Blaming the process is not a cover for incompetence, however. Once problems in the development process are identified, you need to fix them.

> *Managers and developers interested in contributing to a culture of commitment must learn to blame the process, not the people. When schedules slip or budgets are exceeded, they should question what went wrong rather than who screwed up.*

Never promise to do it all. It is also important to remember that when it comes to delivering fast, cheap, and good software, you can achieve any two at the expense of the third. You can save both time and money if you are willing to compromise quality; you can get faster delivery and higher quality if you are willing to pay for it. Time-boxed development, in which software is delivered on a fixed and inviolable schedule, is only possible if all parties are prepared to compromise on budget or quality. When it comes down to the wire, it may become necessary to invest more or to trade functionality, reliability, or other aspects of quality for the absolute guarantee of on-time delivery. Though it may take time, you need to educate clients and upper management on these trade-offs.

At Level 2 in the CMM, processes are said to become predictable. Sometimes this is achieved by reaching a level of predictable mediocrity. Software quality management tends to put the emphasis on getting processes under control—standardizing and regularizing procedures and narrowing the range of options. Certainly this is one route to predictability, but it is not the only one.

It is possible to build a culture of commitment without buying into the whole CMM package, but it requires an initial full commitment from you. So remember: Be careful what you promise. Don't make promises you can't keep.

Know your capabilities and limitations. Don't deny realistic data or punish healthy skepticism. When things go wrong, blame the process, not the people, and then fix the process. Don't expect real commitment to dictated requirements or schedules. And always negotiate schedules, budgets, and requirements.

> *It is possible to build a culture of commitment without buying into the whole process improvement package.*

Ultimately, of course, a culture of commitment is not about commitments to dates or schedules but about our commitments to each other. Genuine commitment is one of the secrets of truly great development teams.

Chapter 37

The Commando Returns: Learning from Experience in the Trenches

David Thielen

Whether intentionally or not, Dave Thielen has been an inspiration to me. When I first met him in front of an audience at a software development conference, we were on opposite sides of a high but invisible fence dividing the putative forces of order from the supposed champions of chaos. Our energetic encounter inspired me to write a column in Software Development *magazine on "coding cowboys" [Constantine, 1992] that broke records for reader response.*

Over the years, Dave has proved himself as a talented developer and manager. Through e-mail and conversations at conferences, I followed his career from Microsoft to game development and beyond. I was surprised when Dave first raised the subject of this chapter at another professional conference. All right. I admit it, I am smiling. I am pleased to see one of the original commando coders returning from the trenches, battle-weary but newly inspired.

—Editor

In the spring of 1992, a panel at the Software Development Conference pitted me against Larry Constantine debating the proper approach to software development management. J.D. Hildebrand, then editor of *Computer Language Magazine*, moderated, keeping the audience under control and the intense but good-natured discussion focused on the issues. At its root, our disagreement reflected the wide disparity in our approaches to management. The panel had been billed as dealing with structured versus unstructured approaches, but someone in the audience described it as the "commando versus corporate mentality."

In case you have any doubt, I advocated the commando approach, fighting the good fight for programmers to be able to do their own thing. Eliminate the designs, the reviews and walk-throughs, the CASE tools, the diagrams, the cost-estimation models, the planning—all the bureaucracy. Just turn your programmers loose and watch them create great products 10 to 100 times faster without the constraints.

Now, after too many additional years in the trenches managing teams of software developers on a variety of projects, I've come to another conclusion. I was wrong and Larry was right. (Boy, that hurt!) The commando approach is less efficient; it results in poorer code that actually takes longer to produce.

> *After years in the trenches managing teams of software developers on a variety of projects, I've concluded that the commando approach is inefficient; it results in poorer code that actually takes longer to produce.*

Has the commando sold out to the corporate mentality? Not exactly. I still think I was correct about a few things back then, but I will save those for last. First, let me dive in and explain where I was wrong—and why I've changed my mind.

LIFE IN A SMALL TEAM

I still believe the best team size is two or three people. Of course, one person alone works most efficiently, but it's critical to have someone with whom you can review your approaches. However, most software projects have gotten too big for this small-team model to work anymore. No matter how good your programmers are, no matter how supportive their environment may be, minuscule teams cannot complete today's massive jobs in any reasonable amount of time.

To add to the challenge, the areas of expertise you need for a project have multiplied. Many times, you need people who are knowledgeable in a host of arcane specialties or skilled in particular areas, in addition to the programmers needed for the core program. You need people who are good at user interface design, COM, multimedia, TCP/IP, HTML, and so on. No one can be an expert in every area. We have simply outgrown the days of the renaissance programmer who can switch from C++ to HTML to graphic design without pausing for coffee.

> *The areas of expertise you need for a project have multiplied, and no one can be an expert in every area. We have simply outgrown the days of the renaissance programmer.*

The case of the Linux operating system demonstrates how productive gigantic, worldwide teams can be (see Chapter 42). With more projects based on large, distributed teams, part-time programmers and telecommuting are going to become a fact of life, especially given the changing job market, where the unemployment rate for good programmers seems to be moving into negative numbers.

With increased team size comes the additional overhead required to keep everyone working toward the same goal and to ensure that the various pieces will plug together properly. Further compounding the challenge for managers is the problem that, simply because you need more people, you end up hiring programmers who may not be as good as you want.

ARCHITECTURE, DESIGN, AND REVIEWS

It used to be that you could put together a good design in your head. The pieces were simple, and the project itself had simple interactions among the parts. This meant that talented programmers could sit down and bang out a good program with no up-front planning and design. The pieces might have a couple of rough edges, but the time saved by not designing up front seemed to more than make up for it in the end.

In many ways, we were working in an industry in its infancy. Every day we were learning how to do things better. In the past, by the time a project was finished, it often differed radically from any original design. But now the projects we work on are much larger, with a significantly greater number of interdependencies. At the same time, our industry has matured so that approaches to problems do not as often change substantially within the time it takes to complete a project.

Without up-front architecture and design, you are almost guaranteed to write code that, as you progress, cannot do what you need it to do. Given the size and diversity of modern teams, you will find that a piece one person is depending on, written by another, does not provide the needed functionality without design.

> *Without up-front architecture and design, you are almost guaranteed to write code that, as you progress, cannot do what you need it to do.*

In those earlier days of commando coding, architecture and design were inefficient steps. As our code began to increase in size, these techniques may have improved productivity, but they could still be ignored, albeit at a cost. For today's larger projects, skipping the architecture and design phase is a good way to guarantee failure. Architecture, design, and systematic design reviews have become critical factors in success.

CALENDAR TIME

Planned schedules are now an essential element for delivering software in a reasonable amount of time. In the past, it seemed easier. You slowly made progress until the weekend before the ship date. Then you and the rest of the team worked straight through the weekend to deliver the final product. Schedules were all but irrelevant in such an environment. In most cases, you pulled through in one last desperate effort. In the rest of the cases, it hardly mattered, anyway.

As projects got bigger, schedules could be useful but most everyone worked on their part with a reasonable sense of urgency. Then, instead of waiting for the last weekend, the entire group went on a death march to finish the project in the final three to six months (see Chapter 18). This was incredibly inefficient and destructive to family life, but it often worked. Besides, many of those young programmers had no family life. But many programmers do have families. In addition, the interdependencies in projects have multiplied to the point where it is critical to know whether a piece will be ready when a programmer needs it. Fewer companies can afford the risk of a death-march effort that may take three months or may drag on until the project and the programmers have to be put out of their misery.

Our industry is shamed by the many software projects that are never completed. Projects fail for various reasons, but with a failure rate that some claim is as high as 75%, it's critical to receive an early warning of potential disaster. You don't want to wait until the last dollar is spent or the day when you must either deliver the software or go out of business. You need to learn as early as possible if you are not going to make it. Schedules let you track the progress both to determine the probable ship date and to determine whether the project should be changed or killed. In other words, the old model that "it's done when it's done" no longer works as a scheduling system.

> *Schedules let you track progress both to determine the probable ship date and to determine whether the project should be changed or killed.*

CODING PROCESS

By coding process, I mean how programmers attack and solve a problem. This is not, by and large, taught in schools. Nor is it covered in books or technical seminars. Everyone is taught the best algorithm to solve certain types of problems or what the API is for certain functionality, not how best to write and test code.

The end result is that everyone comes up with a personal method. This libertarian process may have worked great when no one knew what worked well and everyone was experimenting with different approaches. But we are at the point where it is clear that there are specific practices, such as single-stepping, that all programmers should use.

A generation of programmers has, over entire careers, made independent decisions as to how to program. The more senior developers are generally of an age where, like my father-in-law, they are used to doing things their own ways and have no interest in changing how they code.

Perhaps it's time for programming to grow up. This would require programmers to use the best possible practices for writing and testing their code. We know what constitutes good practice. We know how to structure code that is reliable and easy to maintain. We know the value of such practices as code walk-throughs. Managers need to sell such practices, even over pained and vociferous objections. In my experience, without absolute insistence on using such practices, many programmers will continue to work in a less effective manner.

> *We know how to structure code that is reliable and easy to maintain. We know the value of such practices as code walk-throughs. Perhaps it's time for programming to grow up and use the best possible practices.*

QUALITY PEOPLE

I do retain my belief that the quality of your programmers is the most critical factor in the programming process. Most research shows the difference in productivity between the best and worst programmers to be a factor of as much as 10 or 25 to 1. Nothing can make up for having poor programmers. The most foolish cost-saving tactic is to hire numerous poor programmers instead of a few really good ones.

With that said, I've also concluded that the majority of companies won't spend the money to hire from the top echelon of programmers. Even if all companies tried to do this, not everyone can hire the top 10%. With a shortage of programmers, some companies must end up hiring from the other 90%.

This means each company needs to set up its systems and procedures to take into account the quality of the programmers it has. For the more average programmers who are the bulk of the profession, the amount of overhead to ensure that they are doing the right thing, doing it well, and doing it on time is substantial. Without this overhead, what is done is done wrong, and the final project is almost guaranteed never to be completed.

A company must be realistic about the abilities of the programmers it will attract based upon their pay, the work environment, and how interesting the work is. It must then structure its procedures around the type of programmer it can attract. With too much bureaucracy, progress is slowed; with too little, the job is never completed.

Unfortunately, most companies are not willing to hire the best people. Trying to tell managers that hiring the best programmers is cheaper in the long run—which it is—will not change their minds.

UNREPENTANT STILL

Since I have laid my soul bare on those items where I was wrong, I figure it's only fair to mention some of the matters where I was right. Some things I still believe hold true, even if they may go against conventional wisdom.

In my experience, I have yet to see CASE tools do anything other than slow down a project. I think CASE has taken a good idea—specifying a project—and ruined it by placing the priority on making the specification perfect, rather than getting the key items detailed and then proceeding to code.

> *CASE has taken a good idea—specifying a project—and ruined it by placing the priority on making the specification perfect.*

It is crucial that you give programmers ownership of the pieces on which they are working. Only with ownership will they invest more of themselves and their passion into the project. With this investment, they will do a better job and put in more time to make what they own a success.

After the quality of the programmers themselves, the work environment remains the second most critical factor in productivity. Open work areas and cubicles have been proven time and again to be penny-wise and pound-foolish, lowering rent but also lowering productivity. Closing off windows, requiring set hours, enforcing a dress code, and supporting other stupid human-resource edicts can contribute to lower productivity.

Larry concluded our original debate with a very good comment. He said that having a group of smart programmers who were passionate about their work was the most important part of the process. The other parts—the technical and management structures—merely help a good group be more successful. I agree!

Chapter 38

Persistent Models:
Models as Corporate Assets

Larry Constantine

In the debate over the roles of the stochastic and the structured in software processes, the focus of contention is often on philosophy. Freedom and flexibility duke it out with discipline and deliberation; adaptive agility is contrasted with systematic structure. Lost in the shuffle is the essence of methods and the motivations that led to this divide in the first place. Methods evolved as means to support modeling. Models were invented and introduced into software engineering because they aided and speeded the process. The bureaucratic documentation and rigorous adherence to form came later.

In my experience, the well-intentioned transformation of good ideas into overorganized orthodoxies is an all-but-inevitable outcome of human social activity. From a primordial miasma of method-less exploration emerge the working techniques that become embodied in methodical practice. Eventually, best practices carried to excess generate the counterforces that drive the evolution of a new order. Hegel hit a few nails on the head. It's thesis, antithesis, synthesis. Hacking, CMM, XP. Chaos, order, chaordic (see Chapter 33). Once we recognize the process underlying process evolution, we can step out of the frame and consider what is really important. Models, for instance.

—Editor

The devil may dwell in the details, but it's the big stuff that truly tests us. Large-scale projects have a way of becoming learning experiences—whether we intend them to or not—and often the lessons learned are unexpected ones. When the scale rises above a certain threshold, the name of the game changes (see Chapter 42). I have long been an advocate of model-driven design, not because I have some perverse passion for models but because effective models give you leverage—leverage that helps you build better software and build it more quickly over the full spectrum of projects, from small-scale, time-boxed rapid development efforts to multiyear monsters. A recent model-driven design project highlighted for me some of the special risks and rewards of modeling very large, complex problems. In particular, it got me to thinking about models as long-term investments.

The project in this case was a substantially improved version of a complex programming tool for specialized applications. It was intended to be break-through software that would tax the skills of a dozen and a half developers for well over a year. Although a high-risk undertaking, the project had two big factors in its favor: First, members of the design and development team really knew their stuff. Second, it was to be developed using model-driven design.

After many years of producing a complete line of software tools in this area, the development group had accumulated deep domain knowledge. Much of this knowledge and insight was implicit and undocumented, save for its embodiment in previous software products. Ask these developers a question, and they can almost invariably give you a good answer, but don't ask for something to read on the plane home—the important stuff is nearly all in their heads.

The new system was to be developed through an end-to-end application of usage-centered design, a model-driven approach aimed at maximizing software usability [Constantine and Lockwood, 1999]. The design team began by looking at the roles that users would play in relation to the new product and immediately discovered small but significant holes in the knowledge of the development team. Filling in these holes through site visits and interviews with current customers, the team discovered that a few simple but important capabilities had been neglected in the past while some elaborate features probably were of little value in real-world practice.

> *Through site visits and interviews with current customers, the team discovered that a few simple but important capabilities had been neglected in the past while some elaborate features probably were of little value in real-world practice.*

Combining established knowledge with new insights, the team identified and described 25 different roles that users could play in relation to the planned product. Considering that many fairly elaborate software systems may involve only a handful of distinct user roles, this in itself is a clue to the considerable scope of the project.

Up to this point, the team had taken the low-tech route, working quickly and efficiently with nothing fancier than whiteboards and flip charts despite the size of the user-role model. Once we started to model the tasks to be supported, however, the pace slackened, and we had to turn to technology to help manage the complexity. The initial use-case model was enormously complex, with over 340 use cases. Even with the support of specially developed CASE tools, defining and detailing the role and task models proved tedious and time consuming. Along the way, there were many moments of self-doubt as programmers became increasingly eager to program and as various members of the team questioned the value of pursuing a model-driven development approach.

Eventually, through a mixture of simplification, sophisticated triage, and inspired business decision making, the team was able to prune the problem to some 240 use cases supporting 19 user roles. This move highlighted the first big payoff of model-driven development: clarification and simplification of the problem. Looking at the content and navigation models that described the overall architecture of the user interface, one developer exclaimed that he now realized that such models were the only way to get a true picture of the application as a whole—what was in it and what was not, what was truly needed and what was only nice.

As a result of better organization and more finely tuned, detailed design, the system would be given a vastly superior user interface that would dramatically simplify use by customers. More importantly, when the somewhat skeptical developers recomputed their project estimates, they found that development time for core functionality had actually been reduced as a result of the modeling effort.

DELIVERABLES DELIVERED

The biggest payoff, however, would not actually come until the next round, when another product in the same line was to be redesigned. As the models were completed and the details were filled in, it became clear that they were applicable to more than just the immediate project. This was especially evident for the domain object model that described the core concepts and classes needed in support of the role and task modeling. The major portion of the user role and task models themselves would also be much the same for most software in the product line. Even some of the roles and tasks that had earlier been reduced in scope or excluded from the project were not a wasted effort, since some of these represented specific potential requirements for other products and future extensions.

> *The biggest payoff comes because the models—especially the domain object model—are applicable to more than just the immediate project.*

From this perspective of broad applicability, it is not just the final software but also the models themselves that are products with lasting value. Although intermediate models, such as data models or class diagrams, are often referred to as "project deliverables," they are seldom delivered to anyone beyond the immediate development team. In all too many cases, developers are not used to constructing from models or have little idea of what to do with them, and so the models may merely be "delivered" to ring binders that gather dust on a shelf until they are tossed out in the next office move. Because such models are seen as applicable only to the project at hand, they are considered disposable, and modeling is looked upon as an expense or as part of the administrative overhead.

> *Although often referred to as "project deliverables," in all too many cases, models are merely "delivered" to ring binders to gather dust on a shelf until they are tossed out.*

AMORTIZED ANALYSIS

When one project has to carry the full cost of building a comprehensive set of analysis and design models, that cost can seem prohibitive. When the cost is amortized over a series of projects that will share in the fruits of the modeling process, the accounting picture changes dramatically.

You might think of this perspective as a form of reuse (see Chapter 26), which is certainly an idea in tune with the times. However, the real issue is that such models are corporate assets, with persistent value over time. In fact, I prefer to call them *persistent models,* because, like persistent objects in software, their significance is in their continued existence over time. Persistent models are real assets with a life cycle of their own that may span multiple projects and products.

Analysis and design models are often viewed strictly as a means to an end, but persistent models are the means to many ends. They can help managers shape long-term planning and guide the orderly release of new features or versions targeted to serve varied audiences. As models are elaborated to cover more of the products in a line, they can become substantial corporate assets—core models of the business as well as models of software.

> *As models are elaborated to cover more of the products in a line, they can become substantial corporate assets—core models of the business as well as models of software.*

You can use persistent models to structure the current release and the next and the next. You can extend and modify the models to become the blueprints for similar or related software. You can use them as a sort of "straw model" starting point for a system that is only distantly related. You might launch a design for a claims processing system with a very good solution for another insurance application, for example, beginning with a look at how the new project is different, then adapting the existing models accordingly.

Models as assets are especially promising in certain specialized but quite common circumstances. For example, any group involved in developing and refining a single product or product line through successive versions and releases stands to gain tremendously from the investment in model building. Models can evolve with the changing code. They provide alternative views into the software that can guide developers in choosing the best places and approaches for incorporating new features and capability.

The incremental cost of expanding, refining, or modifying the models to describe updated system requirements and new designs is likely to be relatively small with successive releases. This is especially true for essential models [McMenamin and Palmer, 1984], which are deliberately constructed to be abstract and technology-free descriptions of system capabilities and design. The simplified use cases that form the core model in usage-centered design, for example, have proved particularly easy to adapt to fit even radical changes in underlying technology or basic assumptions.

> *The incremental cost of updating models is likely to be relatively small with successive releases, especially for essential models like the simplified use cases employed in usage-centered design.*

Any group producing applications within a single application domain—currency trading, chemical process automation, personal finance, or whatever—stands to gain much from investing in persistent models. Whether the systems are commercial products in a particular market or are applications for internal use in a given industry, persistent models will be valuable and useful. All applications within a given problem domain will share some common underlying characteristics, whether in user population, in tasks to be supported, or in terms of basic vocabulary and core concepts. To the extent that these commonalties are reflected in persistent models, the models will be transferable from application to application, at least in part and at least as points of departure.

MAINTAINABLE MODELS

Well-maintained models can have hidden value and unexpected payoffs over the long term. For example, a number of programmers have told me that previous design models for applications later proved of great value in coping with the Y2K update nightmare.

Of course, just as code can vary tremendously in how easy it is to maintain and to modify, models can manifest varying degrees of robustness and adaptability. As expected, the medium of expression is part of the story. Models in electronic form, even as the simplest of documents or diagrams, are more readily changed to cover succeeding projects. Ideally, persistent models ought to be constructed using full-featured CASE tools with complete version management facilities. That, of course, is easier said than done when you are using advanced models that are not supported by conventional CASE tools, as is the case with usage-centered design, which is why we had to develop our own tools on this project.

The medium is not the whole message, however. Some models are intrinsically more robust than others, whether embodied as files in a CASE tool or scribbled on newsprint. Models expressed at a higher level of abstraction or that describe software in generalized or generic terms are more likely to survive through the theme and variation of successive releases or varying applications within a common domain. For example, user role models that represent the abstract role played by users in relation with a system are more generalized—hence persistent and transferable—than are profiles of specific users or demographic groups. So-called *essential use cases* that model the intentions of users and the essential purposes of interactions are more likely to hold lasting value through successive projects than task models that describe specific and detailed interaction with a current user interface design. Leaving out the specifics and the details allows you to focus on the essence of a problem and the basic structure of the solution, which are less likely to change from one release to the next, even when differences in the user interface or in supporting internals are substantial.

> *Models expressed at a higher level of abstraction or that describe software in generalized or generic terms are more likely to survive through the theme and variation of successive releases or varying applications within a common domain.*

In other words, for the project I have been describing, part of the long-term value of the models we developed is due to the fact that we were applying usage-centered design. This approach deliberately strives to extract and describe the abstract essence of a problem and aims for a degree of abstraction and generalization that will readily accommodate innovation and change.

Although some models might be of more lasting value than others, the range of potential persistent models is tremendous. It includes data models of all kinds and forms, including entity-relationship diagrams and domain-object/domain-class models along with models of key algorithms, whether expressed as pseudo-code, state-transition diagrams, or structured flowcharts. Persistent models of external requirements include models of user roles and user characteristics; task models ranging from goal hierarchies or work breakdown charts to scenarios, use cases, and essential use cases; and models of user interface contents and content navigation.

Whatever models you use or are considering using, the potential for persistence is probably there. You may even be able to justify expanding your modeling efforts—or using advanced design models for the first time—by arguing for the return on investment over the long haul.

> *You may be able to justify expanding your modeling efforts by arguing for the return on investment over the long haul.*

A superior user interface design, for example, may be of tremendous value even if you cannot implement all of it in the next release. You can come as close as time and budget will allow in the current development cycle, then use the already completed design models to spark the next round. Not only do you start next time with a big leg up on the design, but you also know where you are going well in advance.

Planning and control are, it has been said, the essence of management. Investing in persistent models can provide you with new tools for achieving both while simultaneously enabling your developers to build better software. Just think of persistent models as corporate assets.

Chapter 39

Card Magic for Managers: Low-Tech Techniques for Design and Decisions

Ron Jeffries

Effective process requires effective tools and techniques. Developers and managers are often easily seduced by exotic software and powerful computers, but some of the oldest and simplest technology for problem solving and decision making is also the most efficient and effective. Countless problems in mathematics, engineering, science, and technology have been attacked and solved by people gathered around a chalkboard. Generations of managers and group leaders have learned to make sense of complex situations through "card storming" ideas onto index cards and grouping these into "affinity clusters." Social scientists long ago established that items can be ranked more reliably by shuffling cards than by numbering items on a list. Extreme Programming, the most visible of the newly evolved "lightweight" processes, has generated a renewed interest in some of the oldest tools. In this chapter, Extreme Programming pioneer Ron Jeffries tells us about some of the magic that managers can do with nothing more than a stack of cards.

—Editor

Plain, ordinary index cards can be powerful tools for software developers and their managers. Cards are one of the secrets of success in Extreme Programming (XP) [Beck, 2000]. In XP, cards are used to represent user requirements and for release planning. But cards are in no way limited to XP projects [for example, Bellin and Simone, 1997]. Card-based planning is a powerful technique for communicating, sorting out priorities, and scheduling. Whether in small groups or one-on-one, writing what needs to be done on cards, handling them, and moving them around engages participants in a way that flip charts or whiteboards cannot.

Shuffling cards may sound blindingly dull, but there is magic in the cards. They can be used to help define requirements, decide priorities, schedule activities, and deal with emergencies. A quick overview of XP planning will set the stage for looking at other uses.

> *Shuffling cards may sound blindingly dull, but there is magic in using them to help define requirements, decide priorities, schedule activities, and deal with emergencies.*

PLANNED RELEASE

XP's release-planning practices start with exploration. At the end of exploration, we have a batch of cards with requirements on them, and each card has a cost estimate.

In XP, requirements are called *user stories,* and each story is written on a card. A story is like a use case, but smaller and simpler. It's smaller because each story can be estimated by the programmers as needing no more than a week or so of effort. It's simpler because the story is backed up by acceptance tests that include some of the detail.

After user stories are written, the programmers estimate how long each will take to implement. If the programmers cannot come up with an estimate, either the story is too big and must be broken down or the programmers need to do a simple experiment to learn about how to implement the story. I'll skip the detail on how to estimate, however. The important point is that each story has an associated cost estimate, amounting to just a couple of programmer weeks.

When exploration is finished, release planning moves to commitment. During commitment, the customer decides what will be in the next release by deciding what to do and what to defer. These decisions are made in a deceptively simple way. Since you know the cost of each story in terms of time to delivery and the customer knows what is valuable, the decisions are relatively easy. The process involves laying the cards out against a calendar, choosing to complete the most valuable ones early, and deferring the ones of lesser value until later.

> *Once you know the cost of each user story and the customer knows what is valuable, release-planning decisions are relatively easy. Cards are laid out against a calendar to schedule completion of the most valuable ones first.*

Suppose your team works in two-week iterations and can, altogether, do eight estimated weeks of work in an iteration. Then the customer just picks the most important eight weeks' worth for the first iteration, the next eight for the next, and so on. The magic is not that customers decide about priority but how they decide.

As customers work, they touch and move the cards around. They pick up a few to hold awhile, looking at the rest. They make little batches, saying, "Well, all these go together; there is no sense having one without the others." They wave the cards as they talk. "This one is really important to me. Why does it take so long to implement?" They split the stories right on the spot, negotiating requirements. "OK, the important part is this; I'll write it on a separate card. That's high. The rest of this is medium or low." They slide the cards back and forth, or move some of them off a little ways, out of the schedule but not out of mind. They fondle cards for a little while, getting used to giving them up, then set them down, almost reverently, in the deferred pile.

What is fascinating about this process is that the team doesn't have to push the negotiation. Customers typically accept the costs as given and decide what will provide the best mix of features by the date they want. The result of the XP release-planning process is not just a release plan but a kind of intimacy with the stories and their costs—an understanding and acceptance of reality. And the process goes quickly. You can easily plan a six-month release in less than a day. Cards facilitate the decision process.

The process works so well that I use it all the time. I even planned this chapter with cards. At one point, I took a blank card from the pack to write the first card for iteration planning and placed it on the table. Then I thought of one more thing to say about release planning. Even though the card on the table was blank, I found myself reaching for another one because the one on the table already stood for a release-planning idea in my mind. Cards become the thing they represent, even before anything is written on them. Sometimes you even find yourself pointing to a place where a card might be, referring to it as if it existed.

PLANNED ITERATION

XP's iteration-planning process also starts with exploration. The customer brings in the story cards to be addressed within the iteration and explains each one. The programmers ask questions, often handling the cards as they do so, passing them around, looking at them intently, getting to know them. After the stories are explained, the team brainstorms the technical tasks that have to be done to complete the story. Depending on team size, these may be written on cards or on a whiteboard. Most teams wind up putting them on cards, even if they use a whiteboard to aid group viewing and sign up.

During the commitment phase of iteration planning, programmers sign up for tasks and make individual estimates of how long each will take. A little balancing act often takes place, as people sign up for a bit too much or too little, and sometimes the customer even splits, removes, or adds some stories. After the planning is done, the programmers generally take the story cards with them, plus cards for the tasks they have signed up for, as reminders of what to do.

Through simple, hand-written cards you can collect stories to guide brainstorming of the tasks to be done, help the programmers with creation and acceptance of tasks, and balance the workload.

> *Simple, hand-written cards can collect stories to guide brainstorming of the tasks to be done, help the programmers with creation and acceptance of tasks, and balance the workload.*

GETTING ORGANIZED

Beyond XP, we find other uses for cards. When Ann Anderson, Chet Hendrickson, and I were working on a book on XP [Jeffries, Anderson, and Hendrickson, 2001], we realized after our first round of reviews that we had too many pages and chapters and needed to reorganize the book. We tried working with the chapter files we had in Adobe FrameMaker, but we couldn't get the big picture. We tried working with the book printed out, but even at four book pages per sheet, it was just too hard to handle. We tried working with the table of contents, but even that did not seem to help.

Finally, we made a card for each chapter. We wrote the chapter title and a lead sentence on each card, or sometimes just the chapter name. Then we sat around a table and slid the cards around, grouped them, wrote on them, tore up old ones, and wrote new ones. In a couple of hours, we had a new organization that made sense. Then we went over the cards and signed up for what needed to be done, each picking up the cards we were going to work on.

We had tried and failed with every electronic trick we knew. Then, in a couple of hours with cards, we had the job done and the work allocated.

WRITE ON

Not everyone writes guest columns or books, but most of us have to write reports of one kind or another. If you're like me, sometimes you sit down to write something without an outline. If you need only a page or two, it can work, but even then I sometimes wander off into the wordy weeds. Sometimes I use the outline mode of my word processor to lay out the shape of the article and to reorganize it. Even outline mode is not ideal, however. It isn't easy to switch to a new topic for just a second when you get an idea, grouping things together in different ways is awkward, and getting an overall picture of what you are doing can be challenging.

When I planned this chapter, I wrote my major topics on cards, then added a few separate cards to go with each of the major topic cards. As I worked on one area, I might get an idea for a card in another. I would just grab a card, write a note, and move on. I pushed the cards around on the table, grouped them by topic, stacked them, and sorted them. Cards are tangible and far more flexible than the best software tools. There is something magic about actually writing on the cards.

When I write using an outliner, I often write a lead sentence. The sentence turns into a paragraph, or sometimes two. Without noticing, I slip from working on the organization to working on a specific detail. This can't happen with cards—there isn't enough room. You can write only a single idea on a card, so it's easier to stay on track.

When I am writing, starting from a batch of cards with one idea on each one keeps me focused on the organization instead of the details and helps keep away those memories of my English teacher, Sister Mary Angelica, insisting on an outline to go with each paper.

> *When I am writing, starting from a batch of cards with one idea on each one keeps me focused on the organization instead of the details.*

EMERGENCY

One day on the much-discussed XP project, C3, something had broken badly and the support people were in a bit of trouble. I pulled everyone together and made a list on the whiteboard of what was wrong and what needed to be done. From the group, I drew priorities and estimates, helping them to eliminate the things that didn't have to be done right away. In no time, we had a plan to deal with the emergency.

The process worked, but it was a leadership moment, not a team moment. I had involved everyone, and all had given their answers and estimates, but team members didn't leave with much of a feeling that they had dealt with the situation on their own. It might have been better had I grabbed some cards and sat down at the table with them. I might have started with some cards, but I could have quickly handed them off to other team members, getting everyone more and more involved. Maybe I could have left them better prepared for the next emergency. When an emergency does arise, grab some cards, sit people down, start writing, then mess it up and let someone else grab the deck and take over. Teach someone to fish. . . .

> *When an emergency arises, grab some cards, sit people down, start writing, then mess it up and let someone else grab the deck and take over.*

MEETING PLANS

Setting up a meeting agenda can be difficult, especially when you have a whole group of people trying to define it. Often the meeting planning takes as long as the meeting itself. Different people want to talk about different parts of the agenda. Once items are up on a whiteboard, they can be hard to reorganize. It can be difficult to assess priorities and the time needed.

Try planning a meeting with cards. Write the topics down, give them priorities, and estimate the time needed to address each topic. Think about what will be a good indicator of completion for each topic—an acceptance test, if you like. Think about who has a vested interest in the topic, and use that information to decide who needs to attend and who does not. Once you have the cards and the times, fit them into the time available for the meeting. They probably will not all fit, but you will know this before you schedule the meeting. You can pick the most important ones, schedule smaller meetings before the main one, or deal with it in any number of ways.

JUST TRY

I confess, there is a part of me that doesn't like using cards. I like the continuity of a notebook and prefer using my computer for everything. I can type faster than I write, and typing is more legible. But cards work better. They help me organize my work when I am alone, and they help me communicate and share my work in a team. Cards work better for me than the techniques I naturally prefer, so I make a point of using them whenever I can.

So, try carrying a pack of blank index cards with you, and use them the next time you need to discuss priorities or to organize anything: a project, a meeting, an emergency, a book, or a document. Just write a couple of lines of key information at the top of each card. That way you can arrange them in overlapping piles, to get more of an overview. When you think of something else, add notes on the same card, but generally avoid writing information that will need to change. Handle the cards, move them around, pass them around the room. Pick them up, group them, feel them. And most importantly, feel free to tear up a card. When a card is wrong, or you see a way to improve it, rip it up and do a new one. It feels good!

> *Cards take a little time to get used to, especially if you are a high-tech kind of person. However, cards are a convenient, subtle, and powerful tool that can give you a tangible grasp of a situation as nothing else can.*

Cards take a little time to get used to, especially if you are, like me, a high-tech kind of person. However, cards are a convenient, subtle, and powerful tool that can give you a tangible grasp of a situation as nothing else can. You may be surprised at the card magic that is possible. I know I was.

Chapter 40

Throwaway Software: Delivering through Discards

Dwayne Phillips

We live in a throwaway society, with disposable tableware, disposable diapers, disposable cameras, and even disposable clothing. Aside from the ecological implications, these are all low-budget items. Even with the latest visual development tools and the most streamlined rapid development techniques, however, software is a big-ticket product. Many managers find it takes everything they and their teams can achieve just to meet minimal requirements and deliver something— anything—on schedule. The idea of designing, writing, and debugging code only to throw it away is likely to evoke horror or conjure images of wasteful bureaucratic make-work programs. In this chapter, Dwayne Phillips introduces a process technique that makes rapid iterative prototyping seem conservative by comparison. He argues that managers should look to disposable software as a management tool for delivering better systems and improving the skills of developers.

—Editor

In a world in which software reuse is a headline buzzword, talk of throwaway software may seem misguided. Throwing away software that took time and good money to create does not sound like the road to development success, yet throwaway software is a concept that has real value for software development managers. In *The Mythical Man-Month*, Frederick Brooks [1975] originally proposed the idea of planning to throw away the first version of software. Indeed, sometimes throwing away software helps you deliver better products.

The concept of throwaway software is simple. When you start out, you don't know enough to do it right, but while you are creating the software you learn what users really want, how to optimize algorithms, and how to make your code clean. By the time you finish, you've learned so much that it would be much better if you threw everything away and started over.

Throwaways can be used—and misused—in many ways. You can throw away pieces here and there, then replace them with improvements that add significant value at little cost. Many developers have practiced this approach without thinking about it as a deliberate development strategy. Prototypes are another variation on throwaway software. The most effective prototypes are constructed to prove a concept or demonstrate a design, then discarded. Of course, throwaways can be misused, as when developers substitute disposable software for thinking, designing, peer reviews, and assorted other good practices. The "code first, then think" paradigm has ruined schedules and budgets on countless projects.

The hidden cost of using throwaways is often a certain amount of pride. The first key to properly using throwaways is humility—admitting that we do not know everything and that the code we create is not necessarily worth keeping. Planning is the second key. Planning lets you consider your shortcomings in advance and allow time for learning. You can throw away the first attempt as long as you are smart about it.

> *The first key to using throwaway software is humility—admitting that we do not know everything and that the code we create is not necessarily worth keeping.*

THROWAWAY OPPORTUNITIES

Software development abounds with opportunities for employing throwaways. If someone on your team is having difficulty on a particular task, they probably need some extra time to learn. Grant them a throwaway. Tell them to do their best in two-thirds the time originally allowed. When time is up, let them throw away their work and start over. Allow them the full time for the second pass-through.

Suppose on Monday you assign to a programmer a complex set of subroutines that is due in five days. On Monday afternoon, you check in and find him scratching his head. Cut the time to three days and meet with this programmer and several peers on Thursday. Let him explain how his software works, and have his peers probe what he has done. Contribute ideas on how to improve the software. Then offer him the option of throwing away his software. "If you could do it over again, would you?" If the answer is "Yes," tell him to start over and finish in five days.

This tactic may not always be officially permitted. Some organizations set such high standards that they expect people to know everything. They are in denial about learning on the job. You may have to work around these conditions. Instead of acknowledging that your team is throwing away products, you might just say that the task is taking longer than expected to produce the required quality—which is the truth, of course.

This returns us to the first requirement in using throwaways: humility. Developers must be able to admit they lack knowledge and make mistakes. Organizations need to accept that incomplete knowledge and imperfect work are realities.

I was fortunate that my first job as a team leader both required and rewarded ample humility. Fresh out of graduate school, I knew a great deal about computer vision and software engineering, neither of which were the focus of our project. The team comprised the hottest coding cowboys in the organization. I had to write code as well as manage, and there were many occasions when I had to admit ignorance and ask people how to code certain things in C.

As the project progressed, I became much better at asking for help. Remarkably, the more I asked for help, the more the other team members asked me for help. Asking for help can be difficult, particularly for some of the best developers. Managers can help by setting a good example and by talking about some of their own past failures. Humility may be difficult, but it becomes easier with practice and can be promoted by a safe work environment.

As project managers and team leaders, we need to look for opportunities where throwaways can help. We know our team members and ourselves have weaknesses that can be helped by extra time to learn. Team members may not always recognize some of their own shortcomings. Boundless optimism may be especially characteristic of young professionals. It will be difficult for them to ask for help or to ask for a throwaway. We must lead by watching, finding problems, helping people uncover their weaknesses, and letting them grow.

MANAGED THROWAWAYS

The throwaway opportunities described earlier are the kinds that just happen. Throwaways are even more effective when used on purpose. One tactic is to use throwaways on the hardest part of your project, the area with the most unknowns. It is here where you need to learn the most.

Think about your people and each of the work products they will create during the project. Do they have the necessary knowledge? To what degree? Those areas where knowledge is most limited are of particular interest. You should also consider the impact of each area on the overall project. Those that combine large effects with significant unknowns are good candidates for throwaways.

> *Areas where knowledge is limited or that combine large effects with significant unknowns are good candidates for throwaway software.*

For example, a current project I am helping on is 95% digital signal processing (DSP) software on an embedded system and 5% graphical user interface on a laptop controller. The customer is very picky about user interfaces. The user interface will make or break the product, and there is a high risk of failure.

Here we need at least one throwaway. We have scheduled several sessions with our customer to work through ideas for the user interface. These are taking place early in the project while the DSP people are analyzing requirements. We hope that the second or third user interface will bring customer acceptance for the entire product.

Project management specialists refer to giving extra time and attention to critical and failure-prone parts of a project as *risk management* and *risk mitigation*. Throwaways are a risk management technique.

To be effective risk management, throwaways need planning. Planning is often the difference between success and failure on a project. More important for team members, planning spells the difference between their own personal and professional success or failure.

Without planning, you may assign tasks to people who do not have the required knowledge. They will take twice as much time as expected and may still produce poor software. That will put them behind and lead to unpaid overtime during the rest of the project. People who are always behind and making poor products are failures.

> *To be effective risk management, throwaways need planning. Without planning, you may assign tasks to people who do not have the required knowledge.*

Your plan can include the extra time for learning. The first version of some piece may be pretty bad, but that's okay—you've planned for it. Developers can throw it away and create a better version the second time. People who do that are successes, and a team of successful people cannot help but have a successful project.

The manager's task, then, is to analyze a project to find the hardest parts. Once found, the plan must incorporate extra time on those parts. By giving attention where it is needed, we help our people succeed.

CONTINUING THROWAWAYS

Once you become comfortable with throwaways, you will find additional ways to use them. Software engineering "in the small" and "in the large" presents two basic opportunities.

Throwaways in the small work with critical parts in the source code. Critical parts are those on which the quality of the product substantially depends. As managers, we must find these and optimize them.

We rarely know how to optimize something at the start of a project. Creating and working with the code teaches us what we need to know to do so. For critical parts that need to be optimized, throwaways do the trick.

Using throwaways requires that you follow the modular software concept by separating your software into loosely coupled and highly cohesive modules. Each part does one thing, and all other parts don't care how it does it. This approach can, of course, apply to any form of software, from object-oriented architectures in C++ or Java to structured programs in C, COBOL, Java, and even good old 4GLs.

In the throwaway version, a critical part should be written in a no-frills manner. First, ensure the critical part interfaces with all other parts correctly, and then let the project move forward. Eventually, you will return to the no-frills part, throw it away, and start again from scratch using what you learned along the way to build an optimized part. It is important not to try to improve the no-frills part by patching it, which will only make a mess. Once it is finished, you can drop the optimized part into the software. Since the interfaces are already correct, the optimized part should work with the rest of the software.

> *The throwaway version of a critical part is first written in a no-frills manner. Eventually, you return to it, throw it away, and start again from scratch to build an optimized part using what you learned along the way.*

One application of this technique was in a project that ported a couple dozen components to a vastly different hardware platform. Management expected a big reduction in processing time, but the project team didn't know how to bring about that improvement. So, the first step was to port the components with as few changes as possible. Only after that was done did we look for speed.

One component used repeatedly was found to be taking about 70% of the processing time. We threw it away and wrote it afresh, with all our efforts focused on speed. This reduced the execution time of the major application from 4 hours to 30 minutes. This use of throwaways in the small is an application of an old rule: Make it right before you make it faster [Kernighan and Plauger, 1978].

Throwaways in the large apply to the work products or deliverables of major phases in a project. In my experience, designs are the best candidates for throwaways. A design is a solution to a problem, and there are always countless ways to solve a given problem.

At the start of a project, you may have an idea of how to solve the problem, but you don't know the best way to solve it. Therefore, you may need to plan for a disposable design.

> *You may have an idea of how to solve a problem but don't know the best way to solve it; you may need to plan for a disposable design.*

The disposable design process is simple. Start with a set of project goals. Create a design that meets the requirements. Examine this design in light of the goals. Where does it fall short? What could you do differently to reach the goals more effectively? Then throw away the design and do it again.

Once more, this process requires planning. You must record your goals before you start the project. Then you must allow time to design more than once. This lets you throw away a design, but, of course, this is far less costly than throwing away a product.

A few years back, I worked on a design that met all the requirements but missed one goal: cost. The first design would have worked but required buying an extra memory card. The trouble was that the software was for a supercomputer, and a memory card cost $250,000. We threw away the design and started over. The second design was much easier to devise, as we had learned so much on the first one. We concentrated on memory issues and found ways to avoid buying more hardware.

Modern CASE tools make the throwaway design approach more appealing than ever. The tools support rapid iteration, making three or four designs possible in the same time it used to take to do two.

TOWARD DISPOSABILITY

If you're a project manager, you need to be able to see where throwaways will help before a project begins. You should study preliminary project plans or concepts to see the critical parts to be optimized and to set goals to critique and improve designs.

Using throwaways lets us learn while creating software. The result is better software, although at some cost to our egos. So, first we need humility, since learning only takes place when we admit we do not know everything. Second, we need to put away some of our cowboy habits and plan our projects more thoroughly. We must look at the entire project to identify what will be difficult and possibly deadly and then provide the necessary time.

Whether you call it prototyping or software risk management, it is still the same simple approach: Learn while doing, throw away poor software, then do it right the second time.

Chapter 41

Unified Hegemony: Beyond Universal Solutions

Larry Constantine

It seems altogether fitting to finish out this section of the book by considering the genuine giants of the models and methods world. Beside these ambitious behemoths, most other pretenders to the process throne pale by comparison. An earlier generation of methodologists may have set out to conquer all worlds, but my peers and I eventually learned our lessons, carving out more manageable pieces of the methodological whole. I have long argued that one size does not fit all, and, on a panel in Germany in 1993, Michael Jackson, one of the leading early proponents of universal methods, confessed that he had come to realize that different scales and domains of application demanded different approaches.

Of course, there is always another generation of computer professionals and software visionaries to seek success in world domination. If in operating systems, why not in operational methods? If in central processors, why not in development processes?

—Editor

It is virtually impossible to be an informed manager of software development today without being aware of the *U* word. It is on the covers of books, in articles in our trade magazines, and prominently featured in the titles of conferences and conference presentations. Where once the marketplace of ideas was enamored with objects, now it seems ready to devour anything claiming to be unified. The acronymic derivatives of the *U* word do a dizzying dance before our eyes—UML, UP, RUP, USDP—and we wonder whether we should celebrate our emancipation, bemoan our homogenization, or snicker cynically at the exaggeration.

Perhaps this trend is merely the technological echo of the zeitgeist abroad in the larger world. A divided Germany has reunified. The Europeans have their Union. Even in the often divisive world of competitive sports, "A World in Union," the inspirational theme song debuted at the World Cup in South Africa in 1996, now opens Rugby Union matches around the globe. And today, theoretical physicists stand poised (as they have for decades) on the threshold of a grand unification, the theory of everything that eluded even Einstein.

In the smaller universe of software development (there are only about six million of us developers worldwide), the leading theme songs are UML (Unified Modeling Language) and UP (Unified Process). These purport to give developers and their managers a common notation for representing their ideas and a universal process for translating ideas into software. A few stalwarts notwithstanding, hardly a skeptical voice is raised and scarcely a dissonant note is heard amidst the unison chorus heralding the arrival of this new age of software development unity. No one wants to be the grinch who stole unification, but a truly rational management perspective demands consideration of some of the problems as well as the benefits of unified this or unified that.

> *Hardly a skeptical voice is raised and scarcely a dissonant note is heard, but a truly rational management perspective demands consideration of some of the problems as well as the benefits of unified this or unified that.*

As I write this, the issues in unification are fresh in my mind because in 2000, my company sponsored an international confab on the convergence between usage-centered design and UML/UP. Experts from three continents converged on tiny Rowley, Massachusetts, and spent five days wrestling with the problems and solutions and providing the inspiration for this chapter.

NOTEWORTHY

The fact is that UML and the tools that support it have much to offer software development managers. A single common notation means that results from diverse development teams and projects are more readily shared and compared. Skills also become more portable and transferable when new hires do not have to learn a proprietary scheme of representation.

The need for a common means of modeling software has been recognized by many, and I have long been an outspoken advocate for uniform conventions and consistency, particularly in the matter of notation. Electronics engineers around the world can read each other's diagrams, but the programming priesthood long shunned uniformity, with each sect portraying its problems and picturing its solutions in its own hieroglyphics.

Well before unification was a cloud in Grady Booch's eye, methodologists Meilir Page-Jones, Steven Weiss, and I teamed up to tackle the problem of creating a common notation for modeling object-oriented systems, one that combined (unified) notation for object-oriented and procedural programs. Far less ambitious than UML, our notation also bore a more modest moniker. Though now little more than a historic curiosity, the Uniform Object Notation (UON) [Page-Jones et al., 1990], along with other pioneering notations, contributed to the dialogue and left an enduring legacy that can be seen today in UML.

SOUR NOTES

In the eyes of many, one of the great strengths of UML is that it is comprehensive, which, alas, it is not. Despite its size and complexity, much is left out of UML. Not surprising, considering its origins among the gurus of the object-oriented paradigm, UML provides little or no support for describing software that is not built solely from objects. Ironically, although use cases are at the very heart of modern software development practice and figured prominently in the evolution of UML, the current version provides no explicit and dedicated scheme for structuring the narratives that define use cases. Its most glaring fault, however, is that it completely omits any vocabulary for discussing and designing the very *raison d'être* of modern software: the user interface. When it comes to designing this critical aspect of software-based systems, no specific diagrams or notation are provided: not interface content models, not context navigation maps, not abstract prototypes.

> *Despite its size and complexity, much is left out of UML. Notably, it omits any vocabulary for discussing and designing the very* raison d'être *of modern software: the user interface.*

Weak in its support of use cases and lacking in support for user interface design, UML is proving in practice to be a particularly poor match for usage-centered and task-driven design approaches that employ more sophisticated notions of use cases and tie them directly to the design of user interfaces. Although many groups have attempted usage-centered design with UML and its supporting development tools, most have either given up on the notation and tools or devised admittedly awkward work-arounds and substitutions. (For example, one company casts structured use cases as Activity Diagrams and constructs abstract prototypes of user interfaces with notes added to Class Diagrams.)

Despite its numerous omissions or oversights, UML is still complicated. One of the most popular books on the subject is, not surprisingly, the slim primer by Martin Fowler [1997], *UML Distilled,* a kind of *Reader's Digest* introduction to the language. UML has been roundly criticized by Brian Henderson-Sellers and others of the OPEN movement for having notation that is often arbitrary and far from intuitive [Henderson-Sellers and Unhelkar, 2000].

In the near term, the shortcomings can be overcome through various work-arounds as long as efficiency and ease of use are not paramount. Not being evangelical adherents or doctrinal purists, many developers blithely mix tools and notations in practice. Document templates can be created for structuring use cases, which are then attached as notes to UML diagrams. Generic database systems and drawing tools can be cobbled together with scripts into ad hoc tool suites.

In the long run, of course, change will occur, but the message to the UML people and the vendors of UML-oriented tools must be clear: Support real-world practice in usage-centered and task-driven design or lose business. Managers should not have to choose between best practices in design and development on the one hand and a standardized notation supported by tools on the other.

METHODICAL PROCESS

The Unified Process started life as a method but was renamed midstream, perhaps because its corporate mentors recognized that putting *Rational* in front of *Unified Method* would have yielded an amusing but commercially unwise acronym, or perhaps because methods and methodologies of the past have left a bad taste in the mouths of many managers, who are the real customers for the Process.

Although the arguments for a common notation are straightforward, the case for a uniform process seems harder to make. Notation and modeling are far more rigorous and better understood than process. When it comes to process, every development group is its own distinct story. A 5-person Web shop and a 300-programmer tools vendor are likely to differ in far more than just size. A four-month, time-boxed project producing a new release of a mature payroll application has little in common with a multiyear effort producing a novel programming system for automation tools. The cultural dynamics in a department full of ex-engineers all writing embedded C++ code are poles apart from those in a mixed team of graphic artists, content creators, information architects, database analysts, HTML coders, and Java wonks.

> *Although the arguments for a common notation are straightforward, the case for a uniform process seems harder to make. When it comes to process, every development group is its own distinct story.*

In short, it seems almost axiomatic that no single model for the software development process can work across the board. The brilliance of ISO 9001 is that it does not specify any particular process but only requires a process that is documented and practiced as documented. In all fairness, the Unified Process was intended as a template, a comprehensive guidebook that could be cut down, edited, and tailored to suit varying projects, constraints, and cultures. Nevertheless, to prepare a digest for your readers, you have to read the book; to tailor a slimmed-down subset of the Unified Process, you have to understand pretty much the whole darned thing. The growing interest in "lightweight" methods, such as Extreme Programming, reflects widespread frustrations with the heavyweights of the industry. The bureaucratic thoroughness that might be appropriate for a multiyear project by a defense contractor is probably nuclear overkill for a nimble-footed dot-com start-up.

If these are the problems, why, then, should anyone try to unify processes, and why would anyone be interested in the result? Comfort. A standard and widely recognized process—or the claim to have one—puts both managers and customers at ease. Whatever concerns your customers have, the reassuring answer becomes just, "Oh, we use the Unified Process." After all, it covers everything. For managers, great comfort and confidence come with an approach that not only is supported by software and courseware but also tells everyone on a project just what they should be doing and when and to whom they hand off what. Whether the process is right, appropriate, or efficient is secondary to its ritualized reassurance and formulaic nature. A plug-and-play process that comes on a CD-ROM is almost irresistible. Just buy the CD, send your people to some courses, and you, too, can join the UPpies!

> *A standard and widely recognized process—or the claim to have one—puts both managers and customers at ease. Great comfort and confidence come with an approach that not only is supported by software and courseware but also tells everyone on a project just what they should be doing and when.*

Whether the process is truly unified or not, the storyline is most definitely not. The exact content and scope of the Unified Process remains a somewhat elusive matter. There are books on the Rational Unified Process [Kruchten, 1999] and on the Unified Process [Jacobson et al., 1999], and most readers find little in common between these exegeses. Then, too, there is the official Rational Unified Process, which is a commercial product residing on a CD-ROM, in training courses, and in the minds of marketers. Like all commercial products, its content is whatever those good folk want it to be.

Indeed, Rational has achieved such a commanding lead in both the tools and process areas that RUP has become almost synonymous with UP. One-stop shopping for tools, training, consulting, and performance support has strong management appeal. End-to-end integration of tools and performance-support infrastructure, to the extent that it works as advertised, offers powerful advantages to developers and their managers. Rational has, in a sense, become the Microsoft of process unification: a force to be reckoned with irrespective of the merits and opinions. For decision makers, going with the clear market leader is often the safest and simplest route. If things go well, obviously you had the wisdom to choose the best. If things go badly, you escape blame because you went with the winner.

> *Going with the clear market leader in processes is often the safest and simplest route. If things go well, you had the wisdom to choose the best; if not, you escape blame because you went with the winner.*

The management decisions may seem straightforward, but adding to the UP learning curve for developers—and to the need for training—is a maddening insistence on inventing new names for old ideas and redefining established terms that already have widely accepted meanings. As one might expect of anything pretending to unify complex development processes, UP, like UML, borrows freely from almost anywhere and everywhere, often without credit. So-called *logical prototypes*, for instance, are easily recognized as interface content models in disguise, on which they were based, though scarcely an acknowledgment is in sight. You may think you understand what a storyboard or a scenario is, but such terms get usurped for idiosyncratic usage in the UP.

MODERN LANGUAGE

One manifestation of the hubris of contemporary methodologists is their insistence on calling their congeries *languages*. Today's developers are offered not a unified modeling notation but a Unified Modeling Language, not a pattern collection but a pattern language. (That the pattern people have merely emulated Alexander's original sin of hubris does not justify it.)

Natural and unnatural languages might, indeed, have some lessons to teach us in our search for unification. In a twist of multilingual irony, English, not French, has become the *lingua franca* of commerce and travel. As *L'Académie Française* fights a rear-guard action to keep the mongrel hordes of foreign words at bay, English has no academy, no border patrol, and happily embraces all comers, giving it the richest vocabulary of any natural language.

Only the French would claim French to be a logical language, but logical languages have been devised. Esperanto, perhaps the best known of the many artificial and rational languages, has been around since 1887, but Zamenhof's dream of a world united by a common language seems more distant than ever, and only a tiny minority (less than two million worldwide) are fluent speakers of Esperanto.

UML is no Esperanto. It is best described as a collection of disparate models and the notations for their expression supporting object-oriented analysis and design. If it is a language, it is hardly a universal one, because it has no vocabulary for user interface design and is limited to object-speak.

REALITY CHECK

So, is the revolution over? Has a new and united world order in notation and method arrived? Should working managers "UP-grade" their processes and teach their developers to mumble UML? Perhaps. The CDs and courses are surely selling well, but, as the Germans quickly learned after reunification, the reality of the doing is somewhat different from the selling.

Being a columnist, consultant, and conference presenter affords me abundant opportunities to get the inside stories of companies that have bought the big *U*. If my sources are at all typical, scant little has changed since the era of early CASE tools. Many companies seem to be using UML tools not to design but to document. Often the claim to be using the Unified Process translates, on careful listening, into not much more than owning the CD-ROM and using the vocabulary in casual conversation. Even among the serious and dedicated users, an increasing number express frustration with the overhead involved in using the tools and the methods and the difficulty within both when trying to follow best practices for product usability. In practice, then, the good intentions and worthy goals of unification have to be weighed against the failures of UML and UP to offer well-developed models or methods for task-driven user interface design and efficient and in-depth support for the full range of modern development processes and practices.

> *Many companies seem to be using UML tools not to design but to document. Even among serious and dedicated users, an increasing number express frustration with the overhead involved and with the difficulties when trying to follow best practices for product usability.*

The salvation of the unified agenda is that UML has a built-in mechanism for introducing variations on its uniform themes. For many but not all problems, the solution may be to define new elements and concepts as so-called stereotypes of existing notions and notations within UML. The UP, to its credit, invites customization within certain limits. At some point, however, customization within the framework of UML and UP becomes a procrustean process. Buying a smaller bed or getting a more comfortable frame may sometimes be a better option.

PART VI

Leadership and Teamwork

S tepping down from the lofty levels of process and philosophical pursuits, the closing section returns to the issues of people that opened this collection of essays. Nearly all software of any significance is the work of more than one person. Modern software and Web development is completely dependent on teamwork, on teams of developers, however loosely or well coordinated. The quality of teamwork depends on many factors, first among them the quality of team leadership, which receives special attention here.

Chapter 42

Scaling Up: Teamwork in the Large

Larry Constantine

When I was young, I was often told to think big. Nowadays we are told to think small. As other chapters in this book attest, we are working in an era of small, select, high-performance project teams and rapid iterative development on compressed time scales. Managers are counseled to assemble elite teams of a few highly skilled developers and to scale applications down to be completed within brief cycles or tightly constrained time boxes of 90 to 120 days. Projects bigger than six-by-six, that is, six developers working for six months, are doomed, according to current thinking among the gurus of smallness. Best to avoid such projects altogether.

Not everyone, however, has quite as much freedom to pick and choose as do those industry leaders who counsel small teams and small increments. So, how do you practice teamwork in the large?

—Editor

Small may be beautiful, but not every application fits into one tight package, and not every project can be neatly dissected into digestible six-month chunks. Some enterprise information systems are big monsters no matter how you look at them. Then again, you may have been promoted to inherit a team of two hundred developers and a mandate from top management to use them well. Maybe you just finally got that big break on a really big contract.

Even if you are only part of a three-person team cranking out intranet apps, you might learn something from thinking big. Just as the insanely short delivery cycles of Web-time development (see Chapter 19) can teach us about making effective use of time even when we have more relaxed schedules, the challenges of large-scale projects offer lessons that can be of value even when applied "in the small." In short, there may be many reasons to look at the big picture of large-scale development.

> *There may be many reasons to look at the big picture of large-scale development; the challenges of large-scale projects offer lessons that can be of value even when applied "in the small."*

You will note that I have nicely sidestepped the issue of what constitutes large-scale software projects. How many programmers make for a big project? It's all relative, of course. To a manager experienced in leading a technology point team of three or four programmers, coordinating a department of nine might seem overwhelming. In contrast, to someone schooled in the massive scale of such historic and fabled efforts as IBM's OS/2, the 200-developer team that created the first Windows NT might look downright lean and mean.

Some managers have suggested that a large project is any project that is sufficiently bigger than anything you have done before so that you have no idea how you are going to manage it, and this view goes to the heart of the matter. The issue for the software manager is not the absolute size of the team or the source-code file but the effect of scale on the problems of management.

In this chapter I want to explore some of the ways in which key issues of technical teamwork and technical leadership change with scale and what this might mean for software projects of almost any size. Part of the question of scale is a matter of numbers, such as the number of people participating in a project, but part of the question is really about complexity. Whether your development team is growing or not, odds are that your applications have been growing more complex. Many issues stand out in sharper relief when the scale goes from modest to enormous, hence there can be value in looking at a humongous project.

MILLENNIAL MANAGEMENT

If you want to learn about technical teamwork on a truly grand scale, then I urge you to get a copy of the five-part public television series "21st Century Jet." This joint British-American PBS production is must viewing for anyone seriously interested in the art and craft of technical management. The video is the story of the making of Boeing's 777, hailed as a triumph of both engineering and engineering management. It is not only a dramatic and engaging tale; there also are many lessons for software development managers. PBS (*http://shop.pbs.org*) sells the five videos packaged with a book [Sabbagh, 1996] in their "Business & Finance" section. It could be the best $110 you or your company ever spent.

No one would doubt that the "triple-seven" team led by Boeing's Phil Condit and Alan Mulally was big. Consider a team of 10,000 people scattered around the globe. Mulally and his management team made sure that these people were more than just a team in name. Boeing managers were convinced that to achieve a real breakthrough on a tight schedule and budget, they would need teamwork of the highest order, and that would require radical restructuring of the way their people worked together. Their approach had many aspects, but the pieces that seem particularly relevant to complex software projects are these:

1. Face-to-face team building

2. Consensus-based collaboration

3. Interface management through models

4. Design reuse

Team Building

The highest performance is achieved when a mere group is transformed into a real team, with a strong rapport and shared sense of purpose that can come only from working together closely. Tom DeMarco and Tim Lister call such teams "gel-teams" because they have gelled into a cohesive working unit [DeMarco and Lister, 1999]. Whatever you call them, teams that draw on a shared history and a common culture of work are simply more efficient and effective. If the team's reservoir of shared values and experience is not already full, it must be filled through some deliberate process, and that process is team building. Whether it takes place at an organized retreat or is shoehorned into the brief remarks and introductions at a kick-off meeting, team building is compressed experience that helps build a shared history and culture.

Team building becomes both more crucial and more challenging as the size of the team increases. A sense of teamwork that seems to flow naturally from working closely together with a handful of colleagues may have to be deliberately cultivated when the handful grows to fill an auditorium or beyond. Yet, how do you cultivate a sense of "teamness" when there are thousands of people on your team?

I have been teaching team building and high-performance teamwork techniques for many years, and for all those years I have also been saying that to build a team there is no substitute for face-to-face contact. No matter how large your team or how widely it is dispersed, it is imperative that everyone be gathered together in one room at least once during the life of the project. Whenever I say this it always triggers off a chorus of yes-buts: "Yes, but there is no time for team building on such a tight schedule." "Yes, but it's impossible with 150 programmers and designers working in three different states." "Yes, but the travel expenses would break the budget." The litany of excuses is endless.

> *To build a team, there is no substitute for face-to-face contact. No matter how large your team or how widely it is dispersed, it is imperative that everyone be gathered together in one room at least once.*

The Boeing people took the maxim of team building literally and allowed themselves no excuses. Boeing organized the 777 personnel into individual design-build teams, each of which was jointly responsible for the architecture, engineering, and construction of an entire subsystem. However, they also gathered in all the members of the entire triple-seven team from around the world, assembling nearly 10,000 people in one place. They did this more than once during the project. There is only one space in the entire Boeing empire large enough to hold that many people, an assembly hangar said to be the largest building in the world. Some of the scenes from these meetings are awe-inspiring. This was no crowd of soccer fans cheering on their team, this was the team!

Perhaps it is part of our deeply rooted mammalian heritage, but there is no substitute for meeting face-to-face. Not without reason, important deals are ultimately sealed with a handshake, even though hordes of lawyers may have created reams of signed documents.

The truth is that, even for so-called virtual teams of developers sharing work over the Internet and meeting by video conferencing or for geographically dispersed multinational teams spread across 11 time zones, face-to-face contact as part of a team-building process is invaluable. Or perhaps I should say especially for such teams it is invaluable.

Consensus

There is a telling moment in the original broadcasts just after the 777 management team finishes wrestling with a tough trade-off. They must decide between using an exotic lightweight alloy that has been found to develop harmless but visible cracks or taking a significant hit in take-off weight using conventional alloys. Mulally emerges from the meeting and remarks that this consensus decision making really works. In fact, the building of consensus and the full involvement of people at all levels in the technical decision making was a cornerstone of the 777 project management approach. Each design-build team had to meet its own schedule and objectives, putting a premium on incorporating construction input into engineering and on carrying out tasks collaboratively and concurrently.

Although it may be more common to see large teams marked by some form of top-down dictation of design and business decisions, consensus-based decisions have real advantages as the project scale increases. Not only does consensus make fuller use of skills and expertise, thus leading to better decisions, but it functions as a form of continuing team building that assures higher levels of commitment and participation from all the team members. As an individual team member, I see the work as mine because I agree with the tack taken and can see how my contributions have been incorporated.

> *Consensus-based decisions have real advantages as scale increases. Consensus makes fuller use of skills and expertise and functions as continuing team building that assures higher levels of commitment and participation.*

Interfaces and Interaction

One of the technological innovations of the 777 project was a comprehensive integrated computer-aided design (CAD) system that modeled virtually every feature and aspect of the aircraft as it evolved. It is easy to see this computer system as merely part of the engineering-support infrastructure, but it also served important management functions.

As the number of people on a team or the number of pieces in a product increases, the number of interfaces and potential interactions rises even faster. Among 10 people, there are 45 possible interfaces; among 10,000 there are nearly 50 million. In a tight-knit little group, project communication and coordination can be accomplished just by raising your voice enough to be heard in the next cubicle. It is another story altogether when thousands of engineers and designers must keep each other posted on work progress and the consequences of particular decisions. What seems obvious and natural on the small scale must become deliberate and structured in the large.

In addition to direct lines of communication and interaction among different 777 subteams, the computer models became a common reference point for managing the interfaces among the myriad activities in the design and configuration of the thousands of mechanical, electrical, hydraulic, and other subsystems.

Every decision, every solution, every modification was reflected in the common models, which made the impact on other parts of the project and the product apparent. Widely separated groups were connected through their interactions with the computerized models.

> *Models serve as a common reference point for managing the interfaces among myriad activities. Widely separated groups can be connected through their interactions with computer-based models.*

Another telling moment in the process arose when a fuel-dumping tube could not be installed within a wing because a fastener was already in that spot. The crisis actually highlighted the importance of the CAD models as a tool for managing the interfaces, since the problem occurred because the fastener was not in the computer models, which did not represent details down to the level of individual fasteners. Expensive redesign might have been avoided through more thorough modeling at an earlier stage.

This process of coordination through interaction with development artifacts can also be seen in some large software development efforts. More than 10,000 programmers worldwide have been involved in the creation and maintenance of the one-and-a-half million lines of code in the current version of Linux. It is the source code itself that constitutes the meeting ground for these contributors. Of course, an even better comparison with the 777 approach would be a large software project coordinated through a single set of integrated design models rather than connected by the final code.

Design Reuse

The 777 engineers also avoided making more work for themselves and for the actual builders of the aircraft through reuse. For example, although each of the eight doors on the aircraft was somewhat different, they were designed to use a maximum of common subassemblies and components. Reuse of designs results in not only fewer unique subassemblies or components that must be designed and built but also fewer interactions to be accounted for and tested.

Shared design models can promote reuse by making design problems and current solutions visible across a project. I suspect this is even more true in software than in hardware because of the greater homogeneity of the fundamental components of software.

FLYING SOFTWARE

It may be tempting to dismiss the 777 experience as irrelevant to software engineering and management because the 777 is an aircraft, not a program, but the real picture is more subtle than that. The 777 is a so-called fly-by-wire system, meaning that the actual control is accomplished by computers that mediate between the cockpit and the plane itself. These complex navigational, control, and display systems had to be programmed, so the 777 story is partly a software engineering story. In fact, a colleague recently told me that insiders describe the 777 as two-and-a-half million lines of Ada flying in close formation—not so much an airplane as a complex software system packaged and shipped in an airframe!

Boeing managed the development of those two-and-a-half million lines of Ada with the same engineering discipline and management finesse as the rest of the project, but there is an ironic footnote to the story. At the insistence of the major customer, the entertainment subsystem was subcontracted to an outside group of software developers. Schedule slippage and the unreliability of that software almost delayed the delivery of the entire plane.

My own flying experiences attest to the difference between the kind of disciplined, team-based software engineering that hardware companies like Boeing practice and the kind of semiorganized hacking that passes for programming in many other parts of the industry. On five of the last eight trans-Atlantic flights I've made, the software-controlled in-seat entertainment system has failed catastrophically at some point. Fortunately, the fly-by-wire software functioned without a hitch, and the plane always landed just fine.

Chapter 43

Sustaining Teamwork: Promoting Life-Cycle Teams

Peter H. Jones

Teamwork, whether on a large scale or a small one, is the accepted formula for software management success. Nearly everybody believes in teamwork, and most of us would probably like to believe we are good team players. On the other hand, the lip service paid to team-work, to collaboration, and to building and sustaining buy-in is often quick to be abandoned once a project gathers steam and the pressure builds up. Meetings that were mandatory become desultory, consultations that were frequent become rare, and communication dwindles to chance exchanges in the halls. In this chapter, Peter Jones offers some tips on how to get better results by sustaining teamwork over the full duration of a project. Go, team!

—Editor

Teams and teamwork of all kinds have long enjoyed a great deal of good press in software development. Cross-functional teams in particular are often viewed by management experts as one of the few long-lasting management trends. In practice, however, we often find projects lag behind in team technology, result-ing in uncoordinated development, misinterpreted requirements, and myriad everyday problems. In *Team Talk,* Anne Donnellon [1996], writes, "There is no solid evidence that teams at the professional and managerial level have delivered on their promise . . . companies, teams, and individuals are finding the transi-tion to teams very slow and very painful." Despite this gloomy pronouncement, teamwork makes sense for software development. Developing software remains a complex undertaking, and large projects require the knowledge and skills of many people. With numerous project activities, deliverables, and work products, team coordination becomes a full-time job for project managers.

GOOD SOFTWARE TEAMS

In Donnellon's view, effective teamwork "requires the continuous integration of expertise," meaning that team members of varied skills must work together continuously. With the complexity and scope of large software projects, you might expect to find members of state-of-the-art teams continuously sharing their learning and expertise. However, in many software projects, teams aren't managed in a way that supports such continuous collaboration or integration of expertise. Instead, a typical software project often maintains good intentions of teamwork through the front end, but no further. In the typical project, goodwill suffuses team members in abundance during kick-off, and roles are claimed for the development effort. The project manager gathers the team members, offers a pep talk, and expects teamwork to just happen. Soon afterward, team meetings become smaller and smaller, as more members move into individual assignments and skip perfunctory project meetings. Eventually, team members only meet as a group for crisis management or other "special occasions." The potential for high performance dissipates quickly after the initial organizing session. Somehow, the projects are accomplished, but the full potential of software teamwork is never achieved.

> *Often, after an initial organizing session, the potential for high performance dissipates quickly. Projects are finished, but the full potential of software teamwork is never achieved.*

At the 1998 Team Spirit Conference, several large companies discussed their difficulties with managing technical teams. For various reasons, software developers often don't want to work in true teams. A common rationale was that teams defeat the "hero programmer" image that has successfully enhanced many developers' careers. High-performance teams require senior engineers to mentor and depend on other team members. Many of these would-be leaders do not see nurturing the team as part of their job. Taking credit for a key algorithm, being an acknowledged expert, and other technological wins are intellectual perks in this profession. Development managers must deal with pervasive initial doubt and cynicism about team processes. Establishing a conducive environment for teamwork helps developers overcome these doubts and fears. You must establish the team environment first in your projects by fostering team continuity throughout the project life cycle.

TEAMING THROUGH THE LIFE CYCLE

Significant expectations and traditions work against high-performing teams in software projects. Although teams have evolved as a modern organizational tool in product and systems shops, they are often managed by traditional project management and human-resources approaches. Managed as groups of individuals, members are optimized within their roles, not as a collective team. Moreover, many developers are comfortable working autonomously and enjoy working alone, shunning as counterproductive the coordination required in teams. After the front-end work is complete and the need for consensus is reduced, developers retreat into the engineering world, safe from interruptions by other team members or from product managers, marketing people, users, and customers. The facts of normal development life seem to work against team integration. However, projects stand to gain substantively by keeping teams intact, and not just for progress or checkpoint meetings. Why should we allow the synergy gained from months of teamwork to disappear? How can we maintain team continuity?

MAINTAINING TEAM DEVELOPMENT

One structured approach to team development that has been adopted by many information technology organizations is the joint application design (JAD) session. JAD brings together an entire team, usually along with end users and customers, to work through requirements and initial design. The JAD approach also may include other whole-team sessions, such as project planning, decision making, and constructing group deliverables to carry facilitated teamwork beyond initial JAD sessions into the entire development life cycle. The team design cycle thus extends from project scoping and definition to packaging and validating final deliverables.

However, experience from many organizations indicates that it takes time and repeated success for such full-cycle teamwork processes to take hold. The first steps in instituting team development across the life cycle are the hardest, requiring design activities involving the whole team.

> *It takes time and repeated success for full-cycle teamwork processes to take hold, and the first steps in instituting team development across the life cycle are often the hardest.*

DESIGN AND BEYOND

Whenever a group first meets, you have an opportunity to engage all members in initial participation and to set expectations for sustained interaction. In kick-off meetings or initial sessions, use agendas that focus on team goals as well as project goals. Effective leaders don't focus just on the task; they also emphasize good team processes. Declare your intention of full participation and knowledge sharing. Then back up these expressed values by encouraging contributions from everyone, perhaps using an independent facilitator to elicit participation and avoid biasing participation with your authority. Gaining buy-in and building communication through active participation is not only for team building; it's just good practice in project teams.

Continuous teamwork enables meaningful full-team involvement beyond front-end analysis. In any project life cycle, after an initial analysis phase teams shift focus into product and system design. During product design, your team's needs will differ among the various participants, and the once-integrated team will break up into special interest groups. However, approaches emphasizing software usability can help sustain continuous integration of expertise. For example, a continual user focus requires team members to communicate and share impacts, updates, and ideas that might eventually improve the product. Usability design methods use the team's knowledge and expertise throughout development and reflect learning, new assumptions, and product changes visibly in prototypes.

One effective usability method is participatory design. By involving users in specified design sessions, the team establishes a relationship with its most critical team members: its customers. Teams benefit from continuous knowledge integration by maintaining user involvement beyond the front end and including users in full-team or parallel activities. Participatory, user-focused design relies on front-end analysis, supporting requirements specification and conceptual design.

> *By involving users in design sessions, the team establishes a relationship with its most critical team members: its customers.*

Various participatory methods can foster long-term participation. These include Joint Essential Modeling (JEM), a JAD-like technique developed for usage-centered design [Constantine and Lockwood, 1999]; team sessions for developing scenarios and use cases; cooperative prototyping; implementation planning and work process analysis; and user acceptance and usability evaluations.

Scenario-driven design methods can draw from the whole team's experience to describe system use. Scenarios help create a shared understanding of business processes, application use, or users' real work to bring product ideas to life. Couched in the language of users but applicable to systems and processes, scenarios bridge the gaps among product managers, developers, and users. Scenarios form models of an envisioned product applicable to real work. By starting with user and product knowledge, scenarios add descriptive detail to requirements and design. Although typically used as a front-end technique, scenarios can be developed anytime during the life cycle, for differing purposes. For requirements, scenarios integrate knowledge your team gains while proceeding through concept evaluation, design, and planning. Through reviewing, revising, and testing against prototypes, scenarios evolve throughout design and into implementation and delivery. Scenarios make excellent test scripts by reflecting critical functions users expect from the system. You can use more detailed scenarios as scripts for performing system or acceptance testing and for usability evaluation. Planning and conducting scenario activities helps your team maintain continuity and knowledge sharing throughout the project.

Visual prototyping demonstrates the power of scenarios. More than just a method for representing requirements and design, prototyping supports product and development management well into implementation and testing. Prototypes embodying various degrees of detail are useful throughout the life cycle. Demonstration prototypes, or "page turning" presentations, can explain requirements and proposed enhancements to executives in order to sustain project funding. Interactive prototypes can help you design and evaluate user interface alternatives. These are refined based on user feedback, then serve as visual specifications for engineering. Used throughout design, the same interactive prototype can help the team visualize new product features for future product enhancements. Enhancement definition often parallels development and engages the entire project team. Higher-fidelity interactive prototypes, or alpha versions, are used for evaluation, resulting in team involvement and continuous integration of learning.

> *Used throughout design, the same interactive prototype can help the team visualize new product features for future product enhancements.*

SUSTAINING PARTICIPATION

The type of life cycle dramatically affects the level of teamwork during implementation. A rapid application development (RAD) approach requires more subteam sessions that are brief but focused on fast iterations of work products. Incremental and iterative life cycles, for larger projects, require team decision making and evaluation, with many more sessions than a traditional "waterfall" life cycle. These more complex life cycles require you to coordinate parallel project activities. You need to schedule team sessions to let subteam leaders coordinate development issues and manage integration and testing needs. The larger team gathers for review and at decision-making points, especially where increments or phases require feedback or management decisions.

A waterfall life cycle presents challenges for sustaining teamwork. Team members will often expect to work in relative isolation to meet milestones with discrete deliverables or modules. The high levels of interdependence typically required in rapid or iterative life cycles may be absent. The waterfall life cycle assumes that continuous integration of expertise is not necessary, that individual contributions are sufficient to meet the project schedule.

So what's the best approach for sustaining teamwork throughout a long development life cycle? Aside from user involvement, project team management, and collaborative design, several other activities can help maintain the team's continuity and knowledge sharing.

Design and product reviews. Prototypes, data and process models, code, and architectures must be reviewed, sometimes by the entire team.

Technical design decisions. As engineers respond to requirements feasibility and sizing, the overall team assesses information and supports decisions.

Feedback from customer evaluations and market research. Feedback often shows up throughout design and even development, offering value to the team.

Even delivery phases require teamwork, such as planning for alpha, beta, and system evaluations; conducting testing and reporting results; and decision making. As the delivery phase continues through rollout, team sessions can begin to review customer feedback and manage change control.

UNEXPECTED TURBULENCE

Some common software tools, such as e-mail and CASE tools, that are typically adopted to enhance productivity may actually disrupt effective teamwork.

E-mail is often overused by project teams. Management by e-mail might seem efficient in reducing the need for face-to-face meetings and in allowing team members to respond instantly to pressing issues, but e-mail can dilute the dialogue and learning that take place in teamwork. For complex design issues, e-mail doesn't support creative problem solving. Instead, it tends to reduce issues to quick appraisals. E-mail contributes to isolation by encouraging cryptically drafted communications. Personal intent, nonverbal communication, and context—which help maintain team identity—are missing in e-mail communications. After the next extensive series of e-mail exchanges that seem to only muddy the waters or exacerbate the problems, consider whether a team meeting might not have taken less time.

> *E-mail might seem efficient in reducing the need for face-to-face meetings and in allowing team members to respond instantly to pressing issues, but e-mail can also dilute the dialogue and learning that take place in teamwork.*

Using CASE tools in collaborative analysis and design work can complicate interaction and reduce team cohesion. Although some CASE tools, especially integrated project support environments, are promoted as team-based, they can introduce management problems, especially for organizations new to CASE. Introducing CASE into development requires leadership in organizational and cultural change and surfaces training and integration issues. Even if a "CASE culture" already exists and individuals have used the tools effectively, issues of design control can arise. Design teams requiring full participation have difficulty when a person or subteam has control of the CASE tools. The capturing and interpretation of analysis and design models as well as program structures fall to those managing the tools. Conflicts among team members can arise when control resides with one or a few analysts who are burdened with coordinating and communicating effectively with the team in this (traditionally) non-team design work. Although prototyping tools can raise similar issues of control, prototypes are more often adopted and critiqued by the full team.

The evolution of software development practices has not yet led to state-of-the-art "teamware." Communication and coordination tools lag behind CASE technology. You are more likely to find world-class team technologies in well-funded sports teams or single-mission teams in the military. However, the greatest productivity gains are realized through improving the human side of the equation and usually not through using the latest tools. Sustaining project teamwork over the entire software development life cycle promises enormous payoffs.

Chapter 44

Managing from Below: The Russian Embassy Method

John Boddie

Programmers are neither artists nor engineers. Many of them combine some of the best—and worst—traits of both, which renders the management methods that might be useful with artists and artisans and those that work for engineers and technicians equally ineffective at times. Managing the creative chaos of a project staffed with competent but counterdependent programmers has been likened to herding squirrels. If the analogy is valid, the task is impossible, yet many project managers somehow keep their brilliant software squirrels happy, in the yard, and delivering good code.

Our industry's best managers of the software process have been successful software developers themselves and are every bit as competent and creative as the people they lead. They bring their considerable abilities in understanding problems and innovating solutions to bear on the problems of management, and they are inventing new approaches to fit the special conditions of modern software development.

Some of the best managers heading the best development teams have learned ways to lead lightly but effectively. Some practice their skills as boundary riders, patrolling the borders of projects to protect their developers from external demands and outside distractions. They intercept those intrusions—so vitally important to others but adding nothing to the product—that come in a steady stream from upper management, clients, marketing, and similar sources. Other good managers carefully mentor and monitor their less experienced charges, coaching apprentices toward mastery of the craft. Still others take on the support and administrative functions that no one else wants to do anyway, filling out time sheets, completing documentation, or even commenting the code.

This willingness to do whatever it takes to assure the success of the project, this ability to find unconventional ways to establish control and shape the results, is the hallmark of true technical leadership. Software development has been enriched by these leaders in leadership more than we usually acknowledge.

—Editor

Certain quotes stay with you. In *Up the Organization*, Robert Townsend [1970] said, "The Russians have the best system. The real head of their typical embassy is a third assistant attaché, who is completely free of social obligations and can therefore devote himself fully to running the operation." That struck me as sound when I first read it about twenty-five years ago. As I developed more skill in managing software development teams, the Russian Embassy method has consistently yielded good results for me. Some whose first experience with the method was as members of my project teams have subsequently moved on to management positions, and they tell me that it has also worked well for them.

A development team is usually successful because of what happens within the team, not because of what happens in the organizational layers above it. Upper levels can help the development team succeed by providing resources and defining objectives, but they contribute little to the nuts and bolts of software development work. In the world of software, when project managers attempt to "direct" their "subordinates," projects tend to have problems. I experienced many of these problems before I understood what I was doing wrong.

> *Upper organizational levels can help software development teams succeed by providing resources and defining objectives, but they contribute little to the nuts and bolts of the work. In the world of software, when project managers attempt to "direct" their "subordinates," projects tend to have problems.*

I adopted the Russian Embassy method out of necessity. I was in charge of a project that had a tight schedule and a project team that was a hastily assembled group of part-time consultants. Because people were continually joining and leaving the project, I realized I needed to do two things if we were to have any chance of success. First, I had to be responsible for continuity of project elements. Second, I had to be responsible for communicating the essential values of the project to the people who worked on the team. I believed I had to do whatever was necessary to help the members of the team develop a shared understanding of what these values meant. There was no way to do this if I sat in my office or occasionally met the team over morning coffee. Management from the top was clearly unworkable in this situation. I needed to be in the middle of things and manage from the middle out.

Continuity and values are currents that flow through a team in different directions at different times. Project plans and PERT charts only reflect a hope that the people working on the project will successfully make the continuing series of small course corrections needed to keep things moving in the desired direction. Continuity depends on people working together, often at a low level of detail. The manager can and should supply a map, but the crew seldom sails in a perfectly straight line.

Essential values give a sense of direction to the task and provide the basis by which team members will come to judge themselves and their performance on the project. These values are reinforced and internalized continually as team members ask themselves, "What's important here? Of all the things I could do, which one should I do?" Ease of use might be critical for one project and industrial-strength quality might be critical for another. Whatever the essential values, they need to be communicated. It's important to understand that essential values are not groupthink—each team member will find his or her own way of applying them to individual tasks. Values provide the points of reference for the actions of individuals.

In order to fulfill her responsibilities for ensuring continuity, the manager needs to swim in the same currents as the team. She must have a meaningful role that provides direct benefit to each team member. The context where she works to ensure continuity must also allow her to communicate the essential values of the project as a natural part of the work process, otherwise these values are likely to be viewed as one more example of management posturing. Establishing such a context requires more than leaving the office and walking around among cubicles. It requires active participation in tasks that have tangible deliverables.

> *In order to fulfill responsibilities for ensuring continuity, the manager needs to swim in the same currents as the team and have a meaningful role that provides direct benefit to each team member.*

The Russian Embassy method is a tacit recognition that a manager's points of control exist at different levels of project organization. While control over who joins the team, who is asked to leave, and what steps are required to get an additional budget allocation are located near the top of the project pyramid, other points of control, such as monitoring defect rates or growth in the number of database tables, are typically found at lower levels. It is these lower-level points of control that have the most direct effect on team members, and these are the points of control that are most useful in establishing an effective software construction process.

If a first-level manager allows information from these lower-level points of control to be edited and filtered before it reaches her, she is, in effect, surrendering a significant measure of her managerial effectiveness. In the worst cases, such isolation can lead to outright lying about critical details during the course of the project, an aspect of project management described by Robert Glass [1993] in "Lying to Management."

The Russian Embassy method should not be confused with micromanagement. The third assistant attaché establishes control by taking on selected roles at particularly effective points. A good example of an effective point of control in software development is the defect rate. A manager who is directly involved in the process of defect identification, tracking, and analysis can deal with quality issues at a point where corrections can be made in ways that solve current problems quickly and prevent their recurrence. In the process, the manager will get an accurate picture of problems facing the development team and problems that the team is creating for itself.

> *A manager who is directly involved in the process of defect identification, tracking, and analysis can deal with quality issues at a point where corrections can be made in ways that solve current problems quickly and prevent their recurrence.*

MIDDLE-MANAGEMENT ROLES

I found that my projects ran most smoothly when I took on the administrative roles of scribe and project librarian to put me in close contact with design, defect rates, and system integration efforts. These roles provide an opportunity for continuity since they are represented in all phases of a project. An alternative might be to select a leadership role in the testing effort and define testing to embrace all facets of the project—from requirements development through post-implementation support.

As the manager, I could start meetings or individual discussions by proposing ways to do projects or technical things, such as partitioning the data or identifying appropriate tools. Even better, I could direct team members to prepare initial proposals, providing an early opportunity for team members to have a real ownership stake in the project's outcome. No matter what the source of the initial proposals, the challenge to each working group was to improve upon initial ideas or replace them with something better.

Some team members were uncomfortable at first in criticizing my proposals while I was acting as scribe and taking notes. However, once it was recognized that praise (not only from me but from other members of the team) went to the individuals or groups generating real improvements in ideas, members of the team shed their reticence to criticize with amazing speed.

> *The administrative roles of scribe and project librarian put you in close contact with design, defect rates, and system integration efforts. The manager acting as scribe can help keep meetings focused and can reinforce essential values by asking questions related to such things as quality, delivery time and cost, and user acceptance.*

Many people feel that managers should not attend inspections, walkthroughs, or similar team activities. For many managers, this may be good advice. However, the manager acting as scribe can help keep meetings focused and act to reinforce the essential values of the project by asking questions related to such things as quality, delivery time and cost, and user acceptance. By taking the scribe's responsibility for summarizing and reporting what happens, the manager encourages the quick feedback that is so vital to project continuity.

As scribe, at the end of each meeting I would read back a brief summary of why the meeting was called, what was discussed, what was decided, and who were given action items. This gave the team members an immediate opportunity to correct any misunderstandings I had. The summaries were written up and posted for review, and I would sometimes get additional comments based on these. There is no magic in this practice; it is simply good meeting management. However, my presence and contribution made it clear that open and effective communication was highly valued in the project. Just like the third assistant attaché at the Russian Embassy, my role as "the manager" became less visible, but my influence over the day-to-day actions of the team increased because I was an integral part of what was going on.

To use the Russian Embassy method, the manager must truly believe that the team and individual members can improve on her initial proposals. The manager must communicate this belief by her behavior. The manager's pride in accomplishment comes not from the strength of her own technical or organizational ideas but from the way that the team responds to and synthesizes new approaches from them. This does not mean that the manager is prevented from questioning proposed improvements but that the manager treats her team members as peers rather than as subordinates when discussing specific technical or organizational proposals.

> *To use the Russian Embassy method, you must truly believe that the team can improve on your initial proposals, and you must communicate this belief by your behavior.*

The scribe also has the responsibility for updating the project log and posting meeting reports and other project information for everyone to read. This needs to be done daily. Putting out an internal project report every day may sound like a gimmick, but providing team members with even a general description of what everyone else is doing pays real benefits in ensuring that nothing slips though the cracks. Daily updates also gave me the opportunity to recognize good individual performances publicly. Hardly a programmer alive resents seeing his or her name at the front of a sentence that continues with ". . . just completed a really nice piece of work."

LEADING FROM THE LIBRARY

When I assumed the responsibility of acting as project librarian, I was in an ideal position to enforce the standards used for the project, including design and code inspections, development and execution of test cases, and collection and collation of defect reports. Since these standards coexisted with the underlying emphasis on improvement as a core value in daily activity, the end result was better quality without all of the usual "Total Quality" sloganeering and accompanying cynicism.

The potential benefits of either being the project librarian or treating the project librarian as a peer of technical team leaders are often overlooked by managers. If you consider that the project librarian is one of the few people on a project team who will have regular contact with every team member, the opportunities for using the position for more than clerical drudgery become obvious. The project librarian will have a good grasp of the progress in programming and testing. He will be in a good position to spot points of difficulty that might otherwise remain hidden, such as the fact that a module has been edited and returned to the library twelve times in five days.

> *Managers often overlook the potential benefits of becoming the project librarian or treating the project librarian as a peer of technical team leaders.*

If you do the scribing and library-ing right, you'll be performing like a good third assistant attaché at a Russian Embassy. Mind you, you will be working your tail off, but you will be supporting your team, not managing it as The Boss. Because I was involved directly with what work groups were doing, my reports to my managers and peers were accurate, and there was no need to disrupt work to gather information. All reports, including budgeting, were posted for the team to review, furthering the sense of project continuity.

In addition, my work as scribe and librarian enabled me to detect problems as they were developing, allowing me to put on my "boss" hat and remove obstacles or obtain needed resources in a timely manner. In one case, I detected serious concerns from comments during a design inspection. I formed a review team and told them to stop what they were doing and figure out what would happen if the transaction mix shifted toward additional direct customer inquiries. We concluded there would be enormous service delays, yet there was little we could do within the given hardware constraints. The user was persuaded to provide additional funding for a hardware upgrade early in the process, and when we finally went live, the bigger iron was in place.

This team had the advantage of not having to go through a lengthy education process to bring me up to speed before I took action. If I had been acting as the ambassador rather than as third assistant attaché, team members might have had to wait a week before getting an appointment with me.

PUTTING PEOPLE FIRST

Leading from the position of third assistant attaché is less radical than it may seem. It has long-established parallels in the mentoring activities that are common in many organizations. It is the logical extension of the realization that a manager can succeed only if the people she manages succeed.

The Russian Embassy method explicitly places the process considerations of first-line management above the measurement and control considerations. By taking on a meaningful, direct role in the production of the product, the manager is better able to influence the nature and content of interactions within the team than would be possible from a traditional position of authority. As a scribe, the manager is in an ideal position to detect breakdowns in communications between team members and to follow up to ensure that such breakdowns are not a recurring problem. As a program librarian, the manager can see how her project is coming together and can provide accurate feedback to the team with regard to items on the critical path.

Occasionally, difficult actions are required, such as removing a nonproductive team member. In my experience, the Russian Embassy method makes it easier to take such actions without causing major disruptions to the team. Because I have been functioning as part of the team, there is never a question as to whether I am taking the action because I was misinformed or didn't understand what was going on. I have also been able to accurately gauge the impact of my actions on the team and on the current work effort because I understand the way the team has actually been working in practice—which is often quite different from the way the team appears on an organizational chart.

Every successful project produces not only a product but also a process of changes in the people on the project. The Russian Embassy method ensures that the manager will devote the most significant part of her time to the people on the team. Lao-tzu said, "When the best leader's job is done, the people say, 'We did it ourselves.'" It's a great feeling to work on a project that generates this sentiment, even if you are a third assistant attaché.

Chapter 45

On Becoming a Leader: Advice for Tomorrow's Development Managers

Larry Constantine

Keynote addresses offer both special challenges and special opportunities for the speaker. Many times, they are occasions to reflect or to provoke or both. Although this chapter did not appear in the "Management Forum" column, as the closing session of the very last Software Development Management Conference held in Washington, DC, in 1999, it seemed a fitting way to round out the book.

—Editor

Some of you are managers, some of you aspire to be managers, and some of you would rather sink into the slime than ever become one. But all of you are potential leaders. In a world of fast-changing politics and economics, global connectivity, Internet commerce, enterprise solutions, distributed technologies, and virtual teams, what does it take to be a leader? With the technologies and the acronyms spinning faster than the pages of the calendar, it can be hard to know what direction to turn, much less where, how, when, and whom to lead.

The patterns to be mastered, I believe, lie at the intersection of technology and people, which is the interface where things get especially messy and particularly interesting. I have some trepidation about offering advice on management. Advice to managers is cheap and abundant. Best-selling management books crowd the newsstands and the online booksellers. What could I possibly add to this surplus of sagacity? After all, I am, like most people in this profession, a technologist at heart.

So, it is from this perspective as a fellow nerd that I will attempt to offer a few tips, in the hopes you will find among them something interesting, something useful, perhaps something you have not thought much about before.

1. Lead by Looking

Many years ago I had the wonderful experience of being supervised by a brilliant and charismatic man who absolutely dominated every meeting he attended. That is not to say that he dominated the airtime. No, this man would wait and watch, saying nothing until finally, when others had finished their rapid repartee, their quips and quotes, their bright ideas and brisk arguments, he would speak up, always somewhat speculatively but invariably with insight. His power had many sources, of course, but his wisdom came from us, and he gave it back generously.

Real leadership requires an acute sensitivity to whom is being led where—and what they need to get there. The best leaders spend much of the time just watching, taking it all in. They avoid jumping to conclusions or leaping to premature judgments. They try to understand what is needed and why. They keep on learning, from minute to minute as well as from year to year.

> *The best leaders spend much of the time just watching, taking it all in. They try to understand what is needed and why. They keep on learning, from minute to minute as well as from year to year.*

So keep your eyes and ears open. You might learn something. Of course, it requires patience to pull this off, something I did not learn until I was into my second half-century. So, be patient with yourself, too.

2. Lead by Example—Others Are Watching

Never forget that any leader is always being watched. Set the standard with your own attitude and performance. If you demand thoroughness, practice it. Do you want developers to model before they program? Then use models in your own problem solving. If you expect openness to new ideas, listen and consider, even when your first reaction is to discard a notion as outlandish or impractical. If you want to promote teamwork, be a team player. If you want good communication, learn to communicate well. This admonition is probably obvious to the point of platitude, but it can be darned hard at times to practice what you preach. As you practice and learn, you not only set an example but also extend your own repertoire of leadership.

3. Lead with Questions

Perhaps you remember the popular bumper sticker from the 1960s that read simply "Question authority." Now that it may be you who is the authority, the questions should continue, but be aware of the kind of questions you ask.

Questions are the most misused construction in human language. Questions can seek information, but as often as not they are disguised statements—intended for effect or proffered to manipulate. The parent asks, "What are you doing?" when the kid knows it is all too obvious to both of them that he is painting the walls with mud. When Dad asks, "Do you think I'm some kind of idiot?" any kid with half a brain knows enough not to answer, "Yes, Dad. I just haven't figured out which kind."

The best questions are honest attempts to learn or to make learning possible. Good consultants know that asking the right question is often the shortest route to better solutions. "Good question," someone says, and the mental wheels begin to churn. Often, the best answer to a client's question is another question. Statements declare, questions allow for discovery. It's the old Socratic method you no doubt recall from that teacher you so admired.

Many managers think that they assert authority by their pronouncements and fiats. Ultimately, however, the statements a manager makes may be far less important than the questions he or she asks.

> *The best questions are honest attempts to learn or to make learning possible. Good consultants know that asking the right question is often the shortest route to better solutions.*

4. Lead from Below

You are in a high-tech field, and you must keep in mind the kind of people you are managing. Some software development managers have likened their jobs to herding squirrels—except the squirrels are very smart and get paid extremely well.

The best and brightest in our field, those engineers and technologists who excel at innovation and creative problem solving, are seldom the kind of people who shine as brightly when it comes to the routine tasks of everyday business. Good managers of these inventive independents take over the support functions. They provide administrative and practical support that frees their people to do what they do best. Technical management is not about pronouncements from on high; it's about support from below, about filling out forms and completing the documentation. One crack project manager took on the task of commenting the team's code, in the process adding another level of quality assurance.

Good managers want their engineers solving problems, not wasting time with time sheets or scrubbing coffee mugs. But, of course, if you are seen wiping out the microwave, others may follow your lead. So, go forth and enable. Liberate your people. And empty the trash.

5. Pair Up for Problem Solving

Humans are social creatures. Yes, that's true even for the introverted nerds like us who often seem to prefer the company of machines to that of our fellow human beings. We are all at our best when we multiply our individual abilities with the contributions of colleagues.

Extreme Programming, newest of a long lineage of accelerated development models, uses paired programming to get more and better code in less time, but paired programming is not new. Decades ago, P. J. Plauger taught me that two programmers working at one computer and collaborating on the same code were almost invariably more productive than both working alone. They spell each other, check each other's work, inspire each other, fill in each other's weak spots, and crank out better code with fewer defects. The same formula works for learning a programming language or mastering a new piece of software—you learn not only from the system or the material but also from each other. A dynamic duo who work well together can be worth any three people working in isolation. They bring to the joint endeavor more eyes to spot problems and more brains to solve them. Not everyone can work this way, but for those who can, paired programming is a simple reorganization that can yield dramatic results.

> *A dynamic duo who work well together can be worth any three people working in isolation.*

6. Support Synergy

Teamwork. It's another word so overused that many would just as soon never hear it again. However, effective teamwork is the amplifier that multiplies productivity and creativity. Books and books have covered the myriad tricks of technical teamwork. I am even told that there are some useful pointers in my own books [Constantine, 1995b; 2001]. However, the best advice I can offer is simply not to defeat good teamwork by rewarding and recognizing only outstanding individuals and spectacular solo performances. Ours is an industry of heroes and of heroic efforts to deliver new products and services on time. Indeed, the culture of heroism may be an impediment to our maturation as a profession. We have come to expect heroes and heroism to keep rescuing us from our folly, and we miss the fact that dogged and unheroic efforts may be what carry the day.

Good team players—ones who quietly and without fanfare promote the well-being of the team, who consistently come through for others, and who fill in where needed—are real treasures. Good team players elevate the performance of everyone. The success of all may hinge more on them than on the bright stars who often get all the attention.

7. Manage Meetings

Nearly everyone hates meetings, and no one hates meetings more than technical people, but meetings are another manifestation of the pervasiveness of our social wiring. We gather to swap stories and hear the inside news, to inspire and to share problems. Never underestimate the importance of these social functions. At work, however, the best meetings are working meetings. Like projects, they have a plan and a purpose and deliverables that are more than just paper to be filed. They get real work done. When your people learn that your meetings actually accomplish something, they will stop making excuses to be elsewhere.

> *The best meetings get real work done. When your people learn that your meetings actually accomplish something, they will stop making excuses to be elsewhere.*

Your meetings will work better and be less work if you don't lead them yourself. Savvy managers know the research: letting others lead meetings leads to better decisions and more productive problem solving. It also creates a stage on which others can practice their meeting management skills.

The very best meetings, like work itself, are guided by the precept first taught me by Aussie consultant Rob Thomsett. Have fun and do good work. Both are essential—in meetings, in work, and in life.

8. Improve by Inspection

Many of the very best working meetings are convened to inspect or review work and thereby improve it. Over the years I've learned that stepping back and taking a look at your work is by far the best way to make it better. Systematic reviews and inspections—we used to call them *structured walk-throughs*—are simple to start and inexpensive to conduct, but the payoff is enormous. Requirements reviews, design walk-throughs, usability inspections—there are a whole array of techniques for varied purposes that can help your team deliver better products in less time. As a bonus, teams that regularly practice inspections will learn to avoid the mistakes in the first place, thus improving the process as well as the product.

The most important review of all is the review you do at the end of any project—whether a success or a failure—to see what can be learned from it. In this, be sure to put your own leadership under the microscope, too; even management can be improved by inspection.

9. Slow Down to Speed Up

IBM's motto in the 1960s was simple: "Think." Now, of course, we are told by others to ignore grammar and "Think different." *Thinking,* of course, is the operant term. It is the essence of what we do as professionals and as managers. Your development life cycle may not have a "pause-and-think" step, but it should.

The race is for the swift, we are told. Under the pressure of deadlines and the risk of spectacular failure, we are tempted to rush, skipping over or shortening what may seem to be the less essential activities—like planning or design. Or thinking. Resist that temptation. The more pressure that you are under and the higher the stakes, the more important it is to be systematic and thorough, the more important it is to think.

Few of us will ever get to watch the bomb squad at work, but we have all seen them in movies. The explosives experts charged with disarming some lunatic's time bomb work under immense time pressure. If they fail to finish in time the penalty is enormous. Still, they do not work frantically, tearing off covers and clipping wires in desperation. Methodically, deliberately, they step through the procedures that experience has taught them are most likely to lead to success.

> *Explosives experts work under immense pressure, but they do not work frantically. Methodically, deliberately, they step through the procedures that experience has taught them are most likely to lead to success.*

So, too, in software engineering. The greater the pressure to produce, the greater the importance of knowing what you are producing. Thinking saves time. Modeling saves time. All the time spent solving the wrong problem or producing unworkable solutions is time completely wasted. When the clock is ticking and the customers are screaming, it can take great discipline to work systematically, but chaotic scrambling only gives the appearance of progress.

10. Make Connections

Its called *networking,* and I am not talking about Fast Ethernet or TCP/IP. Social networks—old boy networks along with new girl ones—are another reflection of our inheritance as social creatures. Long ago, like many a newcomer to the profession, I resented the fact that so much seemed to hinge on who you knew rather than what you knew. But the reality is that we all prefer to work with those we know and trust. So be known and be trustworthy.

The answer is not to become a suck-up salesman or to think that superficial social skills can make up for a lack of technical talent. The answer is to understand how human connections are a part of every manager's job.

One project on which I worked produced a design so good and so innovative that some people in the company tried to kill the project. They argued that it would make other products in the line look bad. Fortunately, my counterpart in the client company was not just a brilliant designer; he was also a skilled politician who found a way to make an end run around the opposition. Were it not for his willingness and ability to "play politics," the project might not have gone ahead.

A young friend of mine, who quit university studies in part because she was tired of all the academic politics, soon found politics every bit as rampant in business and industry. In fact, no matter what you do or where you work, politics are part of the game. So learn to play.

11. Work with the Best

On a panel at a major conference not long ago, a colleague argued that the secret of success in software development is just hire the best, most experienced, most productive developers—the top 10%—and then get out of their way. I confess that I myself have on occasion offered similar advice in the past. It is an easy formula for success: with the very best people, it may be hard *not* to succeed. I also admit that I have grave reservations about this elitist approach. In some ways it is too easy, almost absolving managers of their responsibilities for process, for infrastructure, for learning their craft. More importantly, however, it is an example of what is known as a *fallacy of composition,* since the formula can work only for the few, not the many. We cannot all hire just the top 10% of developers, an unsubtle point of elementary arithmetic that nevertheless somehow managed to escape my earnest colleague. Someone, you see, has to work with the rest of us. The average developer is, truth be known, just average.

In management and teaching there is, I believe, a higher calling. Good managers bring out the best in the people whom they manage. The best managers transform those people into the best. That is the sort of thing that motivated me to create structured design and then again when Lucy Lockwood and I created usage-centered design. We wanted to make it possible for ordinary people to achieve extraordinary results.

> *The best managers bring out the best, transforming the people whom they manage into the very best.*

A good manager helps people to exceed themselves.

12. Work Yourself out of Work

One manager I knew, a real people-oriented leader, was brought in above an internal candidate who thought himself deserving and ready for the position. Warned of the potential problem, the new manager called this man into her office and announced that she was going to teach him to take over her job. She started immediately to share what she knew about managing people.

Over the years I have been lucky to have had good mentors who took it on themselves to help me become more of what I could be. So have you, or you would not be where you are; none of us makes it entirely on our own. Behind every so-called self-made person is a host of people who, by accident or design, contributed to the making. You may be talented and you may be tenacious, but you have also been helped, as have we all. As the refrain in the Muppets' *Fraggle Rock* theme song says, "Pass it on!" Pass it on and prepare the next generation to rise even higher. Like good parents and good consultants, good managers work themselves out of a job. Ultimately, managing is about leaving those you have led no longer in need of your leadership.

13. Paint Pictures

The vision thing has gotten so hackneyed and overworked that I hesitate to mention it at all. Still, inspiration—the ability to inspire—remains a vital part of leadership. So, paint pictures of the possible for the people you hope to inspire, but leave the details blank for them to complete. And don't be upset if your seascape is transformed by them into the majesty of mountains.

Visionaries offer direction, dictators give directions.

> *Paint pictures of the possible for the people you hope to inspire, but leave the details blank for them to complete.*

14. Think Systems

When I was studying at MIT's Sloan School of Management, back in the dark ages of computing, general systems theory was a subtext running through much of the curriculum. I learned, as much by osmosis as by course work, to see systems and to think systems. Being able to see the whole, the system that is more than just an assemblage of components, was a fundamental discipline of management even before MIT's Peter Senge popularized it in his books for managers. You need this ability to think in wholes if you are to be able to paint a grand enough canvas for those you would inspire. You will also need the skill to help you play effectively within the political systems that enfold you and your projects. But most of all, as you begin to see, literally, how everything is a system, you will begin to understand—then alter—your part in the interlocking structures of those systems.

Remember, you cannot see the big picture as long as you are inside the frame. Step out, and you realize that, although the whole is more than the sum of its parts, likewise, the part is more than merely a fraction of the whole.

15. Take the Long View

One of the two great joys of growing older is that you get to see things repeat. The other is that growing older beats the hell out of the alternative. From seeing things happen more than once you begin to discern some patterns in the process. You realize that most "revolutionary" products are not revolutionary, that true paradigm shifts are few and far between, and that even those innovations that might be fundamental are unlikely to transform much of anything. Realism should not become an excuse for pessimism, nor should you allow yourself to be seduced into deep cynicism, but you should, as you mature as a manager, find yourself taking more and more with a sizable grain of salt.

In the process, your sense of déjà vu will be heightened and you will more often realize we have been here before. My 93-year-old father-in-law objects to the term *Web browser*. He argues that they do not enable you actually to browse anything. They are slow, primitive, uncooperative beasts connected to a bewildering refuse heap of so-called information that is largely uninteresting and only occasionally and marginally useful. Amen. From browsers, he and I started talking about the early telephones, with their two-handed operation, the handle you had to crank to place a call, and the static-ridden transmission that worsened with distance. There is a pattern in this. As I explained to him, URLs are the magneto cranks of the World Wide Web. Today's browsers are the boxy wooden wall phones of the Internet.

We are always being told of the increasing pace of change, most especially in technology, and many readers of this book will admit to feeling overwhelmed with the accelerating flood of new information and new technology. Taking the longer view, you realize that no matter what technology or school of practice you master, it will eventually be made obsolete by something better—or at least by something different.

> *Taking the long view, you realize that no matter what technology or school of practice you master, it will eventually be made obsolete by something better—or at least by something different.*

Psychologist Sheldon Kopp put it most succinctly and poignantly: nothing lasts! Remember this when you find yourself fighting change. And commit yourself now to a lifetime of learning.

The pace of change has another side to it, however: the human dimension. Jacob Nielsen, for one, is fond of painting enthusiastic pictures of the explosive growth of the Internet, charting the growth in Web sites, the even faster growth in available pages, and the incredible increase in the index he likes to refer to as the "impact" of the Web. And these are on logarithmic scales! I once asked him to superimpose on his "gee whiz" graphs the curves representing the increase over time of the computational speed of the human brain or the growth in channel capacity of the human peripheral nervous system. Both are, of course, perfectly flat.

As technologists, we may be reluctant to acknowledge it, but technology ultimately changes little if anything when it comes to the basic pursuits of the human species. From the campfire to HDTV may seem like an enormous leap, but, like our ancestors, we are still just sitting around in the dark, telling each other tales and passing on our insights in fables. Internet auctions may be dazzling to investors, but they are just another way to trade goods with our neighbors. We use aircraft and cars much as we did carriages and canoes and before that, our feet—to visit our friends and relations, to carry the things we need and want, to see places beyond the horizon. Through all the technological transformations of our own making, we remain fundamentally tribal creatures. Virtual meetings in cyberspace may capture the imagination, but when it comes to actually closing a billion-dollar deal, we meet in person to press the flesh and to pass real paper from hand to hand.

> *Through all the technological transformations of our own making, we remain fundamentally tribal creatures. Virtual meetings in cyberspace may capture the imagination, but when it comes to actually closing a billion-dollar deal, we meet in person to press the flesh and to pass real paper from hand to hand.*

Years ago, I met a man who had developed some of the earliest workable forum software that allowed people separated in both time and space to carry on a discussion of sorts. He was a passionate advocate of social change and truly believed that such software would transform the world by equalizing access and finally enabling true direct democracy. In free-form face-to-face groups, the available time always ends up divided unequally among the participants. Most discussions are driven by the few who dominate the limited airtime. Unfortunately, human nature is more powerful than software. To his chagrin, I predicted that research on electronic forums would show the same kind of distribution of message length and total contributed messages as found in face-to-face groups. It did.

Taking the long view also means looking beyond the current cost-cutting mania of the bean counters and the management pundits. You start thinking about investing, not cost control—about investing in people, investing in processes. Enhancing the skills of your team is not a training expense; it is an investment in human capital, an investment in them as people.

To be the best manager, you must always think in terms of ROI—return on investment. The question is not how much you spend but how much you get for your expenditures. What is it worth if extra time off, larger monitors, or nonstandard software increases the productivity of your crew or increases their likelihood of sticking around when the next headhunter knocks? I don't know. Look at the ROI.

16. Master Technology

Most of us in this business are geeks. Admit it. Me, too. We love technology and technological toys. It is okay to be a geek, so own it. It is a part of you and always will be. As a technical manager, being a geek is both an advantage and a weakness. It is an advantage if you know just enough to carry on a conversation with those who truly know what they are talking about. It is a problem if you get caught up in actually doing the technical stuff yourself, which means you are not doing those managerial things for which others are counting on you. So indulge yourself just enough to get it out of your system.

Most of us would probably prefer to think of technology as good or as a force for good, but technology is neutral. Many people might expect computer-supported cooperative work (CSCW) software to promote collaboration and open communication, but when MIT researchers studied the impact of Lotus Notes on organizational culture, they found that within more rigid and bureaucratic companies it merely reinforced the prevailing lack of sharing and cooperation.

As technology managers, we must always remember that technology is used by people for human ends. Do not be seduced by technology as solution. Technology in itself solves nothing. Like all tools, technology has no soul and cares nothing about how it is used. The same technology that can fuel a revitalized economy can be the basis of exploitative or unscrupulous economic practices. The technology that can give faster access to goods and services to those who possess it can also increase the gap between the technological haves and the have-nots. The technology that gives instant access to a wealth of data can also make it impossible to find anything. The same media that spread truth spew forth falsehood, trivia, filth, and hate.

> *We must always remember that technology is used by people for human ends. Technology in itself solves nothing. Like all tools, it has no soul and cares nothing about how it is used.*

When you hear or read utopian fantasies of a technologically transformed world, remember this: In the wonderful world of technology in which you and I live and work, it is all too easy to come to believe or to act as if this were the real world. It is not. While we talk enthusiastically about universal Internet access, one-half of the people in the real world have never used a telephone and more than one-third of the world has no electricity.

This state of affairs is not about technology, it is about decisions—economic decisions, ethical decisions, social decisions, and personal decisions. As managers who will be called on to lead people and to make decisions, you cannot avoid your responsibilities in this larger scheme of things. Even not to decide is a decision. Ultimately, the difference between irrelevant technology and meaningful technology, between technology as good and technology as evil, is in the day-to-day decisions we all make—or fail to make.

And so I close not with advice but with admonition, with a line from the movie *Running on Empty:* "Go out and make a difference."

References

Albrecht, A. J., and Gaffney, J. E. 1983. "Software Function, Source Lines of Code, and Development Effort Prediction," *IEEE Transactions on Software Engineering, 9* (6): 639–647.

Beck, K. 2000. *Extreme Programming Explained: Embrace Change.* Reading, MA: Addison-Wesley.

Bellin, D., and Simone, S. S. 1997. *The CRC Card Book.* Reading, MA: Addison-Wesley.

Brooks, F. 1995. *The Mythical Man-Month, Anniversary Edition.* Reading, MA: Addison-Wesley.

Brown, S., and Eisenhardt, K. 1998. *Competing on the Edge.* Cambridge, MA: Harvard Business School Press.

Callahan, G. 1997. "Developing Your Intranet Strategy," *Software Development, 5* (2) February.

Carnegie Mellon University, Software Engineering Institute. 1995. *The Capability Maturity Model: Guidelines for Improving the Software Process.* Reading, MA: Addison-Wesley.

Cockburn, A. 2001. *Writing Effective Use Cases.* Boston: Addison-Wesley.

Collofello, J., and Buck, J. 1987. "Software Quality Assurance for Maintenance," *IEEE Software, 4* (5), September/October.

Constantine, L. L. 1992. "Cowboy Coders," *Computer Language, 9* (8), August. Reprinted in Constantine, L. L. *The Peopleware Papers.* Upper Saddle River, NJ: Prentice-Hall, 2001.

Constantine, L. L. 1995a. "In Training," *Software Development, 3* (4), April. Reprinted in Constantine, L. L. *The Peopleware Papers.* Upper Saddle River, NJ: Prentice-Hall, 2001.

Constantine, L. L. 1995b. *Constantine on Peopleware.* Englewood Cliffs, NJ: Prentice-Hall.

Constantine, L. L. 1998. "Abstract Prototyping," *Software Development, 6* (10) October.

Constantine, L. L. 2001. *The Peopleware Papers.* Upper Saddle River, NJ: Prentice-Hall.

Constantine, L. L., and Lockwood, L. A. D. 1994. "Fitting Practices to the People," *American Programmer, 7* (12), December.

Constantine, L. L., and Lockwood, L. A. D. 1999. *Software for Use: A Practical Guide to the Models and Methods of Usage-Centered Design.* Reading, MA: Addison-Wesley.

Constantine, L. L., and Lockwood, L. A. D. 2001. "Structure and Style in Use Cases for User Interface Design," in van Harmelan, M. (ed.) *Object Modeling and User Interface Design.* Harlow, England: Addison-Wesley.

Cooper, A. 1999. *The Inmates Are running the Asylum.* Indiannapolis, IN: Sams.

Cusumano, M., and Selby, R. 1995. *Microsoft Secrets.* New York: Free Press.

De Geus, A. 1997. *The Living Company: Habits for Survival in a Turbulent Business Environment.* Cambridge, MA: Harvard Business School Press.

DeMarco, T., and Lister, T. 1999. *Peopleware Productive Projects and Teams, 2nd ed.* NY: Dorset House.

Dijkstra, E.W. 1968. "Go To Statement Considered Harmful," *Communications of the ACM, 11* (3), March, pp 147–148.

Donnellon, A. 1996. *Team Talk.* Cambridge, MA: Harvard Business School Press.

Fowler, M., and Scott, K. 1987. *UML Distilled: Applying the Standard Object Modeling Language.* Reading, MA: Addison-Wesley.

Gibson, W. 1984. *Neuromancer.* New York: Ace Books.

Gibson, W. 1986. *Burning Chrome.* New York: Arbor House.

Glass, R. 1993. "Lying to Management," *The Software Practitioner, 3* (5), September-October.

Gottesdiener, E. 1999. "Decoding Business Needs," *Software Development, 7* (12), December.

Henderson-Sellers, B., and Unhelkar, B. 2000. *OPEN Modeling with UML.* Boston, MA: Addison-Wesley.

Hock, D. 1999. *Birth of the Chaordic Age.* New York: Berrett-Koehler.

interactions. 2000. Special issue, ACM interactions, May-June 2000.

Jacobson, I., Booch, G., Rumbaugh, J. 1999. *The Unified Software Development Process.* Boston: Addison-Wesley.

Jeffries, R., Anderson, A., and Hendrickson, C. 2001. *Extreme Programming Installed.* Boston: Addison-Wesley.

Jones, C. 1995a. *Patterns of Software Systems Failure and Success.* Boston: International Thomson Computer Press.

Jones, C. 1995b. *Software Quality—Analysis and Guidelines for Success.* Boston: International Thomson Computer Press.

Kauffman, S. 1995. *At Home in the Universe: The Search for the Laws of Self-Organization and Complexity.* Oxford, England: Oxford University Press.

Kelly, K. 1995. *Out of Control: The New Biology of Machines, Social Systems and the Economic World.* Cambridge, MA: Perseus Publishing.

Kernighan, B., and Plauger, P. J. 1978. *The Elements of Programming Style.* New York: McGraw-Hill.

Kruchten, P. 1999. *The Rational Unified Process: An Introduction.* Reading, MA: Addison-Wesley.

Landauer, T. 1995. *The Trouble with Computers.* Cambridge, MA: MIT Press.

McConnell, S. 1996. *Rapid Development.* Redmond, WA: Microsoft Press.

McMenamin, S., and Palmer, J. 1984. *Essential Systems Analysis.* Englewood Cliffs, NJ: Prentice-Hall.

Mogilensky, J., and Deimel, B. L. 1994. "Where do People Fit in the CMM?" *American Programmer, 7* (9), September.

Page-Jones, M. 1995. *What Every Programmer Should Know About Object-Oriented Design.* New York: Dorset House.

Page-Jones, M. 2000. *Fundatmentals of Object-Oriented Design in UML.* Boston: Addison-Wesley.

Page-Jones, M., Weiss, S., and Constantine, L. 1990. "Modeling Object-Oriented Systems: A Uniform Object Notation." *Computer Language, 7* (10), October.

Petzinger, T., Jr. 2000. *The New Pioneers: The Men and Women Who Are Transforming the Workplace and Marketplace.* New York: Touchstone Books.

Roetzheim, W. 1999. "Customized Process Improvement," *Software Development, 7* (3) March.

Sabbagh, K. 1996. *Twenty-First-Century Jet: The Making and Marketing of the Boeing 777.* New York: Scribner.

Sabherwal, R. 1999. "The Role of Trust in Outsourced IS Development Projects," *Communications of the ACM, 42* (2).

Schrage, M. 1989. *No More Teams: Mastering the Dynamics of Creative Collaboration*. New York: Doubleday.

Standish Group. 1995. *Application Development Trends*, January. Arlington, MA: Cutter Information, Inc.

Stevens, W. P., Myers, G. J., and Constantine, L. L. 1974. "Structured Design," *IBM Systems Journal, 13* (2). Reprinted in *Turning Points in Computing*, Special Issue IBM Systems Journal 38 (2–3): 231ff, 1999.

Thomas, D. 1995. "Component-Based Software Construction: Making the Transition from Craft to Engineering," New York: Object Management Group, Inc.

Thomsett, R. 1996. "Double Dummy Spit, and Other Estimating Games," *American Programmer, 9* (6), June.

Townsend, R. 1970. *Up the Organization*. NY: Knopf.

Yourdon, E. 1992. *Decline and Fall of the American Programmer*. Englewood Cliffs, NJ: Prentice-Hall.

Yourdon, E. 1996. *Rise and Resurrection of the American Programmer*. Englewood Cliffs, NJ: Prentice-Hall.

Yourdon, E. 1997. *Death March*. Englewood Cliffs, NJ: Prentice-Hall.

About the Authors

EDITOR

Larry Constantine is Director of Research and Development for Constantine & Lockwood, Ltd., the international consulting and design firm he co-founded, and Adjunct Professor of Information Technology, University of Technology, Sydney (Australia). A pioneer methodologist who developed many of the fundamentals of modern software engineering practice, Constantine is also the co-developer of usage-centered design. In wide demand as a speaker and trainer, Constantine has taught in 19 countries and keynoted numerous major conferences worldwide. He has more than 200 published papers and articles and his 16 books include *Software for Use* (Addison-Wesley), written with Lucy Lockwood and winner of the 1999 *Software Development* Jolt Award for Product Excellence, and *The Peopleware Papers* (Prentice-Hall, 2001). He can be reached through his company's Web site, www.foruse.com

AUTHORS

John Boddie directs the data migration practice for DMR Consulting Group, a division of Fujitsu. After a long career working with software architecture, wagering systems, process control, and operating systems development, he now concentrates on improving the basic but undervalued practices that must be executed successfully in the data processing arena. He is the author of three books, most recently co-authoring with Phil Metzger the third edition of the classic *Managing a Programming Project* (Prentice-Hall, 1995).

Gene Callahan has been developing, managing, and writing about software projects for the last fifteen years. He has written for *Computer Language,*

Software Development, Dr. Dobb's Journal, Java Developer's Journal, Reason Magazine, National Review Online, and other print and Web magazines. He is finishing a book, *Economics for Real People,* due out in 2001, and is an adjunct scholar at the Ludwig von Mises Institute.

Peter Coffee, Technology Editor of *eWEEK,* serves as a columnist and member of the editorial board at the national news outlet covering eBusiness technology and practice. Before joining *eWEEK* (then *PC Week*) in 1989, he spent ten years at Exxon and The Aerospace Corporation; he holds degrees from MIT and Pepperdine's Graziadio School of Business. He has spent more than a decade as a prominent analyst of emerging computing and communications technologies, and is author of the highly praised books "How To Program Java" and "Peter Coffee Teaches PCs." He can be reached at peter_coffee@ziffdavis.com

James Emery is Professor Emeritus of Systems Management and former Associate Provost for Computing at the Naval Postgraduate School in Monterey, California. As Associate Provost, he was responsible for developing the School's IT strategy, operating a central computing facility, building and operating a complex network, and developing administrative applications. He is also Professor Emeritus at the Wharton School of the University of Pennsylvania, and has 10 years' experience in the private sector and government. His teaching and research interests include application software development, IS strategies, and economics of information systems. He has published and lectured widely in these areas.

Dennis J. Frailey is a Principal Fellow at Raytheon Company, an Adjunct Professor at Southern Methodist University, an Instructor at UCLA Extension and the University of Texas Software Quality Institute, and a Senior Consultant with The Process Group. Dr. Frailey has been a software developer since 1962 and is widely recognized as a speaker and educator in the fields of software productivity, software metrics, and software project management. He has been a keynote speaker at several prominent conferences and is particularly proud that his students consider him "the most reasonable Ph.D. around." He can be reached at frailey@acm.org.

Ellen Gottesdiener, Principal of EBG Consulting, Inc., is a consultant, facilitator and trainer helping people to collaboratively capture and verify business, user, and technical requirements. Ellen is an expert in using facilitated workshops for software development projects. She has presented at numerous industry conferences and authored numerous papers on requirements, workshops, methods and modeling. She is a pioneer in business rule-driven requirements workshops. She can be reached at ellen@ebgconsulting.com or through her web site, http://www.ebgconsulting.com.

Sylvain Hamel, with a background in avionics and computer systems, has been developing embedded system software for more than 15 years. He is currently a software engineer involved in software process improvement and software development at Bombardier Transport, Mass Transit Division, North America (St-Bruno, Québec). He is also a graduate student at École Polytechnique de Montréal. He can be reached at shamel@transport.bombardier.com

Jim Highsmith is director of Cutter Consortium's e-Project Management Practice, president of Information Architects, Inc., and author of *Adaptive Software Development: A Collaborative Approach to Managing Complex Systems,* (Dorset House), Jolt Product Excellence Award winner for 2000. He has 30 years experience as a consultant, software developer, manager, and writer. Jim has published dozens of articles in major industry publications and his ideas about agile software development have been featured in *ComputerWorld.* In the last ten years, he has worked with companies in the around the world to help them adapt to the accelerated pace of development in increasingly complex, uncertain environments.

Ron Jeffries is a consultant specializing in agile software development processes, especially the discipline of Extreme Programming. He has helped many teams adopt XP and adapt it to their particular situations. He has presented keynotes, papers, and tutorials at software conferences across the world. Ron is the author, with Ann Anderson and Chet Hendrickson, of *Extreme Programming Installed* (Addison-Wesley, 2001), nominated for the 2001 *Software Development* Magazine Jolt Award. Ron is associated with Object Mentor (www.objectmentor.com), and can be reached at ronjeffries@acm.org.

Capers Jones, Chief Scientist and Founder of Software Productivity Research, Inc. (an Artemis company) specializes in software project management, software cost estimating, and collection of productivity and quality data on a global basis. He is the author of twelve books on software management topics and more than 200 journal articles. He has held positions with IBM in software management and research and with ITT as Assistant Director of Programming Technology.

Peter H. Jones, Ph.D., is a management consultant with Atos Origin and principal of Synchro Systems Design. Dr. Jones engages large organizations and start-ups in developing innovative software products and innovation practices. Author of *Handbook of Team Design* (IEEE Press, 1998), he conducts workshops and publishes research on innovation, design management, and organizational strategy. Dr. Jones teaches graduate courses and seminars in human-computer interaction and usability, and focuses current research on the tacit knowledge and social factors in software product innovation. He can be reached at peter@poetics.org

Naomi Karten has delivered seminars and presentations to more than 100,000 people internationally to help them manage customer expectations, enhance their communications and consulting skills, and build trusting, supportive relationships. Before forming Karten Associates in 1984, she earned a B.A. and M.A. in psychology, and gained extensive IT technical and management experience. Naomi's books include *Managing Expectations: Working With People Who Want More, Better, Faster, Sooner, NOW!* (Dorset House, 1994) and *How to Establish Service Level Agreements* (Her latest book-in-progress is titled *Communication Gaps and How to Close Them.* Naomi's web site features numerous articles on managing expectations, communications, relationship building, gathering customer feedback, and related topics. Reach her at nkarten@compuserve.com, www.nkarten.com

Norm Kerth, President of Elite Systems, is a leading expert and consultant in the areas of specification and design methodologies with emphasis on object-oriented technologies. He has special interest in turning around failed projects and is a leader in the emerging area known as Patterns. An international speaker and master teacher, his most recent book is *Project Retrospectives: A Handbook for Team Reviews* (Dorset House, 2001), already being heralded as a classic. His e-mail address is nkerth@acm.org

Lucy Lockwood, President of Constantine & Lockwood, Ltd., is a consultant and trainer specializing in software usability and high-performance teamwork. Her work in these areas is widely recognized and she has presented at and keynoted major international conferences. She has published numerous papers on management and technical subjects and is the co-author, with Larry Constantine, of the acclaimed book, *Software for Use* (Addison-Wesley, 1999), winner of *Software Development* Magazine's prestigious Jolt Award as the best book of 1999. She can be reached through her company's Web site, www.foruse.com

Mary Loomis, Senior VP of Engineering at Commerce One, is responsible for all the company's product development organizations. A pioneer in the data modeling, object modeling, distributed database, and object database fields, Dr. Loomis has nearly 30 years experience in a variety of roles, including software engineer, professor, consultant and technical manager. She previously held positions with Hewlett-Packard, Versant Object Technology, GE, and D. Appleton Company, and was a tenured professor at the University of Arizona. She is the author of five books and dozens of articles and has been a regular columnist for the *Journal of Object-Oriented*

Programming. She served as founding chair of OMG's Object Analysis and Design Task Force, which produced the international standard Unified Modeling Language UML. Mary can be reached at mary.loomis@commerceone.com.

Steve McConnell is CEO and Chief Software Engineer at Construx Software. His first two books, *Code Complete* (Microsoft Press, 1993) and *Rapid Development* (Microsoft Press, 1996) won *Software Development* Magazine's Jolt Award for outstanding software development books of their respective years. In 1998, readers of *Software Development* Magazine named Steve one of the three most influential people in the software industry along with Bill Gates and Linus Torvalds. Outside work, Steve volunteers as Editor in Chief of *IEEE Software* and is on the Panel of Experts that advises the Software Engineering Body of Knowledge (SWEBOK) project. He can be reached at stevemcc@construx.com

Ulla Merz, president of P2E—From Practice to Experience, is a consultant and practitioner in software project management. Ulla manages software development projects for clients with special situations. As a technical project manager her focus is on process improvement, creating a productive work environment with attention the individual needs of each team member, and applying the right technology for the problem at hand. Her work has been published in software magazines and she publishes a quarterly newsletter "ProjectPress." Ulla can be reached at ullamerz@aol.com

Meilir Page-Jones is president and senior consulting methodologist at Wayland Systems Inc. in Bellevue, WA (www.waysys.com), where he divides his time among training, consulting, conference presentations, writing, and doing honest work on software projects. He is author of three books: *The Practical Guide to Structured Systems Design* (Prentice-Hall, 1988), *Practical Project Management* (Dorset House, 1998) and *Fundamentals of Object-Oriented Design in UML* (Addison-Wesley, 2000), the first edition of which won a Jolt Productivity award. In addition, he has written many articles on software technology and management, together with Wayland Systems' courses on structured methods, object-oriented methods and software-project management. He can be reached at meilir@waysys.com.

Sue Petersen is an anthropologist by training, a programmer by avocation, and a manager by necessity, owning and operating a small business since 1979. She has written for *Windows Tech Journal, Visual Developer Magazine,* and others. Her main professional interests are database design and software engineering and management. She can be reached at suep@networkboy.com

Dwayne Phillips has been a systems and software engineering with the US Government (currently the Department of Defense) since 1980. He wrote *The Software Project Manager's Handbook: Principles that Work at Work* (IEEE Computer Society, 1998) plus numerous articles on image processing and other topics for *The C/C++ Users Journal* and *The Cutter IT Journal*. He is a regular contributor to The Cutter IT E-Mail Advisor. He can be reached at d.phillips@computer.org

Gifford Pinchot, a speaker and consultant on innovation management, is author of the best-selling book, *Intrapreneuring: Why You Don't Have to Leave the Corporation to Become an Entrepreneur* (Harper & Row, 1985) and *The Intelligent Organization* (Berrett Koehler, 1994), written with Elizabeth Pinchot. Pinchot & Company, the firm he leads, helps companies to reduce bureaucratic obstacles and to design and implement more effective and sustainable business practices. Pinchot has founded four companies including a management consulting company specializing in innovating solutions to business growth problems and Consensus Development, a software firm in the internet security business. A graduate of Harvard University, he has also studied neurophysiology at Johns Hopkins University.

Johanna Rothman observes and consults on managing high technology product development. She works with her clients to find the leverage points that will increase their effectiveness as organizations and as managers, helping them ship the right product at the right time, and recruit and retain the best people. An author and frequent speaker on managing high technology product development, Johanna has written numerous articles and presented at and keynoted major international conferences. She can be reached at jr@jrothman.com

David Thielen is a senior manager at a high-tech company. He is the author of several books including *The 12 Simple Secrets of Microsoft Management: How to Think and Act Like a Microsoft Manager and Take Your Company to the Top* (McGraw-Hill, 1999). He presently resides in Boulder, Colorado.

Dave Thomas is CEO of Bedarra Corporation and a Research Professor in Computer Science at Carleton University. He is one of the early pioneers of OO technology and was founder and CEO of Object Technology International, developers of the unique CFM environment ENVY/Developer; VMs and IDEs for IBM VisualAge for Smalltalk, Java and Micro Edition for Embedded Systems; and the light weight Just In Time Software process. With his unusual breadth of experience, Dave he is a popular keynote speaker known for bringing strong pragmatic views into every presentation and publication. Contact him at dave@bedarra.com

Rob Thomsett, whose career began in 1968, has been consulting and educating in the area of project management, teams, and quality since 1974. Rob has served on the Editorial Board of the prestigious *American Programmer* and is a member of the IEEE Industry Advisory Board. He is the author of numerous technical articles and two books, most recently, *Third Wave Project Management: A Handbook for managing the Complex Information Systems* (Prentice-Hall, 1993). In 1994, he developed the Accreditation Programme for Project Management for the Australian Computer Society.

Michael Vizard has been covering computer technology for more than 14 years. As editor in chief, of *InfoWorld,* he is responsible for the day-to-day management of the editorial department in addition to leading the content of InfoWorld.com and managing strategic editorial partnerships. Prior to joining *InfoWorld* in 1995, Vizard had been an editor at *PC Week, ComputerWorld,* and *Digital Review.*

Tony Wasserman is Vice President, West Coast Labs, for Bluestone Software (acquired by Hewlett-Packard). Previously, he was VP of Engineering for a dot-com startup as well as Principal of Software Methods and Tools, consulting for software companies on a broad range of topics. Tony founded and served as President, CEO, and Chairman of Interactive Development Environments, Inc., where he was an architect of the innovative Software through Pictures multi-user modeling environment. He was a professor at University of California, San Francisco, and a Lecturer at UC Berkeley. A Fellow of both the ACM and IEEE, in 1995 he received the first award for distinguished service to the software engineering community from ACM SIGSOFT and in 1986 received the IFIP Silver Core Award. He has published dozens of technical papers, served as Editor-in-Chief of ACM Computing Surveys, and edited eight books

Karl Wiegers is Principal Consultant with Process Impact (www.processimpact.com), a software consulting and education company, where he specializes in requirements engineering, process improvement, software technical reviews, project management, and measurement. Karl holds a Ph.D. in organic chemistry. He is the author of *Software Requirements* (Microsoft Press, 1999) and *Creating a Software Engineering Culture* (Dorset House, 1996), both of which won Productivity Awards from *Software Development* magazine. Karl has also written more than 130 articles on many aspects of software engineering and management, chemistry, and military history. He is a frequent speaker at software conferences.

Ed Yourdon is an international computer consultant who has worked in the computer industry for over 35 years. One of the original architects of the structured analysis/design methods of the 1970s, he is also co-developer of the Yourdon/Whitehead method of object-oriented analysis/design and the popular Coad/Yourdon OO methodology. Ed is the author of 450 technical papers and two dozen books, including *Death March, Rise and Resurrection of the American Programmer,* and *Decline and Fall of the American Programmer.* His latest book, *Time Bomb 2000,* described the risks and technical aspects of the Y2K problem for the layman; he is working on a new edition of his *Modern Structured Analysis* book.

Edward Ziv manages projects with IconMedialab (www.iconmedialab.com), a global provider of integrated e-business solutions. During eight years with a NJ-based Management Consulting firm, Ed led Business Process Improvement initiatives to map corporate strategies and build supporting technology and processes. He has designed and coded back-office trading systems handling over $50 billion for a Wall Street bank. Ed can be reached at edwardziv@yahoo.com

Index

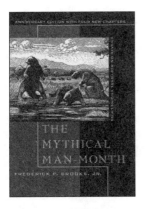

The Mythical Man-Month, Anniversary Edition
Essays On Software Engineering
By Frederick P. Brooks Jr.

With a blend of software engineering facts and thought-provoking opinions, noted industry veteran Fred Brooks offers insight for anyone managing complex projects. These essays draw from his experience as project manager for the IBM System/360 computer family and then for OS/360, its massive software system. Twenty years after the first edition of his book, Brooks has revisited his original ideas and added new thoughts and advice, both for readers already familiar with his work and for readers discovering it for the first time.

0-201-83595-9 • Paperback • 336 pages • ©1995

Beyond Chaos
The Expert Edge in Managing Software Development
Larry L. Constantine

In *Beyond Chaos*, the best of *Software Development's* Management Forum has been incorporated into a single volume, revealing best practices in managing application development. The 45 essays contained in this book are written by many of the leading names in software development, software engineering, and technical management, including Larry Constantine, Karl Wiegers, Capers Jones, Ed Yourdon, Dave Thomas, Meilir Page-Jones, Jim Highsmith, and Steve McConnell.

0-201-71960-6 • Paperback • 418 pages • ©2001

Software Fundamentals
Collected Papers by David L. Parnas
Daniel M. Hoffman and David M. Weiss

David L. Parnas is one of the grandmasters of software engineering. His academic research and industrial collaborations have exerted far-reaching influence on software design and development. Together, his groundbreaking writings constitute the foundation for modern software theory and practice. As a celebration of one of the fathers of modern software engineering, and as a practical guide to the key concepts underlying software development, *Software Fundamentals* is valuable for professionals, especially those who are interested in learning the fundamentals of software.

0-201-70369-6 • Hardcover • 688 pages • ©2001

Managing Software Acquisition
Open Systems and COTS Products
By B. Craig Meyers and Patricia Oberndorf
SEI Series in Software Engineering

The acquisition of open systems and commercial off-the-shelf (COTS) products is becoming an increasingly vital element of large-scale corporate and government software development, offering significant savings in development time and cost whe properly managed. *Managing Software Acquisition* presents th fundamental principles and best practices for successful acqui sition and use of open systems and COTS products. It explore the many opportunities and challenges of this strategy, defines key terms, anticipates potential problems, and discusses the impact of software acquisition on the manager's job.

0-201-70454-4 • Hardcover • 400 pages • ©2001

Technology Acquisition
Buying the Future of Your Business
By Allen Eskelin

With detailed and practical suggestions based on the author's own extensive experience, *Technology Acquisition* facilitates your decision-making process when selecting the right vendo with the right technology, for your business. The book also explains how to implement and operate the technology once the vendor has been selected. By reading this easy-to-follow, step-by-step guide, you will benefit from the author's acquisi-tions experience, and enhance your skillset quickly to follow trends in this rapidly changing industry.

0-201-73804-X • Paperback • 208 pages • ©2001

CMMI℠ Distilled
A Practical Introduction to Integrated Process Improveme
By Dennis Ahern, Aaron Clouse, and Richard Turner
SEI Series in Software Engineering

The Capability Maturity Model Integration (CMMI) is a natura extension of the Capability Maturity Model (CMM). This conc book is the first look at this new standard, which illustrates th benefits of integrating an organization's process improvement initiative to touch areas beyond software (systems engineerin acquisition, staffing, etc.). Subjects detailed in this book inclu the benefits of integrated process improvement, an introductic to the work of the CMMI project, and suggested heuristics on how to choose appropriate models and representations for your organization.

0-201-73500-8 • Paperback • 320 pages • ©2001

Component-Based Software Engineering
Putting the Pieces Together
By George T. Heineman and William T. Councill

Component Based Software Engineering: Putting the Pieces Together is a state-of-the-art snapshot of current perspectives on this emerging development strategy by today's leading experts. With contributions from well-known luminaries including Len Bass, Paul Clements, Martin Griss, and Ivar Jacobson, the book details the plusses and pitfalls of CBSE while revealing its potential for engineering reliable and cost-effective software.

0-201-70485-4 • Hardcover • 880 pages • ©2001

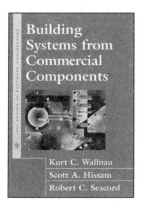

Building Systems from Commercial Components
Kurt C. Wallnau, Scott A. Hissam, and Robert C. Seacord
SEI Series in Software Engineering

Components are growing in popularity as an effective means of saving time and money through software reuse; however, integrating components is a delicate task. This book outlines case studies of the authors' successes and failures that were drawn from their own experiences building large systems for the Department of Defense. With this book as a guide, software architects, engineers, and project managers will be able to build large systems from commercial software components.

0-201-70064-6 • Hardcover • 416 pages • ©2002

Software Product Lines
Practices and Patterns
By Paul Clements and Linda Northrop
SEI Series in Software Engineering

The practice of building sets of related systems from common assets can yield remarkable quantitative improvements in productivity, time to market, product quality, and customer satisfaction. While the benefits of using a product line approach are great, employing this process is not simple. This book helps you face the daunting task of answering the question "where to begin?" By using two fully detailed case studies this book lays out the most important steps necessary to adopting this approach in your organization.

0-201-70332-7 • Hardcover • 576 pages • ©2002

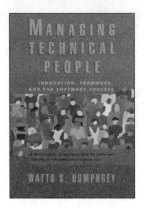

Managing Technical People
Innovation, Teamwork, and the Software Process
By Watts S. Humphrey
SEI Series in Software Engineering

Watts Humphrey's advice on how companies and individuals could improve their software process has been widely adopted. *In Managing Technical People: Innovation, Teamwork, and the Software Process*, he demonstrates the overriding importance of *people* to the success of any software project. He focuses particularly on the critical role of innovative people, and gives concrete advice on how to identify, motivate, and organize these people into highly productive teams.

0-201-54597-7 • Paperback • 352 pages • ©1997

Introduction to the Team Software Process℠
By Watts S. Humphrey
SEI Series in Software Engineering

Software Engineering team members should not have to expend valuable time and energy reinventing ways to organize and run their team. By following a proven process, the team will more quickly be able to focus on the successful completion of the project itself. *Introduction to the Team Software Process℠* details methods to guide the formation of software development teams, to motivate their work, and to enhance their productivity.

0-201-47719-X • Hardcover • 496 pages • ©2000

Software for Use
A Practical Guide to the Models and Methods of Usage-Centered Design
By Larry L. Constantine and Lucy A. D. Lockwood
An ACM Press book

Larry L. Constantine and Lucy A. D. Lockwood turn the focus of software development to the *external* architecture. In *Software for Use: A Practical Guide to the Models and Methods of Usage-Centered Design*, they present the models and methods of a revolutionary approach to software that will help programmers deliver more *usable* software that will enable users to accomplish their tasks with greater ease and efficiency. This book was the recipient of the 1999 *Software Development* magazine Jolt Award.

0-201-92478-1 • Hardcover • 608 pages • ©1999

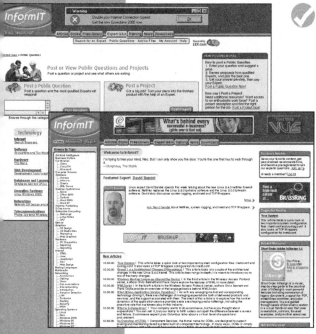

Register
Your Book

at www.aw.com/cseng/register

You may be eligible to receive:

- Advance notice of forthcoming editions of the book
- Related book recommendations
- Chapter excerpts and supplements of forthcoming titles
- Information about special contests and promotions throughout the year
- Notices and reminders about author appearances, tradeshows, and online chats with special guests

Contact us

If you are interested in writing a book or reviewing manuscripts prior to publication, please write to us at:

Editorial Department
Addison-Wesley Professional
75 Arlington Street, Suite 300
Boston, MA 02116 USA
Email: AWPro@aw.com

Visit us on the Web: http://www.aw.com/cseng